Development of Educational Philosophy

DEVELOPMENT OF EDUCATIONAL PHILOSOPHY

Premchand Jogi

CRESCENT
PUBLISHING CORPORATION

Development of Educational Philosophy

Edition: 2021

ISBN 978-81-8342-131-7

Published by :

CRESCENT PUBLISHING CORPORATION
4806/24, Mathur Lane,
Ansari Road, Darya Ganj,
New Delhi - 110002
Phone : 011- 23244131
Mob. : 9711991838, 9999021668
Website : www.crescentpublishingcorp.weebly.com
E-mail : crescentbook@gmail.com

Typesetting by :

Adee Computers
Delhi

Printed at :
G. S. Offset
Delhi

Preface

Education has been traditionally viewed as an endeavour crucial to the progress of a society, and has found immense encouragement in the form of support and endorsement historically. Societies have sought to educate their people for a variety of reasons, which range from production of goods and services satiating curiosity, to enable people to respond creatively to world they live in, or satisfy their aesthetic impulses. Today, as the social, economic and political contexts of the world get increasingly complex, education has widened immensely in its perspective and objectives. As a result, educational philosophy, which encompasses the various schools of thought which contend on the modes, methodologies and strategies of imparting education, has also enlarged its scope and become complex in its present situation.

This book in the series on educational philosophy comentrates its focus onto providing a comprehensive and incisive insight into the development of educational philosophy from its origins throughout the ages, and its contemporary stand on educational issues. Through a detailed discussion of the various schools of thought in educational philosophy, it offers a historical and lucid view of the issue, taking into account the social and political contexts, as well as the needs of societies in particular epochs. It then leads onto an exploration of contemporary philosophy in education, while all the time giving a clear view of the shaping of educational philosophy.

It is hoped that the erudition and insight of the book serve well for all the readers.

Premchand Jogi

Contents

1

Education and Socialism

To state exactly the object of education both the sociological and the biological side must be taken into consideration. That the social phase of education has been largely ignored in the past may be seen from the following definitions taken from the older writers.

Plato says, "The purpose of education is to give to the body and to the soul all the beauty and all the perfection of which they are capable."

Kant defines education as "the development in man of all the perfections which his nature permits." John Stuart Mill "education includes whatever we do for ourselves, and whatever is done for as by others for the express purpose of bringing us nearer to the perfection of our nature."

Herbert Spencer briefly states that "Education is the preparation for complete living."

Rosseau contents himself with the following indefinite generality: "Education is the art of bringing up children and of forming men."

In Horace Mann we see the beginnings of a new idea in education: "By the word 'education' I mean much more than the ability to read, write and keep common accounts. I comprehend under this noble word such a training of the body as shall build it up with robustness and vigor, at once protecting it from disease and enabling it to act formatively upon the crude substances of nature–to turn a wilderness into cultivated fields, forests into ships, or quarries and clay pits into villages and cities. I mean also to include such a cultivation of the intellect as shall enable it to discover those permanent and mighty laws which pervade all parts of the created universe whether material or spiritual.

This is necessary because if we act in obedience to these laws all the resistless forces of nature become our auxiliaries and cheer us on to certain prosperity and triumph. But if we act in contravention or defiance to these laws, then nature resists, thwarts, baffles us, and in the end it is just as certain that she will overwhelm us with ruin as it is that God is stronger than man."

Looked at from the standpoint of society as well as of the individual education means not only the adaptation of the individual to his surroundings, but the training of him to understand his environment and thus the giving to him the power to modify and change it.

Take for example the physical sciences. Education along this line would require an actual understanding for instance of the ways of applying energy–by means of the lever and inclined plane with their modifications–of the nature and modes of action of electricity, the combinations resulting from the union of different chemical elements, etc.

This knowledge could then be used either in new inventions or in handling present instruments and materials.

Again the value of history in education does not consist in the mere knowledge of events or even the exercise of memory on the part of the individual, but in the principles for the guiding of future society that may be drawn from past events.

The power to read is not in itself an education, but the ability, by means of which to gain, for use, the knowledge of facts that have been stored up by other minds. This educative value of reading, this spontaneous making the thought of the author our own, has been largely destroyed by the formal methods of teaching the subject which have created a habit of observing words and their forms, and that only.

Like all things, however, education has been shaped in the past by the economic conditions and needs of society. Long after the sixteenth and seventeenth centuries education was chiefly characterised by a ponderous scholasticism. The artisan, not looked upon as in any sense a 'scholar,' was the only one who with a trained eye and hand could design and make things.

The past century has been a commercial age. It has been marked by great inventions, a vast increase in trading, an enormous production of goods and a growing intricacy of diplomatic relations. A careful survey of present educational methods and subjects of study must convince one that our schools are made to further the interests of the ruling industrial and commercial class of the time.

The technical school that practically serves the purpose of training passably good engineers and mechanics has marked the past few years. It is owing to these technical schools that Germany is to-day becoming able to compete with England both in foreign markets and at home. These best technical schools turn out such a vast number of trained workmen that, underbidding each other in the labor market, their value has decreased until Germany has the cheapest skilled workmen to be found.

Plans are now under way to establish a commercial school at Berlin in which the study of English will be an especial feature. The reason for this is plain. Not only a great portion of Germany's export trade goes to English speaking countries, but English is fast becoming the language of commerce, and a knowledge of it will enable her merchants to push their trade more effectually.

It is interesting also to note the founding of large schools of diplomacy. When modern inventions have put great nations into proximity, and relations are strained, and it has become a matter of nations competing for trade and struggling for territory, it is essential that capital should have trained diplomats to skillfully adjust conditions in foreign markets and political circles and thus guard the interests of the ruling class. Such a school is founded in connection with Columbian University at Washington.

Mr. Gunton says in his magazine that more interest should be taken in these schools because–and here he gives the capitalists' only reason for education–"of the expansion of American trade." It is in this way that education, which should aim at a rounded man and womanhood, is being used for the benefit entirely of the ruling class.

The American manufacturer has heretofore been obliged to draw his designers and workmen of especial skill from foreign schools, but now he sees that it is far more economical to found such schools at home, either private or public, and use them to produce a limitless supply of skilled laborers who, competing with each other, will lower wages.

A recent report of the Bureau of Labor Statistics gives the following as one of the reasons for introducing manual training into schools: "Parents realising that employers will insist that the boy 'start at the bottom in any industry' decide that he must begin to gain the industrial experience which will increase his wages at as early an age as possible, rather than to continue in school to learn the, things which they feel will never be of real use to him."

It is with difficulties such as these that the new education finds itself confronted from the first. Like all revolutionary movements, for that is what in its essence the new education is, it finds the old system which it has outgrown–seeing itself unable to check the new movement–seeking to pervert it to its own benefit. Hence the ruling class see only in domestic science as taught in the schools the means for training more competent servants or in the sloyd work the making of better carpenters.

Our system of industry to-day demands no individuality of the immense body of workmen. It has grown so far mechanical that in the great industrial establishments there is small need for the inventor or artist. This is not contradictory with the statement before of the demand for skilled workmen. Skilled workmen in no way presuppose workmen with any individuality developed.

Our school system has not advanced beyond the demands of the economic conditions. It has the same leveling effect. So many children promoted into a certain grade. The same work and way of doing this work is required of each one. The teacher with forty or fifty children in a grade has little opportunity to study the inclinations of each child. All are made to "toe the same mark." The whole system has become dull and mechanical. The very power of initiative is crushed out of the child.

So entirely commercial is our age that we are not surprised to find our school system run upon that basis. Sufficient school buildings there are not. In many neighborhoods we find from two to three hundred children waiting to be admitted to the kindergarten while many more are attending but half time.

The number of teachers compared with the number of pupils is altogether insufficient. Forty-five or even sixty we have seen enrolled in ward schools under one teacher. These teachers, who are always overworked, are usually utterly unable to teach anything of science. They have never themselves been trained to observe or handle real things and cannot teach the child to see.

Laboratories in physical science may appear to us well equipped considering the condition of the apparatus used in teaching physics or biology or chemistry ten years ago, but the vast majority of the schools are still poorly furnished with the materials for good work in these lines.

But we are passing at present through a period of change, from a time of commercialism and competition to an age of cooperation, and there are present among us the germs for a new growth in education. Already the awakening has begun to be felt.

Beginning as far back as Rosseau, Cemenius and Pestalozzi, an effort was made to put actual perception and observation of things by the senses in place of the mechanical instruction by word. It is not generally known, however, that it is to Robert Owen that we owe some of the first clear statements of the coming revolution in education. He was the first to look upon instruction and education from the point of view of the social organisation.

A recent article in the *Neue Zeit* points out that he brought forward the demand that the intellectual and physical education should go hand in hand. That from the age of eight years up instruction should he united with regular labor in the house and garden. That from the thirteenth year children are to enter into the higher arts and trades and thereby be prepared to further the riches and well-being of society in the most effective manner with the greatest satisfaction to themselves. He comprehended the activity of labor in instruction not only as a necessary pedagogical end, but also as a means to the social production of goods.

The new education and socialism are being developed from the same social conditions. They have as their object the same thing–freedom. Freedom for each one to develop his own methods of thought and his own initiative. To express in material form his inner being. It is recognised that to furnish this inner man and woman with material there must be supplied to them constant contact through their senses with the outside world, for that which is produced is but what has gone in through the senses, modified by each one's individual characteristics and tendencies.

It is for this reason that the new education emphasises the importance of work with tools and materials that the pupil may design and work out his design in a material form. Nature studies also are a prominent feature of the new education. Trips into the country bring the city child into contact with an entirely new phase of life. He sees the seed put into the ground, its growth, the processes by which wheat is converted into flour and bread, the growth of flax, cotton and wool as materials for the manufacture of textile fabrics.

This is in a sense a "return to nature," but not the nature of Rosseau. It is a nature made large by the discoveries of science. Science has opened to us the secrets of the world's formation, the laws of gravitation, the mysteries of the growth of physical organisms and all its secrets have been discovered only by men working in direct contact with the things they tried to reveal.

Education under socialist conditions would produce men and women, not machines. As Marx has said, the end of socialism is "an association wherein the free development of each is the condition of the free development of all," "an economic order of society which together with the greatest possible development of social productive power secures the highest possible harmonious development of human beings."

To-day like the press, the pulpit and the lecture room, so the school is under the control of the ruling class which uses its control for its own advantage. When capitalism has demanded technical skill its schools have produced men trained along that line; when it has required any other quality its schools have produced men with that quality; and when it has found that ignorance, docile and unquestioning, has served its purpose best it has reduced the laboring class to that condition.

To go a step further: as pointed out by Prof. John Dewey, "education should be a process or living and not a preparation for future living." The school to-day is an unnatural life calculated only to prepare one for future work. It has no relation either with the home or society. The life of the average American student is abnormal and returns him to society both scholastic and pedantic. To-day so-called education ends with the class-room instead of all of life being an education. Even the spirit of social solidarity and mutual interest is destroyed by the present system. For one boy to assist another in his task is a thing for which to be punished.

Again, education is far more than the training of the intellect alone. It was a principle of Greek philosophy to unite instruction with music and exercise. Socialism would require and make possible the physical development as well as the mental. Productive work would be united with education. The student studying into the mechanism of the steam engine would be able to put his hands upon one and learn by use its every part.

Following the manufacture of textile goods and the development of industry he would trace it through its primitive forms, the wheel for spinning and the clumsy loom for weaving up through the complicated machinery and vast looms of a modern factory.

Studying the industries connected with the production of foodstuffs, of agriculture in general, he would go out and use the tools employed in the raising of grain and see the growth from the pointed stick with which the savage scratched the ground or the flail that our forefathers used to beat out the and threshing machine of to-day.

The pitable ignorance of our city population of anything to be found in the country, and of our country folk of great manufacturing establishments, and of the majority of our whole population of any part of actual life outside the narrow confines of their own work must be a source of wonder to future generations.

Society would thus be presented to the child in a simplified form. He would begin with the primitive stages through which society passed in savage and barbarous times and gradually ascend in his education to the complex and intricate system of modern industry. Anthropology and etymology would become live and inspiring topics.

For education to be of value it must present a unity in the things taught. Our old system has made each department of science an entirely new and foreign subject to the beginner, having no relation to anything either before or after. For instance, take geology and geography. Few have been trained to see that geography is the study of the present conditions of the earth that represent a certain stage in a long series of stages; that geology is the study of these different stages and the changes in the earth's surface that have resulted in its present physical appearance.

Every teacher should be able to take up subjects of study in due relation to society and the science of society–sociology. So far this unity or synthesis has been a subject of discussion among philosophers, but has received slight notice from the pedagogue.

At the beginning we stated that the object of education is the adapting the individual to his surroundings and the fitting him to change and modify them. These changes should be such as would lead to the progress of humanity. In how infinitely few cases, however, has science been used to benefit the condition of the great mass of the people except when protection for the ruling class demanded that certain steps should be taken. For example, study has put on record much of value in the scientific preparation of food, in the producing of sanitary conditions, and in the prevention of diseases.

Under socialism, with pure food well prepared and healthful surroundings, we shall look to see disease practically stamped out and the life of man extended.

The century has seen great advance in science in medicine, experimental psychology and physiology; yet this knowledge is the monopoly of the few. As shown by Kropotkin in his "Appeal to the Young": "In our society to-day science is only an appendage to luxury which serves to render life pleasanter for the few, but remains absolutely inaccessible to the bulk of mankind." "The philosophers are crammed with scientific truths and almost the whole of the rest of human beings remain what they were five or ten centuries ago, that is to say, in the state of slaves, and machines, incapable of mastering established truths." "We need to spread the truths already mastered by science, to make them part of our daily life, to render them common property."

Again, the discoveries in experimental and physiological psychology must revolutionise many of the old methods of teaching. Genetic psychology, for instance, has shown that the first years of a child's life must be a time of physical activity. The body of the child is not yet under control. It is impossible for him to remain quiet. Yet we remember when school discipline required these little bodies to remain quiet in a seat for four or six hours in a day and our schools are but just beginning to throw off this old discipline and to guide this aimless but necessary activity into useful channels.

Not only the normal but the great number of abnormal will be benefited by the discoveries of psychology. Study has shown what can be done to make the mentally defective useful to society. Likewise with the criminals. The social conditions that have created a large part of them being changed their number would he vastly decreased. The others could be used somewhere in the social organism in productive work. This in no way argues that we should weaken the race by protecting the mentally weak and degenerate. Both would finally become well nigh extinct if not left to perpetuate at will their kind.

Socialist System of Education

The late member of the German diet, Dr. Lasker, delivered a lecture in Berlin, during the seventies, in which he arrived at the conclusion that it is possible for all members of society to have an equal standard of education. But Dr. Lasker was an anti-Socialist, a rigid upholder of private property and capitalism, and the question of education under present-day conditions is pre-eminently a question of money. Therefore an equal standard of education for all is impossible at present. Some may attain a higher education even under unfavorable circumstances, by overcoming many difficulties and by applying an amount of energy that few possess. But the masses can never attain it so long as they must live in a state of social dependence and oppression.

In the new society the conditions of existence will be the same for all. The requirements and inclinations will differ and will always continue to differ, since these differences are rooted in the nature of man. But each individual will be able to develop under conditions equally favorable to all. The uniform equality, imputed to Socialism, is like so many other imputations, sheer nonsense. It would be useless, indeed, if Socialism should strive for uniform equality, for it would then come into conflict with human nature itself and could not hope to see society develop in accordance with its principles. Indeed, if Socialism should succeed in forcing society into unnatural conditions, these new conditions would soon make themselves felt as shackles that would be torn asunder, and Socialism would be doomed. Society develops by innate laws and acts accordingly.

A proper education of the young must be one of the chief tasks of the new society. Every child that is born will be a welcome addition to society. In the child society beholds the possibility of its own continuity, its own further development. Therefore it will also recognise the duty of amply providing for the new being. The first object of its care must, accordingly, be the child-bearing woman, the mother. Comfortable homes, pleasant environment, institutions of all kinds suited to this stage of motherhood, considerate care for her and for the child – these are the first requirements. It is self understood that women will be enabled to nurse their children as long as necessary and desirable. Moleschott, Sonderegger, all hygienists and physicians are agreed that no other nourishment can fully substitute the mother's milk.

Those who, like Eugen Richter, grow indignant at the suggestion that young mothers shall give birth to their children in a lying-in-hospital, where they will be surrounded by every care and comfort that only wealthy persons can afford to-day, and that even they cannot obtain as perfectly as it can be provided in institutions especially equipped for the purpose, should remember that at present at least four-fifths of all children who come into the world are born under the most primitive conditions that mock civilisation.

Of the remaining one-fifth of our mothers again only a small minority are able to enjoy the care and the comforts that should be bestowed upon every woman in this condition. Even to-day some cities have splendid provisions for child-bearing women, and many women gladly make use of these institutions when they feel their time approaching. But these institutions are so expensive that only few women are able to make use of them; others, of course, are prevented by prejudice. Here again we have an example how the bourgeois world everywhere contains the germs for future transformation.

Motherhood among women of wealth and fashion becomes rather peculiar by the fact that these mothers transfer their maternal duties as soon as possible to a proletarian wet-nurse. It is well known that the Lausitz (Spreewald) is the region that supplies the bourgeois women of Berlin, who do not or cannot nurse their infants, with nurses. "The breeding of nurses" is carried on as a trade, since country girls do not hesitate to become pregnant, because they find it profitable, after the birth of their babies, to hire out as nurses to rich families in Berlin. It is not an unusual occurrence that girls have three or four illegitimate children in order to hire out as nurses, and if they earn enough money by this trade they are regarded as desirable wives by the young men of the Spreewald. Regarded from the view-point of bourgeois morality, such actions are despicable; but regarded from the view-point of the family interests of the bourgeoisie, they become praiseworthy and desirable.

As soon as the child will have outgrown infancy it will join companions of its age in common play under common care and direction. Everything needful or desirable for the child's physical and mental development will be supplied. Every observer of children knows that they can be most easily educated in the company of other children. This quality can be successfully applied to the system of education. The play-halls and the kindergarten will be succeeded by a playful introduction into the rudiments of knowledge and the various industrial tasks. They will be succeeded by appropriate mental and physical work, combined with gymnastic exercises and unrestricted motion on the playground and in the gymnasium, the skating-rink and the swimming-pool. There will be exercises, drills and wrestling-matches for both sexes, for the aim will be to bring up a healthy, hardy race that will be normal both physically and mentally. Step by step the children will be initiated into the various practical activities, horticulture, agriculture, manufacture, the technics of the process of production. Mental education in the various realms of knowledge will not be neglected.

The system of education will be purified and improved, just like the system of production. Many antiquated, superfluous methods and subjects, which only serve to hamper the child's mental and physical development, will be dropped. The knowledge of natural things, adapted to the child's understanding, will incite a far greater desire for study than a system of education where one subject conflicts with and contradicts another; for instance, when, on the one hand, children receive religious instruction as taught by the Bible, and, on the other, are taught science and natural history.

The equipment of the schools and the methods and means of education will be in keeping with the advanced stage of civilisation of the new society. All the books and objects required for education and study, food and clothing, will be furnished by society; no pupil will be at a disadvantage with the others. This is another chapter that causes indignation among our bourgeois "men of order." They claim that Socialists seek to turn the school into barracks, and to deprive the parents of all influence over their children. Socialists do not aim at anything of the sort. In future society, parents will have far more time at their disposal than the great majority of parents have to-day. We need but point to the fact that at present many workingmen are employed ten hours daily, and even longer, and that many employees in the postal and railroad service, prison and police officials., etc., as well as mechanics, small farmers, merchants, military men, physicians, etc., must devote an equal length of time to their occupations.

In future parents will be able to devote themselves to their children in a measure that is quite impossible to-day. Moreover, the parents will control the educational system and will determine the measures and methods that are to be adopted and introduced. For then society will be thoroughly democratic. There will be boards of education consisting of parents – men and women – and of the educators. Does anyone presume that these will act contrary to their sentiments and interests? That is done in present-day society, where the state carries out its ideas of education contrary to the wishes of most parents.

Our opponents pretend that it is one of the most agreeable things to parents to have their children about them all day and to be constantly occupied with their education. As a matter of fact, this is not so. Every parent knows that the education of a child is no easy task. Several children facilitate education, but they cause so much work and worry, especially to the mother, that she is thankful when they are old enough to attend school, and she is relieved of their care for a part of the day. Moreover, most parents can educate their children but insufficiently, because they have no time.

The fathers are engaged in their trades or professions and the mothers in their household tasks, and sometimes the mothers are breadwinners, also. But even those parents who have sufficient time usually lack the ability. How many parents are able to follow up the mental development of their children at school and to assist them? Mighty few.

The mother, who, in most cases, might be best enabled to render such assistance, rarely has the ability, because she has not been properly trained herself. Moreover, the methods and subjects are changed so often that they are foreign to most parents. For most children the facilities at home are so insufficient that they have no proper order, comfort or peace for doing their home-work, nor art they helped by anyone. Often the home is small and overcrowded; the entire family are huddled together in a few small rooms, the furniture is scanty, and the child wishing to study lacks every comfort and convenience. Not infrequently light, air and heat are wanting.

The books and school supplies are either wanting entirely or are of the poorest quality. Frequently also the little ones are tortured by hunger, which destroys all inclination for study. Hundreds of thousands of children are put to work at all kinds of domestic and industrial occupations that rob their childhood of its joy and incapacitate them for mental work. Sometimes children must contend with the opposition of narrow-minded parents, who object to it that the children devote time to their studies or to play. In short, there are so many obstacles that it is to be wondered at that the young are so well educated. This is a proof of the health of human nature and of its innate desire for progress and perfection.

Bourgeois society itself recognises a number of these evils and facilitates the education of the young by introducing free public instruction and, here and there, by also furnishing the school supplies. As late as the middle of the eighties the then Minister of Education of Saxony, designated both these institutions as "Socialistic demands." In France, where public education had long been neglected and then progressed all the more rapidly, progress has advanced still further; at least, this is the case in Paris. Here the public-school meal, at the expense of the municipality, has been introduced. Poor children are given the meals free of charge, and the children of parents who are in better circumstances must pay a nominal sum into the municipal treasury. Here we behold a communistic institution that has proved. entirely satisfactory to parents and children.

The insufficiency of our present educational system – it often fails to accomplish the moderate aims it has set for itself – becomes evident from the fact that thousands upon thousands of children are unable to get along at school on account of insufficient nourishment.

Every winter there are thousands of children in our cities who come to school without breakfast. Hundreds of thousands of others are chronically underfed. To all these children public feeding and clothing would be a blessing. In a community that will, by proper care and nourishment, teach them what it means to be human, they will not become acquainted with a house of "correction." Bourgeois society cannot deny the existence of this misery, and so compassionate souls unite to found free-lunch establishments and soup-kitchens, to perform, as a charity, what ought to be performed by society as a duty. Recently a few municipalities have undertaken to feed poor children at public expense. But all this is insufficient and must be accepted as a charitable gift, while it should be demanded as a right.

It is well that the amount of home-work is being reduced in our schools, since the insufficiency of home facilities has been recognised. The child of wealthy parents is at an advantage over his poorer schoolmate, not only because he is privileged by outward circumstances, but also because he is helped at home by a governess or a tutor. On the other hand, laziness and carelessness are fostered in the child of wealthy parents, because their wealth makes study appear superfluous to him, and because demoralising examples are frequently placed before him and he is approached by many temptations. He who learns daily and hourly that rank, position and wealth count for everything, acquires a peculiar conception of human duties and of the institutions of state and society.

When we examine this question more closely we find that bourgeois society has no reason to become indignant over the communistic methods of education aimed at by Socialists, for it has itself introduced such methods for privileged classes, but in a distorted manner. We need but point to the cadet schools, the seminaries and colleges for the clergy. Here thousands of children, some of them belonging to the upper classes, are trained in the most absurd and one-sided way and in strict monastic seclusion for certain occupations.

Many members of the better classes, like physicians, clergymen, officials, manufacturers, large farmers, etc., who live in small towns where there are no higher institutions of learning, send their children to boarding-schools in large cities, and do not see them during the entire year, except at vacation time. It is a contradiction, then, when our opponents decry a communistic system of education and estrangement between parents and children, and at the same time introduce a similar system of education, only in a wrong, insufficient and distorted manner, for their own children.

Only too frequently are the children of the rich not educated by their parents at all, but by nurses, governesses and tutors. A special chapter might be written on this subject that would not cast a favorable light on the family relations of these classes. Here, too, hypocrisy prevails and conditions are anything but ideal, both for the educated and the educators.

In accordance with the entirely altered system of education that aims at the physical and mental development and culture of the young, the teaching force must be increased. The training of the rising generation should be provided for in the same way as the training of the soldiers is provided for in the German army. Here one officer has charge of from 8 to 10 men. If in future a similar number of pupils will be placed under the guidance of one teacher, the desired aims will be attained. Introduction into mechanical activities in the splendidly equipped workshops, and into horticultural and agricultural activities, will also constitute an important factor in the future education of the young. Everything will be taught with a proper variation of occupations and without over-exertion, in order to educate harmoniously developed human beings.

Education must be the same for both sexes and must be given in common to both. Separation of the sexes is justifiable only in cases where the differences of sex make it absolutely necessary. In this manner of education the United States is far advanced over Europe. Here education has been introduced from the primary school to the university. Not only is education furnished free, but the school supplies also, inclusive of the tools for manual training, lessons in cooking, and articles used by the pupils in the study of chemistry and physics. Many schools are equipped with gymnasiums, swimming-pools and playgrounds. In the higher schools the girls are trained in gymnastics, swimming, rowing, running, etc.. – as well as the young men.

The Socialistic system of education will attain still higher results. Properly regulated and ordered and placed under able control, it will continue until the age at which society declares its young men and women to be of age. Then the members of both sexes will be fully prepared to perform all duties and to enjoy all rights.

Then society will be certain of having educated capable, fully developed members, human beings to whom nothing human is foreign, who are as familiar with their own nature as they are with the nature and condition of society, into which they forthwith enter, enjoying full equality. So the excesses of our modern youth that are daily increasing, and that are a natural product of our disintegrating social conditions, will disappear.

Unruliness, lack of self-control, immorality and brutal sensuality, which characterise the modern young men at our higher institutions of learning, our colleges and universities, and that are the result of domestic demoralisation and unrest and of the baneful influences of social life, will not mark the young men of the future. The evil influences of the factory system and the congested dwellings, that cause young people to be self-assertive and unbridled at an age when human beings are in the greatest need of education and of being trained to exercise self-control, will also disappear.

Future society will avoid all these evils without being obliged to resort to compulsory measures. The social institutions and the resulting intellectual atmosphere that will dominate society will simply make the existence of such evils impossible. In society, as in nature, diseases and the destruction of organisms take place only where a process of decay has set in.

None will deny that our present system of education is afflicted with great and serious defects, and, as a matter of fact, these defects are more marked with the higher schools and institutions of learning than with the lower ones. A village school is a model of moral healthfulness compared with a college; a sewing school for poor girls, a model of morality compared with a number of fashionable boarding schools. It is not hard to find the reason for this. Among the upper classes of society every striving after higher aims has been smothered; they are devoid of ideals. Owing to the lack of ideals and loftier aspirations, the unbounded love of enjoyment and the inclination to excesses are disseminated, with their resulting physical and moral deterioration. How can young persons, growing up in such an atmosphere, be different?

A purely material enjoyment of life, carried to extremes, is all they see and know. Why should they strive after higher aims when the wealth of their parents makes every endeavor appear superfluous? The maximum education of the great majority of sons of the German bourgeoisie, consists in their passing the examination for one year's voluntary service in the army. When they have attained this aim, they believe that they have absorbed all knowledge worth knowing and regard themselves as demi-gods. If they have obtained a reserve-officer's certificate, their conceit and arrogance knows no bounds. The influence exercised by this generation, most of whose members are weak in character and knowledge, but strong in servility, characterise the present period as the "age of reserve officers." Its peculiarities are: Ignorance, lack of character, and a servile disposition.

Men fawn on their superiors, and are arrogant and brutal to their inferiors. Most of the daughters of the upper classes are trained to be society ladies, walking fashion plates and silly dolls. They rush from one enjoyment to another, until they grow weary with the boredom of their empty lives, and fall victims to many real and imaginary diseases. When they grow old they become religious fanatics, spiritualists and faith healers, who turn up their eyes at the wickedness of the world and preach asceticism.

In regard to the lower classes, efforts are being made to further diminish their standard of education. The fear prevails that the proletarian might become too wise, that he might tire of his subjection and rebel against his earthly gods. The more ignorant the masses are, the more easily can they be governed and controlled. Large landowners from the East-Elbe province have repeatedly declared in their meetings: "The most stupid workingman is the one most welcome to us." An entire programme is contained in this one sentence.

So present-day society is as helpless and aimless in regard to the question of education as it is in regard to all other questions. What methods, then, does it resort to: It calls for punishment and preaches religion; that is, it preaches submissiveness and contentment to those who are far too submissive and contented already; it teaches abstinence, where poverty compels people to abstain from the very necessities of life. They who brutally rebel against this state of affairs are placed in so-called "reformatories" that are generally controlled by religious influences. That is the limit of the pedagogical wisdom of our society.

The vicious methods of education applied to neglected and demoralised proletarian children become manifest by the frequent cases of abuse and ill-treatment committed by the directors, overseers, etc., in these "homes"(!) Here it has been shown time and again how religious fanatics of the deepest dye have, with a perverted pleasure, ill-treated poor, helpless children with unspeakable brutality; and how many of these horrors may never become known!

Materialist Basis of Education

Among the many contributions the capitalist system has made to the progress of the race, one of the most valuable was the necessity of educating the members of the working class. No right, or privilege, or opportunity is given a lower or under class unless that right or opportunity makes for the benefit and interest of the upper or dominant class.

Two hundred years ago one could find but few workingmen who could read or write. Education was the privilege of the upper class only. It was not necessary for the serf in the field to have a trained mind in order to plow a straight furrow. The skill to swing a scythe or sickle required no mental training or education. But the introduction and development of machinery and the use of steam and electricity necessitated a different type of worker from the unlettered, untutored serf in the field or the woman at the spinning wheel.

To transform the crude ore into a fine steel rail required new skill. To assemble all the various elements together into a mighty engine called for the trained and educated workman. To operate an engine demanded the skilled engineer. In short, the new industrial processes which the capitalist system gave the world necessitated the education and mental training of the workers in order that they might be fit and efficient wealth producers. Capitalism therefore created the economic or material reasons far the need of the great mass of the workers to be educated: It "democratised" education.

While economic and material benefits have accrued to the master class through the education of the workers; while large profits were only possible through a trained and skilled laboring class, yet in this very thing which makes for the triumph of the master class financially, we see a potent and powerful factor in bringing about the political and industrial supremacy of the working class.

Knowledge is Power

Only as the workers have knowledge and intelligence can

they solve the problem of their own political and industrial freedom.

The capitalist masters have educated the workers to their advantage to-day, but for their undoing tomorrow.

The thing that makes for the triumph of capitalism ultimately makes for its own downfall.

Education of the workers for the benefit of the capitalist class means gain and profit only for the few, the upper class of to-day.

Education of the workers for the benefit of the working class means gain and profit for the working class and ultimately for the whole human race.

That which has served the capitalist class will some day serve the working class.

The trained minds that create profits for the masters of to-day will create wealth for the producers to enjoy to-morrow.

The future victories of the working class lie not so much in their numbers, but in the knowledge they possess and the ability to intelligently organise and act together on the political and economic fields.

Men or Machines?

Unsigned, Piedmont edition of *Avanti!*, 24 December 1916, under the banner "Socialists and Education." Comrade Zini's observations and Councillor Sincero's attacks against philosophy are not just isolated polemical episodes: they are necessary clashes between people representing fundamentally opposed interests.

1. Our party has still not settled on a concrete education programme that is in any way different from traditional ones. Until now we have been content to support the general principle of the need

for culture, whether it be at an elementary, or secondary-technical or higher level, and we have campaigned in favour of this principle and propagated it with vigour and energy. We can state that the reduction in illiteracy in Italy is due not so much to the law on compulsory education, as to the intellectual awakening, the awareness of certain spiritual needs that socialist propaganda has succeeded in arousing amongst the ranks of the proletariat in Italy. But we have gone no further than that. Education in Italy is still a rigidly *bourgeois* affair, in the worst sense of the word. Grammar schools and higher education, which are State-run and hence financed from State revenues, i.e. by the direct taxes paid by the proletariat, can only be attended by the children of the bourgeoisie, who alone enjoy the economic independence needed for uninterrupted study. A proletarian, no matter how intelligent he may be, no matter how fit to become a man of culture, is forced either to squander his qualities on some other activity, or else to become a rebel and autodidact – i.e. a mediocrity, a man who cannot give all he could have given had he been completed and strengthened by the discipline of school. Culture is a privilege. Education is a privilege. And we do not want it to be so. All young people should be equal before culture. Using the funds of all citizens, the State should not be financing the education of the children of wealthy parents no matter how mediocre or deficient they may be, while it excludes even the most intelligent and capable children of proletarians. Grammar-school and higher education should be open only to those who can demonstrate that they are worthy of it. And if it is in the public interest that such forms of education should exist, preferably supported and regulated by the State, then it is also in the public interest that they should be open to all intelligent children, regardless of their economic potential. Collective sacrifice is justified only when it benefits those who are most deserving. Therefore, this collective sacrifice should serve especially to give the most deserving children that economic independence they need if they are to devote their time to serious study.

2. Members of the proletariat, who are excluded from grammar schools and higher education as a result of the present social conditions – conditions which ensure that the division of labour between men is unnatural and so retards and is inimical to production – have to fall back upon the parallel educational system: the technical and vocational colleges. As a result of the antidemocratic restrictions imposed by the State budget, the technical colleges, which were set up along democratic lines by the Casati ministry, have undergone a transformation that has largely destroyed their nature. In most cases they have become mere superfetations of the classical schools, and an innocent outlet for the petty-bourgeois mania for finding a secure job. The continually rising entrance fees, and the particular prospects they open up in practical life, have turned these schools too into a privilege. Anyway, the overwhelming majority of the proletariat is automatically excluded from them on account of the uncertain and random life which the wage-earner is forced to lead – the sort of life which is certainly not the most propitious for fruitfully following a course of study.

3. What the proletariat needs is an educational system that is open to all. A system in which the child is allowed to develop and mature and acquire those

general features that serve to develop character. In a word, a humanistic school, as conceived by the ancients, and more recently by the men of the Renaissance. A school which does not mortgage the child's future, a school that does not force the child's will, his intelligence and growing awareness to run along tracks to a predetermined station. A school of freedom and free initiative, not a school of slavery and mechanical precision. The children of proletarians too should have all possibilities open to them; they should be able to develop their own individuality in the optimal way, and hence in the most productive way for both themselves and society. Technical schools should not be allowed to become incubators of little monsters aridly trained for a job, with no general ideas, no general culture, no intellectual stimulation, but only an infallible eye and a firm hand. Technical education too helps a child to blossom into a man – so long as it is educative and not simply informative, simply passing on manual techniques. Councillor Sincero, who is an industrialist, is being too meanly bourgeois when he protests against philosophy.

Of course, meanly bourgeois industrialists might prefer to have workers who were more machines than men. But the sacrifices which everyone in society willingly makes in order to foster improvements and nourish the best and most perfect men who will improve it still more – these sacrifices must bring benefits to the whole of society, not just to one category of people or one class.

It is a problem of right and of force. The proletariat must stay alert, to prevent another abuse being added to the many it has already suffered.

2

Organisation of Education and Culture

It may be observed in general that in modern civilisation all practical activities have become so complex, and the sciences so interwoven with everyday life, that each practical activity tends to create a new type of school for its own executives and specialists and hence to create a body of specialist intellectuals at a higher level to teach in these schools. Thus, side by side with the type of school which may be called "humanistic" – the oldest form of traditional school, designed to develop in each individual human being an as yet undifferentiated general culture, the fundamental power to think and ability to find one's way in life – a whole system of specialised schools, at varying levels, has been being created to serve entire professional sectors, or professions which are already specialised and defined within precise boundaries.

It may be said, indeed, that the educational crisis raging today is precisely linked to the fact that this process of differentiation and particularisation is taking place chaotically, without clear and precise principles, without a well-studied and consciously established plan. The crisis of the curriculum and organisation of the schools, i.e. of the overall framework of a policy for forming modern intellectual cadres, is to a great extent an aspect and a ramification of the more comprehensive and general organic crisis.

The fundamental division into classical and vocational schools was a rational formula: the vocational school for the instrumental classes, the classical school for the dominant classes and the intellectuals. The development of an industrial base both in the cities and in the countryside meant a growing need for the new type of urban intellectual. Side by side with the classical school there developed the technical school, and this placed a question-mark over the very principle of a concrete programme of general culture, a humanistic programme of general culture based on the Graeco-Roman tradition. This programme, once questioned, can be said to be doomed, since its formative capacity was to a great extent based on the general and traditionally unquestioned prestige of a particular form of civilisation.

The tendency today is to abolish every type of schooling that is "disinterested" or "formative" – keeping at most only a small-scale version to serve a tiny élite of ladies and gentlemen who do not have to worry about assuring themselves of a future career. Instead, there is a steady growth of specialised vocational schools, in which the pupil's destiny and future activity are determined in advance.

A rational solution to the crisis ought to adopt the following lines. First, a common basic education imparting a general, humanistic formative culture; this would strike the right balance between development of the capacity for working manually and development of the capacities required for intellectual work. From this type of common schooling, via repeated experiments in vocational orientation, pupils would pass on to one of the specialised schools or to productive work.

One must bear in mind the developing tendency for every practical activity to create for itself its own specialised school, just as every intellectual activity tends to create for itself cultural associations of its own; the latter take on the function of post-scholastic institutions, specialised in organising the conditions in which it is possible to keep abreast of whatever progress is being made in the given scientific field.

It may also be observed that deliberative bodies tend to an ever-increasing extent to distinguish their activity into two "organic" aspects: into the deliberative activity which is their essence, and into technical-cultural activity in which the questions upon which they have to take decisions are first examined by experts and analysed scientifically.

This latter activity has already created a whole bureaucratic body, with a new structure; for apart from the specialised departments of experts who prepare the technical material for the deliberative bodies, a second body of functionaries is created – more or less disinterested "volunteers", selected variously from industry, from the banks, from finance houses.

This is one of the mechanisms by means of which the career bureaucracy eventually came to control the democratic regimes and parliaments; now the mechanism is being organically extended, and is absorbing into its sphere the great specialists of private enterprise, which thus comes to control both régimes and bureaucracies. What is involved is a necessary, organic development which tends to integrate the personnel specialised in the technique of politics with personnel specialised in the concrete problems of administering the essential practical activities of the great and complex national societies of today. Hence every attempt to exorcise these tendencies from the outside produces no result other than moralistic sermons and rhetorical lamentations.

The question is thus raised of modifying the training of technical-political personnel, completing their culture in accordance with the new necessities, and of creating specialised functionaries of a new kind, who as a body will complement deliberative activity. The traditional type of political "leader", prepared only for formal-juridical activities, is becoming anachronistic and represents a danger for the life of the State: the leader must have that minimum of general technical culture which will permit him, if not to "create" autonomously the correct solution, at least to know how to adjudicate between the solutions put forward by the experts, and hence to choose the correct one from the "synthetic" viewpoint of political technique.

A type of deliberative body which seeks to incorporate the technical expertise necessary for it to operate realistically has been described elsewhere, in an account of what happens on the editorial committees of some reviews, when these function at the same time both as editorial committees and as cultural groups. The group criticises as a body, and thus helps to define the tasks of the individual editors, whose activity is organised according to a plan and a division of labour which are rationally arranged in advance.

By means of collective discussion and criticism in which each individual functions as a specialist in his own field and helps to complete the expertise of the collectivity, the average level of the individual editors is in fact successfully raised so that it reaches the altitude or capacity of the most highly-skilled – thus not merely ensuring an ever more select and organic collaboration for the review, but also creating the conditions for the emergence of a homogeneous group of intellectuals, trained to produce a regular and methodical "writing" activity.

Undoubtedly, in this kind of collective activity, each task produces new capacities and possibilities of work, since it creates ever more organic conditions of work: files, bibliographical digests, a library of basic specialised works, etc. Such activity requires an unyielding struggle against habits of dilettantism, of improvisation, of "rhetorical" solutions or those proposed for effect. The work has to be done particularly in written form, just as it is in written form that criticisms have to be made – in the form of terse, succinct notes: this can be achieved if the material is distributed in time, etc.; the writing down of notes and criticisms is a didactic principle rendered necessary by the need to combat the habits formed in public speaking – prolixity, demagogy and paralogism.

This type of intellectual work is necessary in order to impart to autodidacts the discipline in study which an orthodox scholastic career provides, in order to Taylorise intellectual work. Hence the usefulness of the principle of the "old men of Santa Zita" of whom De Sanctis speaks in his memoirs of the Neapolitan school of Basilio Puoti: i.e. the usefulness of a certain "stratification" of capabilities and attitudes, and of the formation of work-groups under the guidance of the most highly-skilled and highly-developed, who can accelerate the training of the most backward and untrained.

When one comes to study the practical organisation of the common school, one problem of importance is that of the various phases of the educational process, phases which correspond to the age and intellectual-moral development of the pupils and to the aims which the school sets itself. The common school, or school of humanistic formation or general culture, should aim to insert young men and women into social activity after bringing them to a certain level of maturity, of capacity for intellectual and practical creativity, and of autonomy of orientation and initiative. The fixing of an age for compulsory school attendance depends on the general economic conditions, since the latter may make it necessary to demand of young men and women, or even of children, a certain immediate productive contribution. The common school necessitates the State's being able to take on the expenditure which at present falls on the family for the maintenance of children at school; in other words, it transforms the budget of the national department from top to bottom, expanding it to an unheard of extent and making it more complex.

The entire function of educating and forming the new generations ceases to be private and becomes public; for only thus can it involve them in their entirety, without divisions of group or caste. But this transformation of scholastic activity requires an unprecedented expansion of the practical organisation of the school, i.e. of buildings, scientific material, of the teaching body, etc.

The teaching body in particular would have to be increased, since the smaller the ratio between teachers and pupils the greater will be the efficiency of the school – and this presents other problems neither easy nor quick to solve. The question of school buildings is not simple either, since this type of school should be a college, with dormitories, refectories, specialised libraries, rooms designed for seminar work, etc. Hence initially the new type of school will have to be, cannot help being, only for restricted groups, made up of young people selected through competition or recommended by similar institutions.

The common school ought to correspond to the period represented today by the primary and secondary schools, reorganised not only as regards the content and the method of teaching, but also as regards the arrangement of the various phases of the educational process. The first, primary grade should not last longer than three or four years, and in addition to imparting the first "instrumental" notions of schooling – reading, writing, sums, geography, history – ought in particular to deal with an aspect of education that is now neglected – i.e. with "rights and duties", with the first notions of the State and society as primordial elements of a new conception of the world which challenges the conceptions that are imparted by the various traditional social environments, i.e. those conceptions which can be termed folkloristic. The didactic problem is one of mitigating and rendering more fertile the dogmatic approach which must inevitably characterise these first years. The rest of the course should not last more than six years, so that by the age of fifteen or sixteen it should be possible to complete all the grades of the common school.

One may object that such a course is too exhausting because too rapid, if the aim is to attain in effect the results which the present organisation of the classical school aims at but does not attain. Yet the new organisation as a whole will have to contain within itself the general elements which in fact make the course too slow today, at least for a part of the pupils. Which are these elements? In a whole series of families, especially in the intellectual strata, the children find in their family life a preparation, a prolongation and a completion of school life; they "breathe in", as the expression goes, a whole quantity of notions and attitudes which facilitate the educational process properly speaking.

They already know and develop their knowledge of the literary language, i.e. the means of expression and of knowledge, which is technically superior to the means possessed by the average member of the school population between the ages of six and twelve. Thus city children, by the very fact of living in a city, have already absorbed by the age of six a quantity of notions and attitudes which make their school careers easier, more profitable, and more rapid. In the basic organisation of the common school, at least the essentials of these conditions must be created – not to speak of the fact, which goes without saying, that parallel to the common school a network of kindergartens and other institutions would develop, in which, even before the school age, children would be habituated to a certain collective discipline and acquire pre-scholastic notions and attitudes. In fact, the common school should be organised like a college, with a collective life by day and by night, freed from the present forms of hypocritical and mechanical discipline; studies should be carried on collectively, with the assistance of the teachers and the best pupils, even during periods of so-called individual study, etc.

The fundamental problem is posed by that phase of the existing school career which is today represented by the *liceo*, and which today does not differ at all, as far as the kind of education is concerned, from the preceding grades – except by the abstract presumption of a greater intellectual and moral maturity of the pupil, matching his greater age and the experience he has already accumulated.

In fact between *liceo* and university, i.e. between the school properly speaking and life, there is now a jump, a real break in continuity, and not a rational passage from quantity (age) to quality. From an almost purely dogmatic education, in which learning by heart plays a great part, the pupil passes to the creative phase, the phase of autonomous, independent work.

From the school, where his studies are subjected to a discipline that is imposed and controlled by authority, the pupil passes on to a phase of study or of professional work in which intellectual self-discipline and moral independence are theoretically unlimited. And this happens immediately after the crisis of puberty, when the ardour of the instinctive and elementary passions has not yet resolved its struggle with the fetters of the character and of moral conscience which are in the process of being formed. Moreover, in Italy, where the principle of 'seminar' work is not widespread in the universities, this passage is even more brusque and mechanical.

By contrast, therefore, the last phase of the common school must be conceived and structured as the decisive phase, whose aim is to create the fundamental values of "humanism", the intellectual self-discipline and the moral independence which are necessary for subsequent specialisation – whether it be of a scientific character or of an immediately practical-productive character.

The study and learning of creative methods in science and in life must begin in this last phase of the school, and no longer be a monopoly of the university or be left to chance in practical life. This phase of the school must already contribute to developing the element of independent responsibility in each individual, must be a creative school. A distinction must be made between creative school and active school, even in the form given to the latter by the Dalton method.

The entire common school is an active school, although it is necessary to place limits on libertarian ideologies in this field and to stress with some energy the duty of the adult generations, i.e. of the State, to "mould" the new generations. The active school is still in its romantic phase, in which the elements of struggle against the mechanical and Jesuitical school have become unhealthily exaggerated – through a desire to distinguish themselves sharply from the latter, and for polemical reasons. It is necessary to enter the "classical", rational phase, and to find in the ends to be attained the natural source for developing the appropriate methods and forms.

The creative school is the culmination of the active school. In the first phase the aim is to discipline, hence also to level out – to obtain a certain kind of "conformism" which may be called "dynamic". In the creative phase, on the basis that has been achieved of "collectivisation" of the social type, the aim is to expand the personality – by now autonomous and responsible, but with a solid and homogeneous moral and social conscience. Thus creative school does not mean school of "inventors and discoverers"; it indicates a phase and a method of research and of knowledge, and not a predetermined "programme" with an obligation to originality and innovation at all costs. It indicates that learning takes place especially through a spontaneous and autonomous effort of the pupil, with the teacher only exercising a function of friendly guide – as happens or should happen in the university.

To discover a truth oneself, without external suggestions or assistance, is to create – even if the truth is an old one. It demonstrates a mastery of the method, and indicates that in any case one has entered the phase of intellectual maturity in which one may discover new truths. Hence in this phase the fundamental scholastic activity will be carried on in seminars, in libraries, in experimental laboratories; during it, the organic data will be collected for a professional orientation.

The advent of the common school means the beginning of new relations between intellectual and industrial work, not only in the school but in the whole of social life. The comprehensive principle will therefore be reflected in all the organisms of culture, transforming them and giving them a new content.

In Search Of The Educational Principle

In the old primary school, there used to be two elements in the educational formation of the children. They were taught the rudiments of natural science, and the idea of civic rights and duties. Scientific ideas were intended to insert the child into the *societas rerum*, the world of things, while lessons in rights and duties were intended to insert him into the State and into civil society. The scientific ideas the children learnt conflicted with the magical conception of the world and nature which they absorbed from an environment steeped in folklore; while the idea of civic rights and duties conflicted with tendencies towards individualistic and localistic barbarism – another dimension of folklore.

The school combated folklore, indeed every residue of traditional conceptions of the world. It taught a more modern outlook based essentially on an awareness of the simple and fundamental fact that there exist objective, intractable natural laws to which man must adapt himself if he is to master them in his turn – and that there exist social and state laws which are the product of human activity, which are established by men and can be altered by men in the interests of their collective development. These laws of the State and of society create that human order which historically best enables men to dominate the laws of nature, that is to say which most facilitates their *work*. For work is the specific mode by which man actively participates in natural life in order to transform and socialise it more and more deeply and extensively.

Thus one can say that the educational principle which was the basis of the old primary school was the idea of work. Human work cannot be realised in all its power of expansion and productivity without an exact and realistic knowledge of natural laws and without a legal order which organically regulates men's life in common. Men must respect this legal order through spontaneous assent, and not merely as an external imposition – it must be a necessity recognised and proposed to themselves as freedom, and not simply the result of coercion.

The idea and the fact of work was the educational principle latent in the primary school, since it is by means of work that the social and State order is introduced and identified within the natural order. The discovery that the relations between the social and natural orders are mediated by work, by man's theoretical and practical activity, creates the first elements of an intuition of the world free from all magic and superstition. It provides a basis for the subsequent development of an historical, dialectical conception of the world, which understands movement and change, which appreciates the sum of effort and sacrifice which the present has cost the past and which the future is costing the present, and which conceives the contemporary world as a synthesis of the past, of all past generations, which projects itself into the future. This was the real basis of the primary school.

Whether it yielded all its fruits, and whether the actual teachers were aware of the nature and philosophical content of their task, is another question. This requires an analysis of the degree of civic consciousness of the entire nation, of which the teaching body was merely an expression, and rather a poor expression – certainly not an *avant-garde*.

It is not entirely true that "instruction is something quite different from "education". An excessive emphasis on this distinction has been a serious error of idealist educationalists and its effects can already be seen in the school system as they have reorganised it. For instruction to be wholly distinct from education, the pupil would have to be pure passivity, a "mechanical receiver" of abstract notions – which is absurd and is anyway "abstractly" denied by the supporters of pure educativity precisely in their opposition to mere mechanistic instruction.

The "certain" becomes "true" in the child's consciousness. But the child's consciousness is not something "individual", it reflects the sector of civil society in which the child participates, and the social relations which are formed within his family, his neighbourhood, his village, etc.

The individual consciousness of the overwhelming majority of children reflects social and cultural relations which are different from and antagonistic to those which are represented in the school curricula: thus the "certain" of an advanced culture becomes "true" in the framework of a fossilised and anachronistic culture. There is no unity between school and life, and so there is no automatic unity between instruction and education.

In the school, the nexus between instruction and education can only be realised by the living work of the teacher. For this he must be aware of the contrast between the type of culture and society which he represents and the type of culture and society represented by his pupils, and conscious of his obligation to accelerate and regulate the child's formation in conformity with the former and in conflict with the latter. If the teaching body is not adequate and the nexus between instruction and education is dissolved, while the problem of teaching is conjured away by cardboard schemata exalting educativity, the teacher's work will as a result become yet more inadequate. We will have rhetorical schools, quite unserious, because the material solidity of what is "certain" will be missing, and what is "true" will be a truth only of words: that is to say, precisely, rhetoric.

This degeneration is even clearer in the secondary school, in the literature and philosophy syllabus. Previously, the pupils at least acquired a certain "baggage" or "equipment" of concrete facts. Now that the teacher must be specifically a philosopher and aesthete, the pupil does not bother with concrete facts and fills his head with formulae and words which usually mean nothing to him, and which are forgotten at once. It was right to struggle against the old school but reforming it was not so simple as it seemed.

The problem was not one of model curricula but of men, and not just of the men who are actually teachers themselves but of the entire social complex which they express. In reality a mediocre teacher may manage to see to it that his pupils become more *informed,* although he will not succeed in making them better educated; he can devote a scrupulous and bureaucratic conscientiousness to the mechanical part of teaching – and the pupil, if he has an active intelligence, will give an order of his own, with the aid of his social background, to the "baggage" he accumulates. With the new curricula, which coincide with a general lowering of the level of the teaching profession, there will no longer be any "baggage" to put in order.

The new curricula should have abolished examinations entirely; for to take an examination now must be fearfully more chancy than before. A date is always a date, whoever the examiner is, and a definition is always a definition. But an aesthetic judgment or a philosophical analysis?

The educational efficacy of the old Italian secondary school, as organised by the Casati Act, was not to be sought in its explicit aim as an "educative" system, but in the fact that its structure and its curriculum were the expression of a traditional mode of intellectual and moral life, of a cultural climate diffused throughout Italian society by ancient tradition. It was the fact that this climate and way of life were in their death-throes, and that the school had become cut off from life, which brought about the crisis in education.

A criticism of the curricula and disciplinary structure of the old system means less than nothing if one does not keep this situation in mind. Thus we come back to the truly active participation of the pupil in the school, which can only exist if the school is related to life. The more the new curricula nominally affirm and theorise the pupil's activity and working collaboration with the teacher, the more they are actually designed as if the pupil were purely passive.

In the old school the grammatical study of Latin and Greek, together with the study of their respective literatures and political histories, was an educational principle – for the humanistic ideal, symbolised by Athens and Rome, was diffused throughout society, and was an essential element of national life and culture. Even the mechanical character of the study of grammar was enlivened by this cultural perspective. Individual facts were not learnt for an immediate practical or professional end.

The end seemed disinterested, because the real interest was the interior development of personality, the formation of character by means of the absorption and assimilation of the whole cultural past of modern European civilisation. Pupils did not learn Latin and Greek in order to speak them, to become waiters, interpreters or commercial letter-writers. They learnt them in order to know at first hand the civilisation of Greece and of Rome – a civilisation that was a necessary precondition of our modern civilisation: in other words, they learnt them in order to be themselves and know themselves consciously.

Latin and Greek were learnt through their grammar, mechanically; but the accusation of formalism and aridity is very unjust and inappropriate. In education one is dealing with children in whom one has to inculcate certain habits of diligence, precision, poise, ability to concentrate on specific subjects, which cannot be acquired without the mechanical repetition of disciplined and methodical acts.

Would a scholar at the age of forty be able to sit for sixteen hours on end at his work-table if he had not, as a child, compulsorily, through mechanical coercion, acquired the appropriate psycho-physical habits? If one wishes to produce great scholars, one still has to start at this point and apply pressure throughout the educational system in order to succeed in creating those thousands or hundreds or even only dozens of scholars of the highest quality which are necessary to every civilisation.

Latin is learnt by analysing it down to its smallest parts – analysing it like a dead thing, it is true, but all analyses made by children can only be of dead things. Besides, one must not forget that the life of the Romans is a myth which to some extent has already interested the child and continues to interest him, so that in the dead object there is always present a greater living being. Thus, the language is dead, it is analysed as an inert object, as a corpse on the dissecting table, but it continually comes to life again in examples and in stories. Could one study Italian in the same way? Impossible.

No living language could be studied like Latin: it would be and *would seem* absurd. No child knows Latin when he starts to study it by these analytical methods. But a living language can be known and it would be enough for a single child to know it, and the spell would be broken: everybody would be off to the Berlitz school at once. Latin appears to the imagination as a myth, even for the teacher. One does not study Latin in order to learn the language.

For a long time, as a result of a cultural and scholarly tradition whose origin and development one might investigate, Latin has been studied as an element in an ideal curriculum, an element which combines and satisfies a whole series of pedagogic and psychological requirements. It has been studied in order to accustom children to studying in a specific manner, and to analysing an historical body which can be treated as a corpse which returns continually to life; in order to accustom them to reason, to think abstractly and schematically while remaining able to plunge back from abstraction into real and immediate life, to see in each fact or datum what is general and what is particular, to distinguish the concept from the specific instance.

For what after all is the educational significance of the constant comparison between Latin and the language one speaks? It involves the distinction and the identification of words and concepts; suggests the whole of formal logic, from the contradiction between opposites to the analysis of distincts; reveals the historical movement of the entire language, modified through time, developing and not static. In the eight years of *ginnasio* and *liceo* the entire history of the real language is studied after it has first been photographed in one abstract moment in the form of grammar. It is studied from Ennius right up to Phaedrus and the Christian writers in Latin: an historical process is analysed from its source until its death in time – or seeming death, since we know that Italian, with which Latin is continually contrasted in school, is modern Latin. Not only the grammar of a certain epoch or its vocabulary are studied, but also, for comparison, the grammar and the vocabulary of each individual author and the meaning of each term in each particular stylistic "period".

Thus the child discovers that the grammar and the vocabulary of Phaedrus are not those of Cicero, nor those of Plautus, nor of Lactantius or Tertullian, and that the same nexus of sounds does not have the same meaning in different periods and for different authors. Latin and Italian are continually compared; but each word is a concept, a symbol, which takes on different shades of meaning according to the period and the writer in each of the two languages under comparison.

The child studies the literary history of the books written in that language, the political history, the achievements of the men who spoke that language. His education is determined by the whole of this organic complex, by the fact that he has followed that itinerary, if only in a purely literal sense, he has passed through those various stages, etc. He has plunged into history and acquired a historicising understanding of the world and of life, which becomes a second – nearly spontaneous – nature, since it is not inculcated pedantically with an openly educational intention. These studies educated without an explicitly declared aim of doing so, with a minimal "educative" intervention on the part of the teacher: they educated because they gave instruction. Logical, artistic, psychological experience was gained unawares, without a continual self-consciousness.

Above all a profound "synthetic", philosophical experience was gained, of an actual historical development. This does not mean – it would be stupid to think so – that Latin and Greek, as such, have intrinsically thaumaturgical qualities in the educational field. It is the whole cultural tradition, which also and particularly lives outside the school, which in a given ambience produces such results. In any case one can see today, with the changes in the traditional idea of culture, the way in which the school is in crisis and with it the study of Latin and Greek.

It will be necessary to replace Latin and Greek as the fulcrum of the formative school, and they will be replaced. But it will not be easy to deploy the new subject or subjects in a didactic form which gives equivalent results in terms of education and general personality-formation, from early childhood to the threshold of the adult choice of career. For in this period what is learnt, or the greater part of it, must be – or appear to the pupils to be – disinterested, i.e. not have immediate or too immediate practical purposes. It must be formative, while being "instructive" – in other words rich in concrete facts.

In the present school, the profound crisis in the traditional culture and its conception of life and of man has resulted in a progressive degeneration. Schools of the vocational type, i.e. those designed to satisfy immediate, practical interests, are beginning to predominate over the formative school, which is not immediately "interested". The most paradoxical aspect of it all is that this new type of school appears and is advocated as being democratic, while in fact it is destined not merely to perpetuate social differences but to crystallise them in Chinese complexities.

The traditional school was oligarchic because it was intended for the new generation of the ruling class, destined to rule in its turn: but it was not oligarchic in its mode of teaching. It is not the fact that the pupils learn how to rule there, nor the fact that it tends to produce gifted men, which gives a particular type of school its social character. This social character is determined by the fact that each social group has its own type of school, intended to perpetuate a specific traditional function, ruling or subordinate. If one wishes to break this pattern one needs, instead of multiplying and grading different types of vocational school, to create a single type of formative school which would take the child up to the threshold of his choice of job, forming him during this time as a person capable of thinking, studying, and ruling – or controlling those who rule.

The multiplication of types of vocational school thus perpetuate traditional social differences; but since, within these differences, it tends to encourage internal diversification, it gives the impression of being democratic in tendency. The labourer can become a skilled worker, for instance, the peasant a surveyor or petty agronomist. But democracy, by definition, cannot mean merely that an unskilled worker can become skilled. It must mean that every "citizen" can "govern" and that society places him, even if only abstractly, in a general condition to achieve this.

Political democracy tends towards a coincidence of the rulers and the ruled, ensuring for each non-ruler a free training in the skills and general technical preparation necessary to that end. But the type of school which is now developing as the school for the people does not tend even to keep up this illusion. For it is organised ever more fully in such a way as to restrict recruitment to the technically qualified governing stratum, in a social and political context which makes it increasingly difficult for "personal initiative" to acquire such skills and technical-political preparation. Thus we are really going back to a division into juridically fixed and crystallised estates rather than moving towards the transcendence of class divisions.

The multiplication of vocational schools which specialise increasingly from the very beginning of the child's educational career is one of the most notable manifestations of this tendency. It is noticeable that the new pedagogy has concentrated its fire on "dogmatism" in the field of instruction and the learning of concrete facts – i.e. precisely in the field in which a certain dogmatism is practically indispensable and can be reabsorbed and dissolved only in the whole cycle of the educational process.

On the other hand, it has been forced to accept the introduction of dogmatism *par excellence* in the field of religious thought, with the result that the whole history of philosophy is now implicitly seen as a succession of ravings and delusions. In the philosophy course, the new curriculum impoverishes the teaching and in practice lowers its level – in spite of seeming very rational and fine, fine as any utopia. The traditional descriptive philosophy, backed by a course in the history of philosophy and by the reading of a certain number of philosophers, in practice seems the best thing.

Descriptive, definitional philosophy may be a dogmatic abstraction, just as grammar and mathematics are, but it is an educational and didactive [sic] necessity. "One equals one" is an abstraction, but it leads nobody to think that one fly equals one elephant. The rules of formal logic are abstractions of the same kind, they are like the grammar of normal thought; but they still need to be studied, since they are not something innate, but have to be acquired through work and reflection. The new curriculum presupposes that formal logic is something you already possess when you think, but does not explain how it is to be acquired, so that in practice it is assumed to be innate.

Formal logic is like grammar: it is assimilated in a "living" way even if the actual learning process has been necessarily schematic and abstract. For the learner is not a passive and mechanical recipient, a gramophone record – even if the liturgical conformity of examinations sometimes makes him appear so. The relation between these educational forms and the child's psychology is always active and creative, just as the relation of the worker to his tools is active and creative. A calibre is likewise a complex of abstractions, but without calibration it is not possible to produce real objects – real objects which are social relations, and which implicitly embody ideas.

The child who sweats at *Barbara, Baraliplon* is certainly performing a tiring task, and it is important that he does only what is absolutely necessary and no more. But it is also true that it will always be an effort to learn physical self-discipline and self-control; the pupil has, in effect, to undergo, a psycho-physical training. Many people have to be persuaded that studying too is a job, and a very tiring one, with its own particular apprenticeship – involving muscles and nerves as well as intellect. It is a process of adaptation, a habit acquired with effort, tedium and even suffering. Wider participation in secondary education brings with it a tendency to ease off the discipline of studies, and to ask for "relaxations".

Many even think that the difficulties of learning are artificial, since they are accustomed to think only of manual work as sweat and toil. The question is a complex one. Undoubtedly the child of a traditionally intellectual family acquires this psycho-physical adaptation more easily. Before he ever enters the class-room he has numerous advantages over his comrades, and is already in possession of attitudes learned from his family environment: he concentrates more easily, since he is used to "sitting still", etc.

Similarly, the son of a city worker suffers less when he goes to work in a factory than does a peasant's child or a young peasant already formed by country life. This is why many people think that the difficulty of study conceals some "trick" which handicaps them – that is, when they do not simply believe that they are stupid by nature.

They see the "gentleman"– and for many, especially in the country, "gentleman" means intellectual – complete, speedily and with apparent ease, work which costs their sons tears and blood, and they think there is a "trick". In the future, these questions may become extremely acute and it will be necessary to resist the tendency to render easy that which cannot become easy without being distorted. If our aim is to produce a new stratum of intellectuals, including those capable of the highest degree of specialisation, from a social group which has not traditionally developed the appropriate attitudes, then we have unprecedented difficulties to overcome.

3

Philosophy of Technology and Education

In this brief discussion is to make explicit the ontologies undergirding the various ways in which technology is discussed in a representative sampling of the contemporary critical literature in education, and by doing so to offer an idiom for discussing a set of issues both pressing yet beset by confusion. When I say "critical" I mean to include those discussions with some reflective component, that is, those at least on some level addressing what technology is in its essence and how, in an ethical sense, educators ought to approach it.

By doing this I mean to exclude from explicit consideration the vast majority of published work on educational technology, namely, narrow technical discussions of how to use particular devices, as well as those restricted to studying the effects of an educational tool or technique in some setting or other. These technical discussions, by and large, contain no account of technology as such, nor do they offer anything of significant prescriptive import.

Like a manufacturer's guide on how to install and troubleshoot a washing machine, such discussions — quite sensibly, given their purpose — assume as unproblematic the end to which the tool is put while also bracketing the most basic questions about what constitutes a machine for washing, whether or not we ought to engage in washing at all, and what, in the end, is washing itself.

My preliminary claim is that most all theoretical accounts of technology — educational or otherwise — may be characterised as adhering in varying degrees to what I will call a *structural ambiguity of common sense*. Our common sense intuitions regarding technological phenomena are, as Heidegger would say, "proximally and for the most part" beset with a deep and internal contradiction. This contradiction amounts to an underlying ambiguity because it represents an oscillating ambivalence in our everyday practices and attitudes.

On the one hand, we experience tools as things that we *use*; we regard them as morally neutral in the sense that they seem to await a human purpose to animate them with moral life. Someone or other is always at the helm, so it seems, and that person or group of persons decides through some willful act the uses to which the tool is put.

On the other hand, however, is an equally prevalent common sense intuition, especially since the advent in this century of science-based "high-tech." In our homes, workplaces and even at play, we are awash in a veritable flood tide of tools ever-more refined and complex. As Don Ihde has put it, our lifeworld has become irrevocably "technologically textured." We may decide which brand or type of telephone to buy, but if we can afford it almost none of us must first determine whether or not to have one at all. It is not up to me personally — or to anyone in particular — whether or not computers are increasingly necessary to mediate everyday human interactions. I become acquainted with the device at work, at home, or in school in order to "keep up."

The other side of the same coin, though, is that technology is perhaps just as commonly regarded as anything-but liberating, as a momentary nuisance or even as a malicious force driven by its own imperatives. We publicly bemoan the "influence" of television on our children, speak of our appliances as "quitting out on us," and fear losing our jobs to robots and teaching machines. The point is that whether we fear and loath it, look toward it for liberation, or merely "go along" with it and allow it to shape our lives, there is an important sense in which we endow it with a certain agency and act as if *it* does things in the world, things that we must react to in various ways. Technologies are thus often regarded as the bearers of intentions and are encountered via what Daniel Dennett calls the "intentional stance".

But all the while we go on *using* tools and techniques, for it — still, somehow — seems that they are simply at mine or someone's service. Hence, the relevant intuitions conflict, and until they are sorted out reflectively, our overall attitude is justly characterised as profoundly ambiguous.

Most of the literature on technology and education reflects this underlying ambiguity. To borrow from the schema Albert Borgmann uses to classify theories of technology generally, the relevant educational literature may be classified into two main groups, corresponding to the abovementioned oscillating poles of common sense and the ontologies implicit in them: "substantive" and "instrumental." In the context of contemporary educational research, important distinctions must be made within both categories. These subdivisions are mine, and reflect the basic *attitudes* taken toward technology in each case, running roughly along the lines of "pro" and "anti."

Substantive theories of technology stem from the common sense intuition that technology is to a great extent an autonomous force, one that shapes us much more than we shape it. It is often called "technological determinism," in the sense that it is technology itself that does the determining of most, if not all, spheres of human activity.

The most famous and perhaps the most uncompromising proponent of substantivism is the French theologian and sociologist Jacques Ellul, who regarded *la technique* as an all-embracing and evil power that has come to enslave all our endeavors, from art and politics to education. The most comprehensive statement of this view in educational theory is provided by C. A. Bowers, who holds that "the technological mindset" — a "unique configuration of thought and social practice that emerged in the West over the last two to three hundred years" — is now so deeply-seated in our culture that it determines most every aspect of contemporary pedagogical practice.

This technological mindset is so pervasive that most every major school reform movement is haplessly contained within it, doomed merely to advance "its" cause. For Bowers, a radical pedagogy worthy of the name must, somehow, step outside this mindset in order to recover — to even imagine — what, for him, would constitute a truly human vision of education. A more subtle version of this view derives from the Frankfurt School and describes the root cause of technology's dominance as a creeping "instrumental reason," a *sub rasa* ideology that increasingly dominates all forms of social and personal life by subverting the legitimacy of public discussion concerning the *ends* of human activity, thereby restricting it to talk about *means*.

Substantive theories of technology, however, invite a radicalism of a very different sort. This group, which I will call the proponents of a "radical instructional design" (RID) theory, might also with justice be labeled "computer romanticists." On the whole, these pro-technology substantivists hold that technology is the key to better schools and better education; it can and will break down traditional barriers to effective and successful school reform. If we humbly labor in the vineyard of instructional programming, following wherever innovation leads, we cannot go astray. As one of these high-tech Jeremiads exhorts: "Some can regret the change, but they cannot reverse it; and others..can welcome it and work to fulfill it."

One of this position's most savvy proponents, Robert Heinich, articulates a paradigm wherein instructional technology is no longer considered part of education and consequently ought to strike out on its own. The mission of preparing teachers informing the institutional life of colleges of education unduly constrains the RID theorist's possibilities. Why think, Heinich challenges, that the best we can do is what teachers — even the very best of them — have done? RID theorists should divorce themselves from schools of education and marry themselves to interdisciplinary technology units on campuses everywhere, realising a paradigmatic and institutional reversal whereby the technologists themselves — unfettered by their erstwhile spouses' teacher-centered inhibitions — pursue all manner of high-tech pleasures.

The normative core of RID theory, however, is by no means restricted to academia, but is widely represented in the recent round of popular books on educational reform. Armed with the conviction that "[t]echnology is the most purely human of humanity's features, and it is the driving force of human society," Lewis Perelman predicts in his book *School's Out* that "the nations that stop trying to "reform" their education and training institutions and choose instead to totally replace them with a brand-new, high-tech learning system will be the world's economic powerhouses through the twenty-first century." Mass schooling as we know it will end in the wake of recent technological innovation. We really have no choice: we either go along and get out front, or we lose our economic competitiveness and decline as a nation.

Neither worshipful nor fearful, the second major category, instrumentalism, builds upon the founding common sense intuition that technologies are merely tools that human beings use in order to achieve the purposes we assign to them. Powerful proof for this is that technologies have always been and are everywhere part of the human story to extend the capacities of given individuals or cultures, for good or ill. The bumpersticker slogan "guns don't kill people, people kill people" hits the mark. Individual or collective human agency is the locus of all valuation and therefore not the device itself, but its causal ensconcement in a social context is the proper target for inquiry.

In education, instrumentalism may be described as pro-technology when it is relatively sanguine about the beneficial uses to which various technologies can be put. A celebrated exponent of this view is Seymour Papert, developer of the widely-used LOGO computer programming language. In his book *Mindstorms* and elsewhere, Papert argues that children learning to program in LOGO, can develop "powerful ideas" for problem-solving that can, he contends, transfer to many other areas of life:

> I have invented ways to take educational advantage of the opportunities to master the art of *deliberately* thinking like a computer, according, for example, to the stereotype of a computer program that proceeds in a step-by-step literal, mechanical fashion...What is most important in this is that through these experiences the children would be serving their apprenticeships as epistemologists, that is to say learning to think articulately about thinking.

Pace some of his critics, however, Papert is no substantivist; he does not believe that the pedagogical benefit of LOGO resides in what it *does to* children, but rather in the kind of control it requires children to take over it. Children should encounter computers in the classroom as "objects to think with," and he argues explicitly against what he calls "technocentric thinking." One must attend to the culture suffusing the classroom first, and on that basis train teachers to use classroom technologies properly.

Instrumentalism is anti-technology insofar as it considers present usage to be overwhelmingly driven by morally suspect motives; technology is problematic, but *only as it is currently employed*. Technology's liberatory potential awaits societal change, usually of fairly major proportions. Most anti-technology instrumentalism in education is Marxist in provenance and takes the form of socio-political critique. Following Andrew Feenberg's philosophical statement of this general position, it might be called a "critical theory of technology" (CTT).

CTT typically regards all other views of technology as so many smokescreens behind which certain social groups, usually identified as the patriarchy, the capitalists, or some other cultural elite, advance their agendas of domination. A focus on the tools themselves aids in maintaining privilege by deflecting critical scrutiny away from the real motive forces of society, the economy and those who control it.

In educational theory, two more or less distinct levels of CTT may be identified. First-level CTT corresponds to a straightforwardly unreconstructed, Marxist analysis. Although I know of no comprehensive statement of first-level CTT in education, Bowles's and Gintis's *Schooling in Capitalist America* suggests that technology, like schooling, essentially functions as a superstructural variable dependent upon the economic base of society and those who control it. And while these authors claim to allow for a certain amount of dialectical interplay between base and superstructure, they nevertheless counsel unequivocally that technology itself is mostly beside the point: "If meaningful educational reform requires a transformation of production relations, as we believe, we must begin by creating a new social structure, not a new technology."

One does not liberate today's oppressive classroom by altering its physical structure, but rather by teaching liberating things for tomorrow's liberated society. Second-level CTT shares with the Marxist view the contention that at present technology serves elite groups and that the task of a radical pedagogy is to uncover how and why this happens. But it differs markedly by not regarding technology as a *neutral* tool in the service of hegemonic power; technology is non-neutral in the sense that, as it is currently constituted, it has demonstrably prejudicial *effects* and, therefore, works to privilege some groups at the expense of others. Elites not only use technology as a club, but use it also to conceal that there is any clubbing going on at all. It provides a perfect weapon — effective yet invisible. And the more value-neutral we regard it, the more invisible it becomes.

Consider ostensibly innocuous notions such as "technological" or "computer literacy." What harm could come from learning to use computers? As it turns out, a great deal: to take just one example, the aim of educating for high-tech fosters a climate of bogus credentialing providing the ideological cover for the disenfranchisement of certain groups.

Yesterday's reading test for custodians is today's "computer experience" for all types of employment. Yet, there are ample grounds to challenge, as Douglas Noble has, the idea that on the whole work in a high-tech society requires any substantive notion of "technological literacy" at all. Given the "user-friendly" trajectory of business machines and the deskilling and further fragmentation of labor in the wake of automation, in the vast majority of cases, working "in contact" with high-tech does not really demand knowing anything much about it. The Burger King cashier indeed "works with" high-tech cash registers, but this hardly entails a higher degree of knowledge about technology. If anything, it demands *less*. Such examples —

and they are legion — add evidence that the drive toward technological literacy seems not to serve any legitimate economic need. Rather, some other agenda, a deep ideological one serving certain identifiable interests, must be driving it. It is not as simple as "change society and technology will follow," for the latter has become too thoroughly interwoven with the former.

As convincing as second-level CTT may sound, however, and as much as it promises to promote what Maxine Greene once called "wide-awakeness" regarding our technological surroundings, as a pedagogy the theory harbors significant dangers. These have mostly to do with this outlook's potential for slippage into a more or less indoctrinating stance. Consistently framing one's role in the classroom as one of unmasking power relations implies that one possesses an unassailable social ontology that one must educate students "up" to.

As one liberates in the name of truth, then, one tends also to disable a more open-ended and, in my view, richer pedagogy — one that remains open to differing interpretations, even ones that challenge at the deepest levels. For instance, one must surely allow for the sorts of dialogical interactions described so well by, among others, Nick Burbules and Sophie Haroutunian-Gordon, where entering into a dialogue while presupposing the correct answer tends to limit the experience.

At times, social critique is appropriate in the classroom, just as is presupposing the right answer is, but not as an overriding ideal; one may feel oneself to possess the truth about important and pressing matters, but the mere transmission of that truth represents a poor notion of what education can be. As I have tried to indicate, the ontologies implicit in instrumentalism and substantivism locate both on opposite ends of the ambiguous spectrum of our culture's common sense. And although it belongs to a much larger work to detail the strengths and weaknesses of each position, certain patterns may already be discerned.

A proper theory of technology in education ought, I think, to take advantage of both position's strengths: the substantive conviction that technology can, in a manner of speaking, take on a life of its own, as well as the instrumentalist impulse to contextualise it within the intentions and effects it mediates. But such a theory will also avoid the excesses and lacunae of the two views: the take it or leave it *en bloc* blackmail of substantivism, and instrumentalism's blinding zeal to name *the* one and only force behind it all. A proper theory of technology in education, then, must incorporate the strengths while avoiding their corrupted counterparts.

Space permits only a hint at the contours of such a theory. As I have argued at length elsewhere, some clues are supplied in the thought of Dewey and early Heidegger. One of the most peculiar properties of technology, both thinkers hold, is that insofar as a tool really functions *as a tool*, it, in a manner of speaking, hides itself in its function, or as Heidegger puts it, it "withdraws" from proximal view. Dewey writes:

> A tool is a particular thing, but it is more than a particular thing, since it is a thing in which a connection, a sequential bond of nature is embodied. It possesses an objective relation as its own defining property. Its perception as well as its actual use takes the mind to other things.

Heidegger's celebrated existential analysis of hammering illustrates this point well. As I hammer-along in order to, say, build my daughter a dollhouse, my project is given significance by the end in view, namely, the dollhouse, making my daughter happy, saving some money by not having to purchase one, and so on. In a sense, I am lost for a time in a miniature world of functional relations, the relays being connected via these "in-order-to's."

For present purposes, the point is that the materiality of the hammer recedes from view in all of this, but only to reveal a dynamic world of meaningful involvements, ever expanding and contracting. I strive to make my daughter happy because being a father demands it, as does my place within the family. Perhaps, as I hammer-along building the dollhouse I am driven by guilt for having forgotten her birthday last week, or by fear that my wife may castigate me for not attending to the child more often.

Ultimately, according to Heidegger, if a resolute questioning pursues these in-order-to's far enough, they lead to a deeper understanding of one's own nature as a finite being, and they highlight what one cares most deeply for. In Heidegger's language, such radical questioning fore-grounds one's "ownmost possibilities for Being." However far down this road I may travel, though, the activity of hammering-along is necessarily ensconced in a web of involvements whose significance is limited only by my capacity, perhaps my courage, for self-reflection.

Technologies, then, in this case even simple ones, if they are encountered in the proper way, can catalyse self-understanding unto unforeseen depths — even as they simultaneously conceal from view significant aspects of one's environing world. This double aspect of technology — both concealing and revealing — is the rock of insight upon which to build not only descriptions of technology in education, but also the beginnings of a normative theory that decisively links technology with educational experience.

If one grants that education, as opposed to training, indoctrination and the like, has much more to do with revealing worlds of involvement than it does with closing them off, one may generate an imperative for educators to orient themselves toward technology such that the latter are allowed to reveal worlds in as open-ended a manner as possible. The substantive conviction that technology is, in a way, telic, thereby unites with the instrumentalist caveat that looking at the tool itself at the expense of its contextuality is misguided.

As philosophers, we can help to provide a more compelling vocabulary for faulting, say, a curriculum too laden with software tutorial programs on the grounds that, while they may well effectively disclose how to accomplish certain tasks, the overall effect may be to shut out much, much more — largely by concealing the predetermined pathways along which such programs must run.

One may learn to factor quadratic equations like a pro while also "learning" that education itself is accumulating information, has end-points, and is generally something to be gotten over with. What is wrong here is not the learning of useful information *per se*, but that one's ability to initiate learning in wider and alien contexts withers away; no sum of microworlds can match the dynamic, ever-expanding and edifying capacity to go on revealing one's own lifeworld. Technological devices are not foes here but they do constitute *problems*. Our task as educators is to make them into enabling ones.

Exploring the Intellectual Foundation of Technology Education

Since the colonial era, Western institutionalised education increasingly has been put into the service of civilisation-building by seeking to advance practical industrial needs. But education has not always had such an explicitly economic orientation. In the early Middle Ages, the purpose of education was conceived of primarily in terms of advancing spiritual well-being, Church- or State-sponsored occupations, and socially "proper" forms of knowledge. Only as European nations embarked upon colonial expansion did education begin to become associated with citizenship, nation-building, practical and secular knowledge, and the advancement of a technological civilisation and private enterprise. As a result, since the eighteenth century, this second school of educational thought has become increasingly dominant in educational thought and practice.

Our contemporary understanding of science and technology education owes much to Enlightenment-based assumptions on the nature of civilisational advancement. These assumptions are illustrated in the writings of formative educational thinkers during the eighteenth and nineteenth centuries, especially the works of Antoine-Nicholas de Condorcet and John Dewey.

In examining their beliefs, I am not seeking to merely provide only an overview of educational thought but to bring into question certain fundamental assumptions embedded in the historical development of technology education. Although I acknowledge the theme of "education for citizenship" as an Enlightenment ideal that helped to generate mass education, I am more concerned with exploring the validity of using technological advancement as a benchmark of civilisational progress—an ideological belief that continues to be implicated within non-critical approaches to technology education. Put another way, I see a problematic conceptual linkage between technology, education, civilisation-building, industrial growth, and human purpose.

Education, Technology, and Condorcet

Throughout the Middle Ages, the Renaissance, and the Reformation, nearly all technological innovations took place on an individual craft basis; knowledge was transferred from generation to generation by apprenticeship. Significant technological advancements, such as the clock, the horizontal axle windmill, gigantic

Gothic cathedrals, the printing press, and better guns and ships, were being developed outside of the universities. But these advancements, by themselves, did not cause Europeans to rethink their then-dominant understanding of human purpose in relation to spiritual perfection. Nor did the outward expansion of the market economy, which has frequently been identified as the most significant force leading to the Industrial Revolution, cause Europeans to rethink their lofty status.

The growth of the market economy is often tied closely to the growth of secular institutions, government bureaucracies, the availability of raw materials, and early trade with, later exploitation of, non-Western societies. All of these elements, it has been argued, somehow worked together to convince Europeans of the merits of industrialisation; that the same development did not occur outside of Europe appears to merely reinforce this perspective. What is generally overlooked, however, is how the Europeans' growing knowledge of distant cultures helped to change their worldview of themselves and their relation to the physical world and other cultures. The Enlightenment was one result of this new orientation; another was the Industrial Revolution; and still another was a growing emphasis on the merits of technology education.

Throughout the seventeenth and eighteenth centuries, higher education in Europe and the emerging power of the United States retained a classical format. The first broadly based engineering university would not be founded until the Ecole Polytechnique was established in France in 1794. During these two centuries, however, Europeans increased their trade and colonial interactions with less technologically advanced cultures, and began to recognise their own cultural superiority in terms of technological achievements. As a result, a fundamental reorientation was beginning to take place concerning the role of technology and the purpose of education in European society.

The French Enlightenment of the eighteenth century built upon the ideas of Francis Bacon and his contemporaries. The Enlightenment was a rejection of both realism and the idea that the greatness of humankind rested in ancient knowledge. While all Enlightenment thinkers believed in certain basic principles, namely, the inherent goodness of humankind, the right to a democratic society, and that civilisation must advance through technological progress to a more advanced state of being, only Jean-Jacques Rousseau and Antoine-Nicholas de Condorcet focused on education to any degree, and Condorcet was arguably the more thorough and influential of the two.

During mid-eighteenth century France, education was targeted at the elite, dominated by the Church, and unavailable for most of the population. The universities of France, as in most of Europe, still regarded law, medicine, and theology as the only relevant disciplines in the classical study framework; the Catholic Church and its cohort the French monarchy retained an ever-weakening hegemony in a declining and battle-weary French state.

Great Britain was becoming a formidable power in Europe, and would further enhance its position by giving birth to the Industrial Revolution in the middle of the century. On the other hand, late-eighteenth century France, like Germany and the United States, was becoming increasingly "backward" by comparison, and education was beginning to be seen as a way to catch up with the British. In 1791-92, Condorcet presented a plan for a universal form of education to the French Legislative Assembly, proposing a "complete national system of secular schools to provide equal opportunity for all children, free, compulsory and universal". His plan was rejected at the time, but he put in place germinal ideas for mass education that later would be used in educational planning in France, Germany, and the United States.

Condorcet, like other Enlightenment thinkers, believed that there was no limit to the learning capabilities of the human mind and that progress meant the perfection of science and technology. He also believed that all "men" are products of nature, with equal rights bestowed upon them to the moral, practical, and intellectual pursuits of reason. Human progress, in his view, rested on an individual's ability to educate and refine himself in those three areas of human action. Since colonisation had proven the "superiority" of Western technology, such knowledge should be spread to all through the liberating power of education.

In 1793, Condorcet wrote his great essay, *Sketch for a Historical Picture of the Progress of the Human Mind*; in it, he argued that the human mind must progress from irrationality to rationality, from superstition to reason, from pre-scientific thought to scientific enlightenment. Progress constitutes ten stages of human development, or "civilisation." The first stage of civilisation is the "savage" tribe, dependent on hunting, fishing, crude weapons, and simple utensils, with little government bureaucracy and only a "small number of moral ideas". Condorcet viewed the African tribe as representative of this first stage of human development, while he placed European-based societies further up the evolutionary ladder:

> Will all nations one day attain that state of civilisation which the most enlightened, the freest and the least burdened by prejudices, such as the French and Anglo-Americans, have attained already? Will the vast gulf that separates these peoples from the slavery of nations under the rule of monarchs, from the barbarism of African tribes, from the ignorances of savages, little by little disappear?

For Condorcet, as a culture moves from one stage to the next, it develops more advanced technologies and bureaucratic political systems, and exhibits more personal freedoms and democratic principles.

Condorcet's tenth stage of civilisation, the last and the greatest, is marked by liberty, equality, democracy and universal education for all. Of all these social developments, education is the most significant to Condorcet because it is the key to all forms of human progress: "With greater equality of education there will be greater equality in industry and so in wealth; equality in wealth necessarily leads to equality in education: and equality between nations and equality within a single nation are mutually dependent". Thus, a "well directed system of education" will result in "progress" in its most basic form and "the absolute perfection of the human race". Through education, the citizen of the masses might, among other things, be taught to manage their own households, to know their rights and to exercise those rights, to be empowered in the face of those who possess authority, to overcome ignorant prejudices, to use reason to overcome superstition, and to advance the technological arts. Furthermore, Condorcet recognised the need for a linkage between science and the technological arts in education:

> If we turn now to the arts, whose theory depends on [the] sciences, we shall find that their progress depending as it does on that of theory, can have no other limits; that the procedures of the different arts can be perfected and simplified in the same way as the methods of the sciences; new instruments, machines and looms can add to man's strength and can improve at once the quality and the accuracy of his productions, and can diminish the time and labour that has to be expended on them. The obstacles still in the way of this progress will disappear, accidents will be foreseen and prevented, the insanitary conditions that are due either to the work itself or the climate will be eliminated.

Given this faith in technology, Condorcet not surprisingly blended his understanding of education, technological progress, and reason with morality and happiness. Human reason and logic, which always work for the betterment of humankind, are responsible for keeping technological development on track. Although technological development might have limits, human reason will solve those problems:

> But even if we agree that the limit will one day arrive, nothing follows from it that is in the least alarming as far as either the happiness of the human race or its indefinite perfectibility is concerned;..we can assume that by then men will know that, if they have a duty towards those not yet born, that duty is not to give them existence but to give them happiness; their aim should be to promote the general welfare of the human race or of the society in which they live or of the family to which they belong, rather than foolishly to encumber the world with useless and wretched beings.

Thus, Condorcet predicted that reason would somehow progress far enough to provide the moral grounding necessary to avoiding overpopulating the world with "useless and wretched beings." Progress, reason, science, technology, and knowledge would collapse into one unified, determining force, since these are the foundations for morality.

Finally, while Condorcet condemned the ignorant prejudices of his day, what he called the "murderous contempt for men of another colour or creed," he was a firm proponent of the civilising mission of the West. He believed that the Europeans had a duty to civilise those "savage nations who still inhabit vast tracts of land". European missionaries and their "superstitions," he predicted, would disappear, as would the existing practices of trade and colonialism for greed and profit. Instead, enlightened, newly appointed European trade representatives would be assigned to colonial outposts to act as "liberators" to the uncivilised lands of the world; teachers to educate the ignorant:

> These vast lands are inhabited partly by large tribes who need assistance from us to become civilised, who wait only to find brothers amongst the European nations to become their friends and pupils; partly by races oppressed by sacred despots or dull-witted conquerors, and who for so many centuries have cried out to be liberated; partly by tribes living in a condition of almost total savagery in a climate whose harshness repels the sweet blessings of civilisation and deters those who would teach them its benefits; and finally, by conquering hordes who know no other law but force, no other profession but piracy. The progress of these two last classes of people will be slower and stormier; and perhaps it will even be that, reduced in number as they are driven back by civilised nations, they will finally disappear imperceptibly before them or merge into them.

Cloaked in Condorcet's colorful prose, the preceding passage advances the notion of European "civilised" cultural superiority. And, although Condorcet condemned the "sacred despots or dull-witted conquerors" of the "oppressed" tribal cultures, he failed to acknowledge the impact of European tyrants. Ironically, the average European peasant was arguably no more liberated than the tribal cultures he criticised.

Condorcet's text was published and widely read after his death in 1794, and his ideas began to be put into practice in the early nineteenth century. But the Enlightenment emerged at a violent time in French and European history, and Condorcet himself was imprisoned as an aristocrat during the French Revolution and died shortly thereafter. Furthermore, the Catholic and Protestant Churches remained powerful stabilising forces well beyond the Enlightenment and into the nineteenth century. Thus, although Condorcet and the other Enlightenment thinkers had only a minor immediate impact on education in Europe, they planted important seeds of change that would ultimately transform the theory and practice of European and American institutionalised education.

Development of Technology education in the United States

The model for what can now be called "mass" education was put into place by the four Western modernising powers of the last two centuries: Great Britain, France, Germany, and the United States. The educational systems developed by these nations helped them to realise Condorcet's vision of education, that is, mass education with a technological orientation.

Although several factors played a role in the emergence of technology education—the development of the nation-state, the expansion of the market economy, the weakness of the Catholic Church, and other tangible factors—the Enlightenment represented a more crucial repositioning of civilisational advancement. Viewed in these terms, the Industrial Revolution was both a practical manifestation of this changing orientation and a foundational moment in history which helped stimulate other nations to modernise. To illustrate these assertions, I will consider some key points in the development of technology education in the United States in the post-Enlightenment era.

Although the United States is more heavily endowed with natural resources than any of its European counterparts, its ascent to economic superpower over the last century owes much to the expansion of technology education, particularly at the university level. Since the American Revolution of 1776, one of the most dominant and recurrent themes in American educational philosophy has been the motif of Condorcet's concept of "education for citizenship," or education as the *right* of the people.

Prominent educational historian R. Freeman Butts notes, "One of the most far-reaching results of Enlightenment theories of education was the development of education for citizenship". Owing much to

Enlightenment thought, this theme has also been linked to other Enlightenment ideals, such as the value of natural science, progress, and technological advancement.

From its beginnings, unlike the German version of education as "enlightenment from above," educational practice in the United States exemplified the principle of "enlightenment from below"—the establishment of a universal, free, and compulsory education program under the control of public organisations. Following the American Revolution, Thomas Jefferson, a former ambassador to France sympathetic to early French Enlightenment thought, became the most formidable spokesperson for a state-supported free and universal educational system, and science was one key component of his proposed educational curriculum.

As a starting point, Jefferson introduced his plan to the Virginia legislature in 1779, where, just as Condorcet would later experience in France, it failed to receive enough votes for approval. Subsequently, American education would remain in the hands of private parties, primarily the Church, until well into the nineteenth century. But Jefferson sparked a debate around the purpose of education, and his influence closely paralleled Condorcet's in Europe. By 1818, he had successfully introduced bills that led to the founding of the University of Virginia and the reorganisation of William and Mary.

American historian Page Smith has characterised the legacy of Jefferson as introducing an ongoing tension between two forms of "consciousness" that have shaped American educational theory and practice. The first, what he calls the "Classical Christian Consciousness," and what the American Constitution was based on, embodies the long-standing tradition of an ordered universe governed by natural laws and laws governing human beings as defined by God Himself. This consciousness held that "the best thought and experience of the race was a precious heritage that must be preserved as a vital part of the consciousness of the new nation". This consciousness was evident in the long-standing dominance of classical education, with its religious underpinnings and elite nature.

Conversely, the "Secular Democratic Consciousness" embodies the values of the Enlightenment and is characterised by a "faith in limitless progress through reason and science" and "the natural goodness of man once he was free from superstition/religion". The Secular Democratic Consciousness, with Jefferson as its leading spokesperson, would eventually become the predominant consciousness, in spite of the dogma of the early classical college system in America.

The new consciousness was initially aided by the pragmatic, skill-oriented teachings of Noah Webster's spelling and grammar books in the late-eighteenth century, the introduction of *McGuffey's Readers* in 1836, and many other similar texts that celebrated American knowledge and sought to create "traditional American values". *McGuffey's Readers* eventually sold 100 million copies and for over half a century served as the "principal reading matter" for rural America; young American's were "dazzled" with such stories as "Washington and His Little Hatchet" and "Woodman Spare That Tree".

The values espoused by the *Readers* were as much Victorian as American, but they served to inspire "patriotic and moral values" and "loudly proclaimed the glories of resourcefulness and the sadness of indolence". Yet, the Classical Christian Consciousness remained dominant in education throughout the nineteenth century, and distinct core curriculums, such as programs in engineering and science, and professional majors did not commonly appear until near the turn of the twentieth century. Smith notes that the debate between these two schools of thought "has, indeed, been continual throughout the history of the republic and goes on scarcely diminished to the this day".

Responding to Jeffersonian and pragmatic ideals, by the middle of the nineteenth century, a rising chorus of voices began calling for a public education system, voices including Horace Mann, James G. Carter, Henry Barnard, Calvin Stowe, Caleb Mills, John D. Pierce, Ninian Edwards, Calvin Wiley, and Charles F. Mercer.

Foremost among these men was Horace Mann, who was one of the first to put into place a free state educational system for primary schools. Writing in 1847, Mann advanced the "natural rights" theme of Condorcet and argued that education was the "*absolute right* of every human being that comes into the world". Mann held that institutionalised, government-supported free education should be the responsibility of each successive generation. Mann's ideas were influential in moving education away from the lingering classical education for the elites to public education for the masses.

Although aspects of Enlightenment science—including the ideas of Descartes, Newton, Copernicus, Galileo, and Kepler—crept into the curriculums of traditional institutions such as Harvard beginning in the early eighteenth century, technological university-level institutions did not appear for another 100 years. Finally, in the early nineteenth century, Rensselaer Polytechnic Institute and West Point were founded.

At first, these schools were regarded as less prestigious than their classical counterparts. By mid-century, however, "catching up" to the European powers became an increasing concern as "the clamor of the modernisers became more insistent, claiming that economic development, industrialisation, and urbanisation required more and more highly trained manpower". Soon, other initiatives were expanding the opportunities for technological university education, and by 1860, Michigan,

Maryland, and Pennsylvania had established agricultural schools.

The voices of modernisation reform grew increasingly stronger from then on, as industrialists pushed more fervently for political changes in higher education funding. By 1862, already twenty institutions could be accurately called "scientific schools," but these were insufficient to meet corporate needs. Industrialists' strongly lobbied Congress for more technically oriented schools, and their efforts resulted in the passage of the Morrill Act in 1862.

The Act granted federal aid in support of state colleges in agriculture and engineering "in order to promote the liberal and practical education of the industrial classes in the several pursuits and professions of life". To encourage the rapid building of these schools, a state was required to found a college within five years of the act to secure a grant. In 1890, a second Morrill Act was passed with similar guidelines. As a direct result of these reforms, by 1880 there were 85 college-level engineering schools in the country; by 1917, there were 126. And the annual number of engineering graduates rose from 100 in 1870 to 4300 by the onset of World War I.

Beginning in the late nineteenth century, one the most powerful calls for modernisation, and one that deserves special attention, came from the educational philosophy of John Dewey. Dewey, who would later be highly influential to Chinese and Japanese educators in the early twentieth century, rallied against the lingering dominance of elite and classical education. Deservedly, Dewey is often credited with leading the final assault on American religious and classical education: "As the nineteenth century turned into the twentieth century the experimentation of John Dewey and his followers made it even more difficult for advocates of a closed intellectual system and conventional body of truth to hold their own".

In addition, Dewey is still regarded today as *the* proponent of democratic education and education for citizenship philosophies.

Building upon the ideals of Condorcet, Jefferson, and Mann, Dewey wrote in his 1900 essay "Schooling as a Form of Community Life" that school should be thought of as a "miniature community, an embryonic society". As such, Dewey recognised the need for a more "cultural" education, one that combined theory and practice, to help create more well-rounded, intelligent, and adaptable citizens:

> When the school introduces and trains each child of society into membership within such a little community, saturating him with the spirit of service, and providing him with the instruments of effective self-direction, we shall have the deepest and best guaranty of a larger society which is worthy, lovely, and harmonious.

These general themes throughout Dewey's writings have been continuously resurrected in educational thought and criticism. Dewey's thinking was, and still is, influential in helping to sustain an institutionalised Western education system that would not merely teach skills for a narrowly defined job or function, but also included education for citizenship and experience.

At the root of Dewey's pedagogy is his philosophy of science, a belief that the scientific methodology can be interpreted or translated into educational theory and practice, as well as in terms of human activity. This point has been de-emphasized in many of the more celebratory accounts of Dewey's pedagogy, but it is equally critical to understanding his broad outlook on educational purpose and progress:

> For more than fifty years Dewey was the chief apostle of modernity in American philosophy as well as in American education. He argued that schools should strive to emphasize moral goals based upon democratic civic and social experience, vocational and practical usefulness, and

> individual development in light of the rapid modernising changes that were taking place in Western civilisation.

Central to Dewey's thinking are the ideas of "logical" reflective thought and objectivity. Everything is subject to objective scientific scrutiny, including morality and values as well as scientific and practical affairs In fact, working from the Enlightenment as a basis, Dewey refers to knowledge and morality as virtually identical concepts: "Actively to participate in the making of knowledge is the highest prerogative of man". For Dewey, these beliefs are *critical* to human purpose, and all stem from his firm commitment to the scientific methodology: "One of the only two articles that remain in my creed of life is that the future of civilisation depends upon the widening spread and deepening hold of the scientific habit of mind".

At a deeper level, Dewey's perspective on civilisational advancement reflects the Enlightenment bias towards progress and "civilised" versus "savage" cultures. Dewey thus might be characterised as Condorcet's interpreter:

> A savage who has been shipwrecked on a river may note certain things that serve him as signs of danger in the future. But civilised man deliberately *makes* such signs; he sets up in advance of any particular shipwreck warning buoys, and builds lighthouses where he sees signs with great expertness; civilised man institutes a weather service by which signs are artificially secured and information is distributed in advance of the appearance of any signs that could be detected with special methods. A savage finds his way skillfully through a wilderness by reading obscure indications; civilised man builds a highway that shows the road to it all.

Although Dewey is saying civilised man uses technology to expand the capabilities inherent in the savage, and is therefore apparently not as harsh as Condorcet, he nonetheless makes a clear distinction between civilised–advanced and uncivilised–primitive based upon relative measures of technological development.

Building "civilisation" is important to Dewey, and throughout his writings there is a recurrent preoccupation with the positive aspects of functional, practical tasks—the core of his educational philosophy. For Dewey, only by engaging in and thereby experiencing functional tasks, with scientific understanding, does education become truly meaningful:

> The occupation supplies the child with a genuine motive; it gives him experience at first hand; it brings him into contact with realities. It does all this, but in addition it is liberalised throughout by translation into its historic and social values and scientific equivalent. With the growth of the child's mind in power and knowledge it ceases to be a pleasant occupation merely and becomes more and more a medium, an instrument, an organ—and is thereby transformed.

The pedagogy of Dewey boils down to what he calls the "project method," or the active intellectual pursuit of a project and its scientific basis. Linking scientific theory and technological practice is the key component in Dewey's recommendations on education. Arousing "intellectual interest" is therefore understood by Dewey purely in terms of scientific interest; the net result being that "Theoretical subjects will become more practical, because more related to the scope of life; practical subjects will become more charged with theory and intelligent insight. Both will be vitally and not just formally unified".

In the end, Dewey's legacy is as a key figure in reflecting the undercurrents of turn-of-the-century industrial America, and informing and predicting the growth of the technical disciplines in modern American education. In the twentieth century, the importance of engineering and other technical occupations is signified by the relative prestige of institutions such MIT and the California Institute of Technology. By 1913, the United States had emerged as an industrial power and had replaced Britain as the world leader in coal mining, machine tools, and chemical and automobile production. By that time, the ideal of education for citizenship was virtually inseparable, in practice, from education for practical occupations in the service of industrial needs.

Current Trends

The current direction of educational thought and practice concerning science and technology is a continuation of the historical precedents outlined in this essay; by World War I, all industrial powers were giving high priority to technology education. The cumulation of this trend in the twentieth century is an overvaluation of increasingly functional, professional, and corporate forms of knowledge. The gradual growth of skill-based technology education in the West grew out of an increase in the perceived need for technological advancement and the industrial power-holders need for skilled workers, especially those in engineering and related technical backgrounds. In the twentieth century, all educational disciplines have been increasingly scrutinised on their "use" value.

In light of the Japanese high-technology competitive advancements and apparent successes in skill-based education, it is not surprising that much contemporary educational literature calls for changes needed to fix the "failing" American education system. Often, the concern in this literature is with developing "correct" educational models that will enhance skill-based learning. Of special importance is more effectively bridging academic and industrial interests, especially in high technology. This is no better illustrated than by the 1995 educational pilot program of the Malcolm Baldrige Quality Award, an award originally designed exclusively for organisational improvement by profit-making companies. The pilot program is headed by both industrial and university representatives, and claims to have been "successfully" tested at all levels of education. The goal of the award is to stimulate educational process improvement using criteria very similar to the corporate quality award. "Education" is defined in practical terms—schools must prove their "effectiveness" through "measurable" results, and "learner-centered" education must account for the "real needs of learners":

> Such needs derive from the requirements of the marketplace and the responsibilities of citizenship. Changes in technology and in the national and world economies are creating increasing demands on employees to become knowledge workers and problem solvers, keeping pace with the rapid changes in the marketplace...A learning-centered school needs to fully understand and translate marketplace and citizenship requirements into appropriate curricula.

Given this foundation for "learning," the underlying emphasis throughout the criteria is the urgent need for building closer ties between education and industry.

It is important to recognise, however, that industrial motivations are also linked to a firm faith in technological progress. Thus, to say that technology education has merely been reduced to industrial needs, as may be exemplified most explicitly by the global proliferation of secondary and post-secondary technical institutes, is to too easily reduce the problem to industrial "interference." Furthermore, although Dewey might now argue that such an approach to education is too rigid and narrow, his definition of "creativity" also falls squarely within the scientific and technological framework—one which might be easily adapted to industrial needs. The fact remains that education and industry have nurtured each other, and it would be difficult to define the contemporary purpose of technology education solely in non-industrial terms.

Rethinking Technology education and Social Progress

Since the late Middle Ages, Western education has become

widespread and institutionalised out of a historical need for skills. The process of developing and practicing mass education thus has been closely linked with the expansion of Western technological development and the pursuit of progress. Consequently, skill-based education has become critical to the survival of all disciplines, and the closer a program of study is allied to servicing the needs of our technology-driven society, the better.

Western education in the West does offer some students the prospect of engaging technology from a critical perspective. A host of humanistic philosophers and social historians in Critical Theory, Cultural Studies, Postmodernism, or other philosophy- and history-based schools of thought have brought into question Western technology and progress. But while the *practice* of technological development in modern Western society marches forward and expands into the third world, the educational attention paid to placing technology into a broader social context is paltry by comparison. Technology studies, as a specific program of study, appears to be just beyond the scope of both the technical and the non-technical disciplines, both of which remain largely content to focus on skill-based education.

Teachers of technology education, in both secondary and higher levels, are in a unique position to directly influence administration, peer, and student perceptions of the role technology in contemporary society. Technology education must seek to go beyond the transmission of the most effective and economic usage of "tools" in modern society to include critical investigations of the social purpose of technology. This means embracing a critical approach to technological issues, considering so-called humanistic and social science perspectives on the role of technology in society, and empowering all students to engage in a critical dialog around technology, progress, education, and the meaning of civilisational advancement.

4

Right to Philosophy of Education

If we raise the question as to what the task of philosophy of education could be, the critical role is one of the obvious candidates. But *how* can philosophy of education be critical? And how can the criticality of philosophy of education be *legitimised*. What, in other words, gives educational philosophy the *right* to be critical?

In this essay I want to explore the critical possibilities for educational philosophy. I will discuss three critical "programs," namely, *critical dogmatism, transcendental critique,* and *deconstruction*. Besides an examination of the critical potential of each program, and of the way in which each program legitimises its right to be critical, I will compare these programs in order to establish which program might best support the critical work of educational philosophy.

Within the scope of this essay, I will not be able to spell out the practical implications for the critical work carried out by educational philosophers. Yet, I hope that my reflections will provide a meaningful framework for further discussion.

Critical Dogmatism

I propose to define critical dogmatism as any style of critique in which the critical operation consists of the application of a criterion. The operation is *critical,* in that it gives an evaluation of a specific state of affairs. The operation is *dogmatic,* in that the criterion itself is kept out of reach of the critical operation and is applied to this state of affairs "from the outside." Critical dogmatism, so we could say, derives its right to be critical from the *truth* of the criterion.

Critical dogmatism is quite common in educational philosophy. Critical work is, for example, carried out by means of a definition of what counts as education. Such a definition is used to evaluate educative practices and theories, which can then turn out to be, for example, non-educative or indoctrinary. Critical dogmatism can also be found in the work of those educational philosophers who see themselves as children's advocates. Here, the basis for critique is the conviction that the child represents a value of its own; a value that must be respected in educational theory and practice. A third example is the work of those educational philosophers who take "emancipation" to be the general criterion for the evaluation of educational theory and practice.

Although I refer to this style of criticism as "dogmatic," there is, as such, nothing objectionable to this approach. That is to say, there is nothing objectionable to critical dogmatism *as long as one recognises and accepts its dogmatic character.* As Hans Albert has expressed in his "Münchhausen trilemma," any attempt to articulate foundations - and in critical dogmatism the criterion founds the critical operation - leads "to a situation with three alternatives, all of which appear unacceptable."

The trilemma forces one to choose between (1) an *infinite regress,* because the propositions that serve as a fundament need to be founded themselves; (2) a *logical circle* that results from the fact that in the process of giving reasons, one has to resort to statements that have already shown themselves to be in need of justification; or (3) breaking off the attempt at a particular point by *dogmatically* installing a foundation.

Albert argues, that the only possible foundation of critique *is* a dogmatic foundation, so that the only possible form of critique is dogmatic critique. Of course, this conclusion raises some problems. If dogmatism appears at the heart of the critical enterprise, the critical operation seems to be immediately subverted. How can critique be effective - or even more: How is critique possible - if its ultimate foundation is merely conventional?

I believe that critical dogmatism is in trouble once it is acknowledged that the criterion itself can only be installed dogmatically. This is not to suggest, that the application of such criteria has never had any positive effects or that any critical work in educational philosophy along these lines has been in vain. But we should be aware of the paradoxical character of this style of critique.

Although this brings critical dogmatism into a difficult position, it does not mean that the possibilities for critique as such are thereby exhausted. What has been argued so far, is the paradoxical character of critique as the application of a criterion that is itself beyond critique. There is, however, a critical style which claims that it can circumvent the paradox of critical dogmatism. This is *transcendental critique.*

Transcendental Critique

Transcendental critique has its roots in the emergence of the scientific worldview. From then onwards, philosophy could no longer claim to provide knowledge of the natural world (physics), nor of a more fundamental reality (*meta*physics). Philosophy thus lost its role as a foundational discipline. It was Kant who put philosophy on a new track -the *transcendental* track - where it became the proper task of philosophy to articulate the *conditions of possibility* of true (scientific) knowledge.

Kant's program was almost immediately criticised for the reflexive paradox it contained. It was Hegel who pointed out the problematic character of the attempt to acquire knowledge about the process of knowledge acquisition. The reason why Kant did not perceive this paradox had to do with the framework of the philosophy of consciousness in which he operated. For Kant, the "Ich denke", was the "highest point, to which we must ascribe all employment of the understanding, even the whole of logic, and conformally therewith, transcendental philosophy."

The work of Karl-Otto Apel can be seen as a (re)articulation of transcendental philosophy that tries to circumvent this "dogmatic element" in Kant's position by making a shift from the philosophy of consciousness to the philosophy of language. The main difference between Apel and Kant lies in Apel's recognition of the fact that all knowledge is linguistically mediated. While Kant assumed that the acquisition of knowledge is basically an individualistic enterprise, Apel argues that our individual experiences must be "lifted" to the level of a language game in order to become knowledge.

The link between experience and language is, however, not established automatically. The question of the validity of our individual experiences has to be answered by means of *argumentation*. Because argumentation only makes sense within a language game, within a "community of communication," Apel concludes that this community is the condition of possibility of all knowledge.

Apel's "linguistic turn" results in the recognition of the *a priori of the community of communication*. Because we can never get "before" the actual use of language in a specific community of communication, any reflection on language can only take place in a specific language game or community of communication. The pragmatic dimension is therefore the most basic dimension of language, for which reason Apel refers to his position as *transcendental pragmatics*.

Although Apel establishes a strong link between transcendental pragmatics and really existing communities of communication - a maneuver which seems to give his project a strong conventionalistic basis - he introduces a critical element that is meant to enable transcendental pragmatics to go beyond convention. This element is the *ideal community of communication* or the *transcendental language game*.

Apel claims that a participant in a genuine argument is at the very same time a member of a concrete community of communication and a counterfactual *ideal* community of communication, a community which is, in principle, open to all speakers and which excludes all force except the force of the better argument. This community "is, at least implicitly, anticipated in all human actions claiming to be meaningful and it is explicitly anticipated in philosophical arguments claiming to be valid." Any claim to intersubjectively valid knowledge therefore implicitly acknowledges this ideal community, as a "meta-institution" of rational argumentation, to be its ultimate source of justification. Communication would lose its meaning when one no longer aims at this ideal.

The idea of the ideal community of communication provides a criterion which makes critique possible. What distinguishes Apel's position from critical dogmatism is that this criterion is not installed dogmatically but by means of a process of *reflexive grounding*. With respect to this process Apel claims that he can circumvent the dogmatic implications of the Münchhausen trilemma.

The first thing that has to be acknowledged, is that the first and the third option of the Münchhausen trilemma hang together. Both are connected to Albert's contention that the process of foundation must necessarily be understood in terms of *deduction*. If we talk about foundations in a deductive style, that is, if we raise the question of the "foundation of the foundation," it is clear that we enter an infinite regress which can only be stopped arbitrarily. Apel admits that if we understand foundations in this sense, we will never find them. But this does not mean that we should give up the idea of foundation as such, only that we need another way to bring foundations into view.

Apel starts from the recognition that the conditions of possibility of argumentation have to be presupposed in all argumentation. But if this is so, then it follows, that one cannot argue against these conditions of possibility without immediately falling into a *performative contradiction*, that is, a situation where the performative dimensions of the argument contradict the propositional content. From this, Apel concludes that *all contentions that cannot be disclaimed without falling into a performative contradiction, express a condition of possibility of the argumentative use of language*. The principle of performative consistency is therefore the criterion which can *reveal* the ultimate foundations of the argumentative use of language, that is, those propositions that do not need further grounding, because, so Apel argues, they cannot be understood without knowing that they are true.

Although Apel articulates the way in which the ultimate foundations of the argumentative use of language can be *revealed*, he does not say much about what these foundations actually are. Yet, it is not difficult to see that what the application of the principle of performative consistency can bring into view are the foundations, or, so we could say, the "meta-rules" of all argumentative use of language. These meta-rules, which include such things as the contention that all communication aims at consensus, that all communication rests upon the validity of claims to truth, rightness and truthfulness, and that these claims can in principle be redeemed, outline the *ideal* community of communication.

Apel's program tries to argue for the possibility or articulating criteria for critique non-dogmatically. More than just another style of critique, Apel suggests that critical dogmatism - at least in so far as it concerns the dogmatic choice for rationality - is an untenable position, because "any choice that could be understood as meaningful already presupposes the transcendental language game as its condition of possibility." From this it does not follow that every decision is rational, but it does follow that a decision in favor of the principle of rational legitimation of criticism is "rational *a priori*," because "reason...can always confirm its own legitimation through reflection on the fact that it presupposes its own self-understanding of the very rules it opts for."

These remarks reveal that the criticality of transcendental pragmatics is motivated by *rationality*. After all, the "sin" of the performative contradiction is a sin against rationality, and it is for this very reason that the contradiction has to be avoided. Rationality therefore gives transcendental critique its "right" to be critical. This becomes clear when we look at the way in which the transcendental style of critique is applied in educational philosophy. In a more strict sense, we can see this style of critique at work in discussions about critical thinking and education. Here the work of Harvey Siegel stands out as a continuous attempt to spot the performative contradiction in any challenge to rationality. In a wider sense, the critical potential of the idea of performative contradiction is used as a form of internal critique, where the main critical work consists of a confrontation of a position or argument with its conditions of possibility.

Transcendental critique presents itself as a "stronger" conception of critique than critical dogmatism, primarily because it claims to be able to articulate its choice for rationality non-dogmatically. Compared to critical dogmatism, I want to argue that transcendental critique indeed is a more sophisticated critical program. But transcendental critique is not (yet) the last word about critique.

Deconstruction

The writings of Jacques Derrida - to which I will refer as deconstruction - articulate yet another critical program. Like Apel, Derrida rejects the possibility of a grounding by deduction. But unlike Apel, the conclusions he draws from this rejection are quite different.

Derrida sees the history of Western philosophy as a continuous attempt to locate a fundamental ground which serves both as an absolute beginning and as a center from which everything originating from it can be mastered and controlled. Since Plato, the origin has always been defined in terms of *presence*. This "metaphysics of presence" includes a *hierarchical axiology* in which the origin is designated as pure, simple, normal, self-sufficient, and self-identical, in order *then* to think in terms of derivation, complication, deterioration, accident, and so forth. This is "*the* metaphysical exigency," that which has been "the most constant, most profound and most potent."

Derrida wants to put this metaphysical gesture into question. He acknowledges that he is not the first to do so. But against Nietzsche, Freud, Heidegger, and all other "destructive discourses" that wanted to overcome metaphysics, Derrida argues that we can never make a total break. "There is no sense," he argues, "in doing without the concepts of metaphysics in order to shake metaphysics. We...can pronounce not a single destructive proposition which has not already had to slip into the form, the logic, and the implicit postulations of precisely what it seeks to contest." While Derrida definitely wants to "shake" metaphysics, he acknowledges that this cannot be done from some neutral and innocent place outside of metaphysics. Derrida wants to shake metaphysics, to put it simply, by showing that metaphysics is itself always already shaking, by showing the impossibility of any attempt to fix being through the presentation of a self-identical, original presence.

One way in which Derrida articulates this impossibility and its predicaments, is through the "notion" of *différance,* which he articulates in discussion with the structuralist semiotics of Ferdinand de Saussure. Contrary to the idea that language is a naming process, attaching words to things, Saussure argues that language is a structure where any individual element is meaningless outside the confines of that structure. In language there are only *differences*. These differences, however, are not differences between positive terms, that is, between terms that in and by themselves refer to things outside the system. In language there are only differences *without* positive terms. From this two conclusions follow.

First of all, the idea of differences without positive terms entails that the "movement of signification" is only possible if each element "appearing on the scene of presence, is related to something other than itself." What is called "the present" is therefore constituted "by means of this very relation to what it is not". This contamination is a necessary contamination: For the present to be itself, it already has to be *other* than itself. This puts the non-present in a double position, because it is the non-present which makes the presence of the present possible, and yet, it can only make this presence possible by means of its own exclusion. What is excluded thereby, in a sense, returns to sign the act of its own exclusion. And it is this apparent complicity, which "outplays the legality of the decision to exclude" in the first place.

If this is what deconstruction can bring into view, we can already get an idea of its critical potential, because at the heart of deconstruction, we find a concern for the "constitutive outside" of what presents itself as self-sufficient. This reveals that deconstruction is more than just a destruction of the metaphysics of presence. Deconstruction is first and foremost an *affirmation* of what is excluded and forgotten. An affirmation, in short, of what is *other*.

There is, however, a complication which concerns the question of *how* deconstruction can bring that what is excluded into view. For if it is the case that in language there are only differences without positive terms, then we have to concede that we can no longer articulate the differential character of language itself by means of a positive term. Difference without positive terms implies that this "dimension" must itself always remain unperceived, for strictly speaking, it is unconceptualisable. The "play of difference," which is "the condition for the possibility and functioning of every sign, is in itself a silent play".

If we would want to articulate that which does not let itself be articulated and yet is the condition for the possibility of all articulation - which we might want to do in order to prevent metaphysics from re-entering - we must acknowledge that there can never be a word or a concept to represent this silent play. We must acknowledge that this play cannot simply be exposed, for "one can expose only that which at a certain moment can become *present*". And we must acknowledge that there is nowhere to begin, "for what is put into question is precisely the quest for a rightful beginning, an absolute point of departure". All this is expressed in the new word or concept - "which is neither a word nor a concept" but a "neographism" - of *différance*.

The reason why Derrida introduces that "what is written as *différance*" is not difficult to grasp. Although "the play of difference" is identified as the condition of possibility of all conceptuality, we should not make the mistake to think that we have finally found the real origin of all conceptuality. The predicament is this: because we are talking about the condition of possibility of all conceptuality, this condition cannot belong to that which it makes possible. Yet, the only way in which we can *articulate* this condition of possibility is *within* this order. Because the condition of possibility is always articulated in terms of the system that is made possible by it, it is, in a sense, always already "too late" to be its condition of possibility.

At this level, the critical potential of deconstruction returns in an even more radical way. The point here is, that because conditions of possibility are always already contaminated by the "system" that is made possible by them, this "system" is never totally delimited by these conditions. *Différance* is therefore a quasi-transcendental or quasi-condition of possibility, because, as John D. Caputo aptly describes, it "does not describe fixed boundaries that delimit what can happen and what not, but points a mute, Buddhist finger at the moon of uncontainable effects."

Deconstruction thus tries to open up the system in the name of that which cannot be thought of in terms of the system. This reveals that the deconstructive affirmation is not simply an affirmation of what is known to be excluded by the system. Deconstruction is an affirmation of what is wholly other (*tout autre*), of what is unforeseeable from the present. It is an affirmation of an otherness that is always to come, as an event which "as event, exceeds calculation, rules, programs, anticipations." Deconstruction is an openness towards the unforeseeable in-coming of the other. It is from this concern for what is totally other, a concern to which Derrida sometimes refers as *justice*, that deconstruction derives its right to be critical.

FROM CRITIQUE TO DECONSTRUCTION

In the preceding pages I have discussed three ways in which philosophy of education might perform its critical role. I have argued that these programs derive their right to be critical from three different sources, namely, truth, rationality, and justice.

I have shown that the existence of critical dogmatism depends on the fact that the critical criterion is itself kept out of reach of the critical operation. Although this situation is rather unsatisfactory, I have presented Albert's Münchhausen trilemma to suggest that a dogmatic installment of the critical criterion is perhaps inevitable. The work of Apel implies a straightforward rejection of this suggestion. Apel shows that it is possible to articulate a critical criterion in a non-dogmatic way, at least in so far as we are concerned with the criteria that govern the argumentative use of language. Apel argues that the principle of performative consistency can bring into view the "meta-rules" of all argumentation. These meta-rules outline the ideal community of communication. What can deconstruction add to this picture?

It is not difficult to see the profound differences between deconstruction and critical dogmatism. Like transcendental critique, deconstruction problematises the dogmatic installment of the critical criterion. As Derrida writes, deconstruction "always aims at the trust confided in the critical, critico-theoretical agency, that is, the deciding agency," for which reason he concludes that "deconstruction is deconstruction of critical dogmatism." Further, deconstruction challenges the idea that there are pure, uncontaminated criteria that we can simply apply. At the basis of our decisions, Derrida argues, lies a radical undecidability, which cannot be closed off by our decisions, but which "continues to inhabit the decision."

The critical distance between deconstruction and transcendental critique is perhaps less easy to grasp. Yet this distance is also substantial. Derrida and Apel agree on the fact that we are always already on the "inside" of language, so that the language game that has made us who we are is, in Apel's words, unsurpassable.

Difficulties arise as soon as we want to say something about what makes our speaking - and more specifically in the case of Apel, argumentation - possible. Although Apel hesitates to give a positive description of the conditions of possibility of the argumentative use of language, he believes that these conditions can be identified by means of the principle of performative consistency. This eventually leads him to the meta-rules that constitute the ideal community of communication.

The crucial difference between transcendental critique and deconstruction lies in the way in which the idea of conditions of possibility is understood. If I see it correctly, Apel has to assume that conditions of possibility control the system that is made possible by them, because it is only on this assumption that the idea of performative consistency makes sense.

After all, a performative contradiction, a propositional sin against the conditions that make the performance of the proposition possible, can only occur when all performances in the "system" are controlled by these conditions. What Derrida brings into consideration, is that conditions of possibility are never totally external to the system. They are always already "contaminated" - if not "controlled"- by the system, and it is precisely because of this, that they cannot have total control over the system. What is possible, so we could say, is always more than what the conditions of possibility allow for. Deconstruction wants to do justice to this unforseeable excess, it wants to keep the possibility for an incoming of the wholly other open.

At this point, it becomes clear that deconstruction poses a serious challenge to the program of transcendental critique. This at least suggests - although further discussion is needed - that deconstruction is a stronger, and, in a sense, more coherent critical program than transcendental critique. What is crucial to see, is that deconstruction puts its challenge to the "iron grip" of rationality out of its concern for what is structurally excluded. It puts its challenge to rationality, in short, in the name of justice.

This leaves me with one final observation. I have argued that what motivates deconstruction is its concern for the unforeseeable invention of the other. In conclusion, I want to suggest that this very concern can also be understood as the central concern of education. It is for this reason that I want to urge educational philosophers to further explore the critical potential of deconstruction. It could well be that deconstruction then will turn out to be the most adequate critical style for a philosophy of education that does not merely want to be critical *about* education, but first and foremost *for* education.

5

Communicative Pedagogy

Educators of very different times and places share a common intuition about the educational relationship. They want it to be — or at least want it to become — an equal and symmetrical relationship. For this reason they refer to this relationship using such terms as "dialogue" and "communication." There is at least one obvious reason for this intuition, grounded in the fact that the educational relationship is a relationship between human beings.

The argument is that the educational relationship cannot and should not be reduced to a merely instrumental, manipulative, or what Habermas calls a strategic relationship, because this would ignore the personhood — or at least the emerging personhood — of the child. Kant has expressed the assumption behind this argument very explicitly in his second formulation of the Categorical Imperative, where he argues that, because "man exists as an end in itself," he must in all actions be regarded not merely as a means but always "at the same time as an end."

Basically, educators have taken up the challenge implied in this intuition in two different ways. On the one hand, there are those who endorse the Kantian maxim but at the same time argue that the child is not yet capable of *real* dialogue and *real* communication. For them this capacity is the very sign of adulthood and therefore it is postulated as the intended outcome of education. Education itself is presented as a kind of trajectory which sets out as manipulation and eventually develops into communication.

The point of this position — to which I will refer as *manipulative pedagogy* — can be made clear by paraphrasing Richard Peters: the child "can and must enter the palace of Communication through the courtyard of Manipulation." Manipulative pedagogy entails the educational paradox — very eloquently put by Kant in his question "How do I cultivate freedom through coercion?" — because in seeing education as a process in which the child is in a sense *made* into a person, the personhood of the child is simultaneously affirmed and denied.

The other position is held by educators who do not merely want to *anticipate* the child's communicative and dialogical competency by treating it, for example, as a useful practical fiction. They want to acknowledge this capacity within the very process of education itself. Consequently, they treat education as *real* dialogue or *real* communication. Here we can also speak of a trajectory from manipulation to communication, but that it is not education itself which is depicted as such. What adherents of this position — which I will refer to as *communicative pedagogy* —argue for, is a replacement of a manipulative understanding of education or a manipulative educational practice by a communicative or dialogical one.

At first sight the manipulative conception appears to make sense as it appears to be supported by what Richard Peters refers to as the "brute facts of child development," which are thought to reveal — and here I paraphrase Peters again — that at the most formative years of a child's development he is incapable of a communicative or dialogical form of life. Although the communicative conception seems to express an empirical impossibility, this has by no means prevented educators from developing, supporting, promoting and practicing some form of communicative pedagogy.

The field is densely populated and contains a wide range of different options, from the dialogical pedagogy of Martin Buber and "critical-communicative pedagogy" of Klaus Schaller, through positions inspired by Socrates, Hans-Georg Gadamer, John Dewey and Jürgen Habermas, to German "anti-pedagogy" and the work of Paulo Freire.

Now the intriguing question is, Why is communicative pedagogy flourishing? Do adherents of communicative pedagogy think that they can ignore the "brute facts of child development?" If so, is there any reasonable ground for this? Or must we conclude that adherents of communicative pedagogy simply act irrationally?

In this paper I will argue that there is indeed reason for some adherents of communicative pedagogy to neglect the "brute facts of child development." This is done in the context of what I take to be the main aim of this paper, namely, to provide a conceptual clarification of the debate on education and communication. I will first specify the difference between manipulative and communicative pedagogy.

Then I will introduce a distinction between two varieties of communicative pedagogy, the *ethical* and the *empirical* variety. After having discussed both varieties, I will show that the crucial distinction is not to be made between manipulative pedagogy on the one hand and communicative pedagogy on the other, but between manipulative pedagogy *and* the ethical variety of communicative pedagogy on the one hand, and the empirical variety on the other. I will then be able to show that only the empirical variety is *not* susceptible to the "brute facts of child development."

From Manipulation to Communication

In a paper entitled "From the educational relationship to educational interaction" Friedrich Kron reconstructs three phases in the development of the way in which the educational relationship has been theorised in German educational philosophy. The interesting thing about Kron's reconstruction is not only that it documents a trajectory from a manipulative to a communicative conception of education. He also offers a conceptual framework for specifying the exact difference between manipulative and communicative pedagogy.

Kron starts with Wilhelm Dilthey, who in 1894 declares that "the science of education has to start with a description of the educator in his relation to the educated, as what is first of all needed is a depiction of the educational phenomenon itself." Although Dilthey acknowledges that "education is a function of society," he adds that this function can only be realised in a *personal* relationship between the educator and the educated.

In this relationship the intentional activities of the educator are thought to coincide with the "educatibility" of the child. Herman Nohl, a student of Dilthey, holds a similar position. For him the foundation of education is situated in the "educative community" between a mature and an immature human being. This relationship exists for the sake of the child, so that he can come "to his own life and form." Where Dilthey — following Herbart — talks about educatibility, Nohl refers to the child's "will to be educated".

Kron argues that this "classical" conception of the educational relationship —which was dominant in

German pedagogy at least until the sixties — has two central characteristics. First of all, the educational relationship is characterised by a *one-directional* or *unilateral intentionality*. Education is seen as an intentional activity, but it is only the educator who has intentions, not the educated. The latter is only "educatible." The second characteristic is what Kron refers to as *negative anthropology*.

The Dilthey-Nohl conception defines the child in negative terms. The child is *not yet* educated, *not yet* rational, *not yet* competent to communicate, *not yet* really intentional, etc. Taken together, these two characteristics depict the educational relationship as a structurally asymmetrical relationship in which the personhood of the immature child is produced by the intentional activities of the mature adult.

In the second phase — in which the philosophy of Existentialism plays a central role — the "idealised" Dilthey-Nohl conception is replaced by a more "realistic" one. The most important theoretical shift occurs with respect to intentionality: the idea of unilateral intentionality is replaced by the idea of "broken" intentionality. It is acknowledged that the educator can fail in his pedagogical activities because the child is not just "willing material." This means that the child's personhood is no longer thought to be exclusively constituted by the intentional actions of the adult.

Educational authority is supplemented by educational impotence, educational love and responsibility by fear and despair. This has repercussions for the anthropological underpinning of education. In a sense, educator and educated are in the same anthropological position. Kron calls it a "radical equality of opportunity" in that the child and the adult are both "thrown into existence." Although the two central characteristics of the first phase are undermined, representatives of the second phase do not come to a theoretical articulation of their position. The reason for this is very well expressed by Otto Bollnow, who argues that the fallibility of education can only be existentially *experienced;* it cannot be put into theory.

This does happen, however, in the third phase, where the leading paradigm is Symbolic Interactionism. From this perspective education is no longer understood as manipulation of the behavior or the behavioral dispositions of the child; education is considered to be a process of social interaction, constituted by the interpretive actions of all participants. This entails a crucial theoretical shift, as the educational relationship is now understood as a *two-directional* or *bilateral intentional* process. This also has anthropological implications, because the child is no longer seen as, by definition, deficient. Bilateral intentionality entails a *positive anthropology*.

Kron's reconstruction offers a conceptual framework for specifying what is at stake in the shift from a manipulative to a communicative conception of education. In terms of this framework it is a shift from unilateral to bilateral intentionality and, correspondingly, from an negative to a positive anthropology. While in the first position, the personhood of the child is thought to be dependent upon the intentional activities of the educator, the second position envisages education as a process constituted by the intentionality of both the educator and the educandee.

Ethical Variety of Communicative Pedagogy

Although Kron gives a clear idea of what is at stake in a communicative conception of education, one crucial distinction *within* the field of communicative pedagogy remains invisible. This is the distinction between what I propose to call the *ethical* and the *empirical* variety of communicative pedagogy.

A fine example of the ethical variety has recently been given by Nicholas Burbules in his book *Dialogue in Teaching*. Burbules characterises his book as a description and a defense of a particular educational ideal, namely, dialogue. Dialogue is described as "a particular kind of pedagogical communicative relation: a conversational interaction directed intentionally towards teaching and learning," which implies that not every interaction between human beings counts as dialogue.

Burbules stresses that dialogue is "non-teleological" in that it has no pre-determined outcome. Also, dialogue "tends toward a decentered and non authoritarian view of learning," as it is not aimed at changing other people but at effecting a change in and by the participants themselves. The communicative foundations of dialogue are found in the fact that language, reason, morality and our social organisation — and here Burbules refers to Bakhtin, Vygotsky, Habermas and Dewey — are thought to be thoroughly dialogical and relational in character.

Although Burbules argues for a dialogical type of education, he is well aware that there is no guarantee that the practice of education will ever conform to this educational ideal. Dialogue might therefore best be understood as a kind of "critical reference point." Crucial for Burbules's position is his claim that it is not an unrealistic or utopian reference point.

> The benefit of communicative norms such as dialogue…is not that they represent abstract ideals to which we should aspire, but that they exemplify *implicit* values that we actually do hold, that are latent in the practices in which we are actually engaged. In this, they function as reminders of standards that are necessarily implied by what we do and by what we say we want.

Elsewhere in his book, Burbules stretches this argument a bit further when he writes that according to Habermas the essential feature of communication towards understanding is that it entails an implicit commitment to certain standards...that can be invoked by either partner in conversation.

Throughout his book Burbules stresses that dialogue depends upon "the commitment that joins interlocutors in an ongoing communicative relation." Therefore, successful dialogue involves a willing partnership and cooperation in the fact of likely disagreements, confusions, failures and misunderstandings. Persisting in this process requires a relation of mutual respect, trust, and concern — and part of the dialogical interchange often must relate to the establishment and maintenance of these bonds.

This shows that the dialogical relation is not exhausted by a cognitive interest; the "affective qualities of concern and commitment that draw us into dialogue" and "the capacity of dialogue to involve us and carry us beyond our intentions" are all aspects of the dialogical relation.

As Burbules's point is that dialogue depends upon "a commitment to the process of communicative interchange itself," it does not come as a surprise that the development and fostering of such a commitment is taken as a crucial step towards a dialogical educational practice. Here Burbules introduces the notion of "communicative virtues," which include such qualities as "tolerance, patience, an openness to give and receive criticism, the inclination to admit that one might be mistaken, the desire to reinterpret or translate one's own concerns...the self-imposition of restraint in order that others may have a turn to speak, and...the willingness to listen thoughtfully and attentively."

Burbules sees the relationship between the communicative virtues and dialogue as a reciprocal one. Whether dialogue will happen, depends upon the communicative virtues of the interacting partners; but it is precisely by means of dialogue that these virtues are developed. On the one hand, this means that the communicative virtues constitute "significant educational aims in their own right." On the other hand, it implies that education itself is a process of "initiation" into dialogical relationships. This is thought of as a "bootstrapped process," because for Burbules it makes no sense to wait for ideal conditions to happen. "We improve by imitating, practicing, and experimenting in the midst of real-time activities."

There can be no doubt that Burbules's position is a specimen of communicative pedagogy. Dialogue is not something to happen *after* the child has been educated; education *itself* should be dialogical. Further, Burbules defines dialogue in terms of a bilateral intentionality, which suggests that it is backed by a positive anthropology. My reason for calling Burbules's position a specimen of the *ethical* variety of communicative pedagogy is twofold. First it should be noted — and this is by no means meant as a disqualification of Burbules's position — that he only gives a "description and defense" of a particular educational ideal.

Burbules's point is that we *ought to* educate in a dialogical way. Although, as I will argue below, his justification for this "ought" is not without importance, this has no effect upon the status of his enterprise. Basically, it is an evocation. This evocation — and this is my second reason — is addressed to the partners in interaction. Burbules makes dialogue totally dependent upon their *commitment*. Dialogue will only happen when at least two human subjects have committed themselves to it. This *ethical* commitment comes first; dialogue is derivative. Taken together, Burbules specifies what we *ought to* do and what *we* ought to do.

Empirical Variety of Communicative Pedagogy

While the ethical variety argues that education *should be* dialogical or communicative, the basic claim of the empirical variety is that education *is* communication. The difference is not a merely verbal one. What lies behind these claims, are two different anthropological presuppositions, or, to be more precise, two different conceptions about the relationship between subjectivity and intersubjectivity. While the ethical variety understands intersubjectivity as grounded in subjectivity, the empirical variety understands subjectivity as grounded in intersubjectivity.

The ethical variety of communicative pedagogy rests upon an intentional conception of human (inter)action which has its theoretical roots in what Habermas refers to as the tradition of the philosophy of consciousness. This tradition takes the individual, conscious subject as the unproblematic unit of analysis and explains social interaction — including educational interaction — as an achievement of the interacting partners.

In this tradition, the individual subject is treated as an independent variable. In the empirical variety precisely this conception of human subjectivity is contested. From the empirical point of view, subjectivity is thought to be in need of an explanation. And the intersubjective, communicative "praxis" is proposed as the independent variable that can do so.

Within philosophy the "intersubjective turn" has, amongst others, been taken by John Dewey, George Herbert Mead and, more recently, by Jürgen Habermas. Habermas has introduced the notion of "communicative action" to refer to the communicative praxis which precedes subjectivity. I have argued elsewhere that the same concept can also be used to characterise the pragmatic position. What should be kept in mind here is that the expression "communication" is not meant to refer to the interaction between subjects; rather, it is meant to refer to the "matrix" that precedes subjectivity. Although this matrix can be understood ontologically, that is, as the source from which subjectivity emerges, the "paradigm of intersubjectivity" at least entails a methodological rule, namely, that intersubjectivity is the explanatory entity.

The claim that education *is* communication should be understood against this background. This means that it is meant as an alternative for those views of education based upon the — in the eyes of the empirical variety problematical —presuppositions of the philosophy of consciousness. I deliberately speak in the plural, that is, about views, as this not only holds for the ethical variety of communicative pedagogy but also for manipulative pedagogy. Both positions presuppose the existence of intentional subjects.

The only difference is that manipulative pedagogy denies that the child already has intentions of its own, while the ethical variety of communicative pedagogy holds that the child should be treated as having real intentions. Although Kron is right in arguing that the difference between the two positions can be specified in terms of unilateral versus bilateral intentionality, we can now add that in both cases intentionality — and thus the existence of intentional subjects — is presupposed. From this point of view, the split is *not* between manipulative and communicative pedagogy, but between manipulative pedagogy and the ethical variety of communicative pedagogy on the one hand, and the empirical variety on the other.

The key question of course is what the intersubjective turn exactly implies for our understanding of education.

The definitive answer to this question has not yet been given; so far there have only been very few attempts to make this connection. I will therefore confine myself to two issues that can shed some light upon the status of the empirical variety of communicative pedagogy.

The first issue concerns the claim of adherents of manipulative pedagogy that education-as-manipulation is the means by which the "Palace of Communication" can and must be reached. What is suggested here is that the community between educator and educandee can and must be brought about by the intentional actions of the educator. However, for the actions of the educator to have any effect upon the child, some form of community must be presupposed. The claim of the empirical variety of communicative pedagogy is that precisely this community is the basis for any interaction at all. In this sense community — or communication — is not only thought to precede all education, but is in fact a constitutive precondition, or what might be called a transcendental precondition, of education.

The suggestion that education has a non-intentional communicative basis, can also be clarified by means of the difference between the intention and the meaning of an act. In the manipulative account, it is presumed that the intentions behind the actions of the educator coincide with their meaning. From the perspective of the empirical variety, it is argued that there is no reason whatsoever to assume such a coincidence between intention and meaning.

The meaning of an act is brought about in the communicative praxis in which this act plays a role. It is therefore intersubjective. Educational actions are not excluded from this, and the adherents of Kron's second phase were well aware of this fact. But neither they, nor the adherents of Symbolic Interactionism were able to articulate this intuition in a non-intentionalistic way.

Empirical communicative pedagogy, however, is able to do away with this "intentionalistic bias," by arguing that intersubjective meaning overrides subjective intention.

This brings me to my second point, namely, whether the empirical variety is threatened by the "brute facts of child development" or not. To begin with, it must be acknowledged that both manipulative pedagogy and the ethical variety of communicative pedagogy are threatened by these facts.

Manipulative pedagogy simply acknowledges this and consequently sees education as a structurally asymmetrical — and paradoxical — enterprise. In the ethical variety of communicative pedagogy, the problem is circumvented. This is most clearly shown in Kron's discussion of Symbolic Interactionism, where it is argued that education has a lower limit in what is known as the "phase of stubbornness." This stubbornness is thought to be the first sign of the intentionality of the child; from there education can supposedly take off. To my mind, Burbules is not that clear about this issue.

From the fact that dialogue is characterised as a bilaterally intentional activity, it might be argued that he is also forced to acknowledge a lower limit in education. But as he argues that the dialogical development of communicative virtues is a "bootstrapped process," it might also be concluded that Burbules holds that dialogue can start from birth onwards.

My reason for arguing that the empirical variety is *not* threatened by the "brute facts of child development" has to do with what is thought to be revealed by these facts, namely, that the child is not yet a full-blown, that is, an intentional subject. The point of the empirical variety is that subjectivity is *not* a constitutive precondition of intersubjectivity and communication. Therefore, it is not affected by the non-intentionality of the child.

This is only a problem for those positions which "need" a subject before they can talk about intersubjectivity and communication. Of course, this does not entail a denial of the "brute facts of child development". What should not be forgotten, however, is that there are no "brute facts" as such. Therefore, it might well be that most of the facts revealed by developmental psychology are, in a sense, produced by, or at least dependent upon, the paradigm of the philosophy of consciousness.

6

Universities and Transdisciplinarity

Education is the strategy that has been developed by our species with a dual purpose: to estimulate societal life and to enhance creativity. This has been achieved through the transmission of accumulated knowledge from previous generations and through living through challenging experiences. In all levels of education and in every society, along history, these two major goals for education are noticeable. Of course, the characteristics of each society determines the style education has taken in that specific society. The prevailing systems of knowledge determine educational practices. A number of case studies illustrate this.

We are recognising great changes occurring in society. The new facilities in transportation, communications and information collecting, storing and processing bring new dimensions to the technology developed since the dawn of modern science. These have evident reflects on the characteristics of modern civilisation, particularly in urban life, in the models of property and production and in economics. Consequently, new perceptions of equity, of security, of recognition and reward have been generated and universalised in modern times. From a colonial posture in the origin of these concepts we move at a very fast pace to seeing the humanity as a whole and recognising a human race, of which the Earth is the home.

And we look for our identity as individuals belonging to a species with many specificities among all the living entities in a planet which is part of an ongoing cosmic process. Indicators of these new perceptions are numerous. Modern education will, necessarily, reflect these new perceptions.

Particularly the universities are out of compass with these recent developments. Universities created in the traditional model in the colonies and recently independent nations are indicators of the inadequacy.

We are looking for new models. This has been common in every stage of mankind in which we see the emergence of new forms of knowledge. Now the character of universality of the educational systems, the incorporation of the traditions to intellectual circles all over the world, and the emergence of new forms of production demand a new organisation for these places of production and transmission of knowledge. Of course, the concept of knowledge is essential for any proposal in this direction.

What follows reflects the transdisciplinary approach to the understanding of ourselves and of our place in the cosmos.

TRANSDISCIPLINARITY

It is important to recognise the need of intellectual support for our behavior which results from a diversity of views. In a moment of strong and widespread indicators of nationalisms, fundamentalisms in human relations, a planetary view is needed.

How did we reach this point? It is interesting at this moment to venture into some etymological remarks. In the main Indo-European languages, the word life comes from two roots. One, traced back to the Latin (*vie, vita, vida*) has a meaning of behavior, which in the XI century has been identified with the of a complex system in evolution from two status, birth and death. In another conception, life comes from *leip* which has to do with the functioning of the body (liver, lipo). In both there is the sense of a dynamics of continuity of the individual and of the species, of survival. The search for nourishment and mechanisms of reproduction are imprinted in the genetic code.

Modern science and technology have created just about everything, except life with the splendourous complexity of continuity and reproduction. Continuity not only of the individual, but of life in the most general sense. Out of these drives, intrinsic to life, we see the rise of altruistic and ecological behavior, which are the warranty of life. Like every living being, *homo sapiens sapiens* is driven toward survival of the individual and of the species which permeates our entire existence, in the span between birth and death.

But unique among all the species, we are provided also with a sense of time, we aim at transcending our existence, going before birth and after death, driven by consciousness and will. Understanding consciousness and will are present in the earliest manifestations of human behavior. Looking for our past and for our future have led to cults and spirituality, in the forms of traditions and religions, and to divinations, in the form of arts and sciences. Knowledge means the acquired ability of surviving and transcending.

Under this dual drive towards survival and transcendence , human behavior has marked an evolution towards the acquisition of knowledge. In this evolution some distortions are noticeable.

The main particularity in this evolution is a contracition with the commitment of preservation of life in the essence of its code: continuity of life through the survival of the individual and of the species. Although it is intrinsic to life the elimination of one individual or of species so that other can survive, under altruistic and ecological behavior, in the human species this is done under the motivation of consciousness and will. The basic question we rise is related to this, that is, the elimination of one life so that another go on. This is the most fundamental issue of individual, social and environmental morality. In this multiplicity we place *ethics* .

What does ethics mean ?

What does it mean an ethical behavior? Again, an etymological exercise show us that ethics, as well as ethos and ethno, refer to the other. It is the recognition of the other which brings the need of an ethics. The recognition of conflicting behavior of the other in oneself, the other in the strange, the other in competing societies and species. To prevail upon the other concur with the drives towards survival and transcendence. The equilibrium in this concurrence is the major and essential issue. My reflections are permeated by this single question.

It has been frequent in the behavior of our species the acceptance that some forms of life are more worthed than others and some are not only useless but in some cases threatening. Some species are dangerous - so away with them! In the same vein, some individuals in a certain species are less productive, give us less of aimed benefits, so away with them! Some indeed bother us, like a mosquito in the middle of the night. So, away with them! And this cascading reasoning can be carried on to our own species: some are less productive, so away with them, some bother us, so away with them. If we use insecticides for mosquitoes that bother us, why not to use guillotines, electric chairs, and nowadays letal injections to eliminate those deviants that bother us.

Summing up, human behavior has been increasingly dominated by the feeling that one individual may be worth more than others. This is the origin of modern social and environmental behavior. I see no way of facing man's social and environmental behavior other than looking into values and generating an appropriate ethics, focused on restablishing concurrence in equilibrium with survival and transcendence.

Scientific knowledge has grown and continues to grow, apparently without limit to its reach, disclosing the mechanics of the universe and giving us the capability of looking into the minute and most elementary components of matter, of touching and shaping the evolution of living forms. This same mode of thought, scientific knowledge, has been used to convince individuals that they are close to absolute truth and boast such a degree of precision and self-confidence that the humbleness of search is replaced by the arrogance of sureness, which intimidates inquiry and praises dogmatism.Most of the distortions in the long search of mankind for knowledge throughout history has been the result of a segregationistic separation between science and traditions.

Something like a *neurosis philosophicus* tries to identify and to emphasize contradictions between traditional knowledge and scientific knowledge. The attribute of "rational" is reserved to the later in a detrimental and contemptuously way for the former.

Ethical responsability has been "rationalised", brought into normative codes, or reserved, in depreciation, to the domain of values and traditions. The renaissance consolidated modes of thought which had originated in the civilisations of the antiquity around the Mediterranean. A new mode of thought was developed in Europe and imposed through the world after the navigations.

The western "civilisatory mission", which started about 500 years ago, resulted in a model of society dominated by science and technology and a consequent economical, social and political order. Modes of production and division of labor and new concepts of property and wealth, are intimately related with underlying philosophy which made all them possible, which was indeed proposed to justify the conquest-colonisation process.

In this process gods, languages, modes of thought, of labor, of property, of health and so on were imposed throughout the globe. Science and ʟhe values associated with scientific and rational thought were often used to relationalise variants of exploitation of human beings by human beings in the process of building up agricultural supplies. The concept of humanity and an ethics for the entire mankind was gradually removed from this thought.

This mode of thought, prevailing since the XVI century was responsible for:

— interpreting differences among human beings as different stages in the evolution of the species;

— explaining unsatisfying basic material needs as ranging from lack of industry to laziness, and the the search for the satisfaction of spiritual needs as lack of scientific rationality;

— and the preservation of natural and cultural patrimony as obstacles to progress. Indeed, progress is a concept associated with the new thought.

All these three characteristics of modern thought lead to a despicable behavior. The associations are clear:

— with arrogance,

— with indiference and inhumanity,

— with irresponsible behavior. These are capital sins and may cause the destruction of the species. They violate the natural wisdom of a species, they dictate the most serious threat to the extinction of *homo sapiens sapiens*.

Phomo sapiens sapiens. We have to restore the dialectical complementarity of theory and practice. But we are frequently trapped by the fascination of the theoretical discourse at the expenses of the recognition of the essence of the practice. This is the essence of transdisciplinarity.

A new ethics

The species can not survive without an ethics which counteract the characteristics of modern thought and appeal to the simple and primary principle of preservation of life and civilisation on Earth. We call this the

Ethics of preservation :

1. *respect* for the other in spite of all differences;
2. *solidarity* with others in the satisfaction their basic needs for survival and for transcendence;
3. *cooperation* with the other in the preservation of the common natural and cultural patrimony.

Can civilisation survive without an ethics for the entire mankind?

Human behavior as action

In the very short span of his presence in the planet, man is threatened by extinction and at the same time is marvelled to find himself as the focus of a process. We propose understanding *homo sapiens sapiens* as a creature in search of wisdom and of the sublime.

Human behavior and life are inseparable. Life is action performed by the individual in and into reality, an action which follows a strategy designed by the individual himself as a result of his will after processing information from reality. We understand reality in the sense proposed by Basarab Nicolescu: *"une realité d'interaction ou de participation."*

Will plus processing of information are the essence of free intelligent behavior which characterises our species and which defines our existence. One exists in the measure one reacts to impulses (information) from reality and willingly processes this information defining strategies for action upon reality. The dynamics of the process

... reality → individual → action → reality → individual →...

is the dynamics of life and we all, as living human beings, are subjected to it. And thanks to it, we all are responsible for modifying reality. To what extent ? To the measure of our sanity.

Action manifests in several ways. Action which leads to survival and satisfaction of needs common to all living beings, as well as action which satisfies man's characteristic needs for explanations, for understanding and for creating. In other words, for tanscending his own existence and projecting himself into the past and into the future.

Reflecting upon the behavior of living species, we see a form of wisdom in nature. This is seen either in the laws which determines a rigorous and predictable behavior, mathematically precise, according to the old paradigms, or in the complexity which defies the basic assumptions of cause and effect and which have to be recognised as inaccessible to our current understanding.

The believe in the first hypothesis lead to the success of the reductionist approach. Going deeper into the phenomena, increasingly narrowing the field of interest and treating them under increasingly limited specific methodological precepts, we do not avoid the needed search for global explanations, thus paving the way to the multidisciplinarian and to the interdisciplinarian approaches. But these are nothing more than recurrent incursions into the unknown with the same or similar methodological instruments, shifting the focus to other categories of questions. We will not be succesful in our search for explanations if we remain the level of classical methods of science and focus our views on functions and their domains and counter domains. In other terms, if we rerstrict our analysis to cause and effect. We need to go a step further, looking into the categories of analysis themselves and understanding the relations between the objects and their dependences within the various categories . This is similar to what has been called functorial analysis by mathematicians. Our proposal calls for an analysis of the dynamics of the full process.

The scheme below is appropriate to describe the relations and interdependence of individuals, societies and nature. The three relate to each other according to survival strategies. We leave it open the explanation for these strategies, be it according to precise laws which sociobiology try to understand or according to a chaotic or to a synergetic behavior.

Relations, such as mating and societal arragements, are well known among individuals of the same species and collective actions obey comportamental patterns dicatated by genetic structure. At the same time, individuals should relate with their environment and with other species through action upon the nature in which they are immersed, as a constituent part of it, and not as mere predators. These actions are essential for their own survival. And collectively, as a society, to keep the equilibrium. These behaviors, represented by the sides of the this triangle, are respectively regulated by the principles of animal physiology, of sociobiology and of ecology.

From the triangle of survival to the triangle of transcendence

At best interdisciplinarian approach, through domains of knowledge known as physiology, sociobiology and biology. But a global view calls for a transdiciplinarian approach. This leads as to the a geometrical metaphor in which we see the triangle as the essence of the phenomenon life. Breaking this triangle, in each of its sides, would lead to the termination of life in the planet. We thus call this the triangle of survival and the universe in which we place this triangle, which in our metaphoric image is the entire plane, reality. Very much like the adventure of Abbott's Square we will probe three and higher dimensional spaces, where we will find the *Omni.*

In the long history of the cosmos, which stands for reality in its totality, life comes relatively late in a diminute part of it. Since then, it has manifested itself as phenomena of various kinds. Other forms of life, in different universes, would probably call for different geometric metaphors. We can hardly conceive the same principles of physiology, sociobiology and ecology in a possible extra-terrestrial equivalent to life.

In this metaphorically plane reality, hominids appeared - by creation or by evolution - about 4,5 million years ago. From the Australopithecus through the Homo sapiens and finally to our own species, *Homo sapien sapiens* , another triangle is superimposed into the triangle of survival, which nevertheless continues to be the essence for the phenomenon life.

When *homo sapiens* came into being, tools, instruments, equipment, techniques came into playing a role in these arrangements. The relations of this new species with natural reality, in which it was equally immersed as a part of it and not as mere observer, can not escape the model given in the triangle of survival. The new species may exhibit other characteristics. Maybe a special development of the neck and the head, manisfeted mainly in a special arrangement of the internal ear, possibilitated standing on two feet and allowed for a more accute sense of observer, and the differentiation of the upper part of the trachea, which allowed for a different arrangement of sounds possibilitating a very sophisticated form of communication.

These characteristics combined with a growth of the cerebral cortex to give origin to a species with a much better control of the body, an acute capability of receiving vast amount of information and of processing this information with an enormous sense of memory, plus the development of a creative form of communication - language - and the development of a sense of past and future. The animal characteristics and the drive for survival became subordinated to intelligence and will. This is the *homo sapiens sapiens* .

These new characteristics superimposed to the triangle of life another one, the triangle of transcendence, responsible for new intermediations between individuals, nature and societies. Each individual of this new species, *homo sapiens sapiens,* which calls himself man, is, the same as any living species, constantly in the process of struggling for his own survival and for continuity of the species.

But in this process man is acquiring mediators between himself, his other kins and nature, such as tools, instruments, equipments, techniques and communication. Some of these indeed deface nature. Other then the agglomerate of natural facts, nature now exhibits new facts, artifacts and mentifacts, facts produced by individual men. Reality is thus modified, enlarged.

Through the senses - which are yet only minimally known and controlled by man - artifacts inform other individuals, while mentifacts inform only the producer himself. Our senses are recognised as capable of recognising what can be explained as materialised. Vibrations, light, sound, waves or particules, not sensed, are capable of producing sensations which are sensed.

High frequencies are not sensed by the senses of humans, but yes for the senses of other animals.

Each individual of the species *homo sapiens sapiens* is provided with an internal characteristic which submits the struggle for individual survival and for the continuity of the species, characteristics of all living species, to himself and to his will. Thus he develops a new characteristic behavior, unique to thés species, which is the power of decision upon his behavior. This is an essential principle, in different traditions called spirit, soul, anima, karma, and several other denominations. Will generates the essential need to explain, to understand and, to transcend one's own existence, to draw from their ancestors and to project into the generations to come. Man thus acquires a sense of past and of future, the sense of time.

The drive towards survival is thus associated with the drive towards transcendence. Both become, together, the essentiality of human life. To eat, to breath and to procriate take another meaning. The purely animal drive towards survival, of the individual and of the species, of nourishing and of mating, is now associated with the drive towards transcending. Nourishing and mating are associated with pleasure and emotions and are impregnated with rituals.

Discovering the other mediates the relation between the individual and society. The search for the other, a mere mechanism for the continuation of the species in all the other species, with man acquires another dimension . The search and discovery of "thee" is the first step for transcending his own space, for projecting oneself, indeed a necessary preliminary step towards transcending one's own existence. The recognition of "thee" and the search for a "common thee" leads naturally to the creation of myths and symbols, of traditions and norms, of wisdom and knowledge, of culture in its broadest sense.

Individuals subordinate themselves to these categories of behavior intermediating their relations with their kinds. These categories dominate relations between individuals and society, as well as between societies of individuals and reality itself. The driving force of survival of the species is thus modified by factors resulting from these mediations. Examples are labor and division of labor, property, power structure and hierarchy.

These new intermediations are the essence of what became known as knowledge, the *matema*. This is recognised in the acquisition of abilities, capabilities, ways of doing, of explaining, of understanding, of coping with everyday needs of survival and of transcendence, and takes the form of distinct ways of communicating, invention of different instruments, acceptance of distinct ways of organising themselves and of dividing labor.

Groups of individuals living in a society, subjected to specific natural conditions, share the same responses to these specificities, the same *matema*. The resulting modes or styles of surving and transcending, which is manifested in communications, instruments and techniques, power and labor structure, myths and symbols, religion and systems of explanations, or what we simply call culture. These forms of behavior are incorporated in the pool of common knowledge which keeps a group of individuals, a community, a society together and operational.

Culture thus manifests itself in different, obviously interrelated, forms and domains. Cultural forms, such as language, mathematical practices, religious feelings, family structure, dressing and behavior patterns, are thus diversified. They are of course associated with the history of the groups of individuals, communities and societies where they were developed.

Cultural diversities are present and impossible to avoid. A larger community is partitioned into several distinct cultural variants, each owing to its own history and responding differently to the same stimulus. Intracultural relations are enriching and at the same time challenging. Humanity at large is partitioned into different cultures, revealing sometimes conflicting forms. Intercultural relations are also enriching and also challenging. Intercultural, and sometimes even intracultural, conflicts are impossible to avoid. To live with these cultural conflicts is the main theme of cultural dynamics. And to reach the capability of living with cultural conflicts is the ultimate goal of civilisation.

The essence of humanity

We will now discuss the meaning of being human or the essence of the human being. The play between the noun and verb, being and being, synhesizes this discussion. The essence of humanity is attained when the two are together in a symbiotic relation. This can only happen in a dimension superior to the flat two dimensional material reality.

The star resulting from the superposition of the two triangles, survival and transcendence, is the metaphoric symbol of the species. It is the substantive aspect of *homo sapiens sapiens*. The metaphor brings the star resulting from the two triangles superimposed as the essence of human species and it stands for the realisation by the human species of its essential needs of survival and transcendence. This geometrical metaphor of the *star of essentiality* is an example of what we referred to a few paragraphs above. All this is immersed in a material reality in which transcendence can not be fulfilled. The material reality is the present, is the moment we are living. Metaphorically, is a two-dimensional universe, here and now.

A further step, towards total wisdom, would be to reach another dimension. The human species gives a step which differentiates it from all other living species towards a third-dimension. To transcend is the effort to go beyond reality and this is a move to another dimension. We can not reach past neither future, but we are driven to them. Both past and future as behavior go beyond reality, are outside the two-dimensional space of the real.

To penetrate this new dimension is man's attainment of spirituality, it is reaching the karma, it is the step beyond the materiality of two-dimensional reality. The drive towards this is the essence of will. Thus man attains his plenitude, reaches humanity, takes possession of his self, only in this enhanced three-dimensional reality. This is our concept of acquiring the full status of a human being.

Is this immersed in a higher dimensional reality? This goes beyond the capabilities of our perception as a species. We can reach the three-dimensional enhanced reality. It is our goal, as individuals and as a species, to attain the full dimensionality of our being humans. We probe into the unknown, into the higher dimensions, which is the domain of omniscience, omnipotence and omnipresence.

7

Multiculturalism and Education

Public schools in the United States once included Protestant prayers and readings from the King James Version of the Bible as central parts of the school day. Little or no effort was made to respect the diverse religious beliefs of non-Protestants. Catholic children were sometimes whipped by teachers if they refused to read from the King James Bible.

In the same schools, history was taught largely without reference to, let alone understanding of, the experiences of American Indians, blacks, and women. And, perhaps more significantly, all subjects were taught to racially segregated student bodies, for whom even an inclusive, culturally respectful civics curriculum would have been overwhelmed by the civics lesson in white supremacy implicit in the way children were distributed among schools.

This traditional model illustrates the problem with a civic education unmodified by multiculturalism. The traditional model withheld respect from different ways of life, and denigrated the contributions of minority groups and women to American civic culture. It also taught morally skewed lessons in civic virtue. When history classes exalted the contributions of the founding fathers with scant discussion of the institution of slavery, the lives of slaves, the Underground Railroad, or the contributions of African-Americans to civic understandings, public schools failed, among other things, to teach students the civic values of democratic dissent and disobedience to unjust laws. In not teaching these democratic values, schools diminished the role of dissenters and restricted the range of reasonable political alternatives that children could understand and embrace.

To cite another, not atypical example, from personal experience: The world history texts in my public school devoted as much space to the heroic acts of righteous Christians in rescuing Jews during the Holocaust as to the slaughter itself of millions of Jews. These texts sent an unsubtle signal to every student who read them that some people count for much more than others in this country. These texts also failed to convey how the historical experiences of minorities can offer American citizens a more adequate understanding of our civic values of "liberty and justice for all."

These purportedly patriotic history lessons were *repressive* and *discriminatory*. They simultaneously restricted understanding of diverse ways of life and denigrated the people who lived those lives. Repression in schooling is commonly identified with banning books and punishing teachers or students for unpopular ideas. But schooling is often repressive, and more insidiously so, by virtue of what it fails to teach. A civic education is repressive when it fails to teach appreciation and respect for the positive contributions by minorities to a society's common culture.

An antidote to this traditional civics curriculum is education that aims to appreciate the social contributions and life experiences of the various groups that constitute society. Such appreciation defines one common conception of multicultural education, a conception compatible with the principles of democratic education. We are a society constituted by many cultures. It is both morally wrong and empirically false to teach students as if it were otherwise.

Some contemporary American educators, however, defend schooling that is multicultural in a different sense. They defend schools designed primarily to cultivate the separatist cultural identities of minorities and to bolster the self-esteem of students based on their membership in a separatist culture. Afrocentrism is a currently controversial instance of such a separatist multicultural perspective, but the perspective is not unique to Afrocentrism, nor is it new to American education. Some all-white schools are designed to serve a similar if less publicly criticised purpose: to teach children a sense of racial superiority, which is taken to justify racial discrimination.

The chief problem with such segregation academies from a democratic perspective is not the inaccuracy of what they teach children about the superior accomplishments of their ancestors, but their attempt to cultivate among these children a sense of superiority based on race. These schools try to teach racial *discrimination*, albeit for differing reasons. Democratic governments cannot prevent private individuals and associations from conveying to children a sense of superiority based on race, religion, gender, or class, but they must not support schools that convey the very disrespect that democratic education should be designed to dispel.

Some educators say that teaching disadvantaged students to identify with the superior contributions of their ancestors bolsters their *self-esteem*, "the favorable appreciation or opinion of oneself." But this way of cultivating self-esteem comes at the cost of undercutting *mutual respect* among citizens, "a proper regard for the dignity of person or position." In a democracy, proper regard for the position of citizens includes the mutual recognition that all persons, regardless of the accomplishments of their ancestors, are entitled to equal political and civil liberties and fair equality of opportunity to live a good life.

Public schooling in a democracy should not therefore forswear the aim of increasing the self-esteem of disadvantaged students. The aim is to be distinguished from recognising and respecting the identification of individuals with particular cultures. This identification is something that public schooling can support, as a way of respecting students with different cultural identifications, and also as a way of recognising the multitude of cultural opportunities that are open to all students as members of a multicultural society.

Imagine a curriculum in which the achievements of Africa and Africans, ancient and modern, are given due place alongside the treatment of other continents and peoples, and in which the links between the history of Africa and the history of African-Americans are made plain. Such a curriculum taught to *all* students puts multicultural education in service to democratic values, not in opposition. Such a curriculum supports rather than subverts one of the most basic lessons of democratic education: that all individuals, regardless of their cultural identifications, have equal civic standing, and are honored or dishonored by their own acts, not by the acts of their ancestors.

For schools to cultivate a sense of self-esteem in students that is sustainable alongside mutual respect among citizens, schools need to help every student succeed academically. Students learn to appreciate themselves as accomplished individuals when schools help them become accomplished learners. This educational task is a lot harder than teaching students to identify with their ancestors. Educational success entails learning something that is worthy of being publicly honored as knowledge and understanding.

The fact that educational success, like self-esteem, is achieved by individuals does not mean that its attainment must be a solitary endeavor. Quite the contrary. Some of the most successful teaching occurs in cooperative and diverse learning groups. The self-esteem that is compatible with civic equality cannot be acquired by group identification.

We have identified two ways that schools have failed to meet the challenge of securing common values and respecting cultural differences. The traditional civics curriculum imposes a cultural singularity that is false to the pluralism of American life and disrespectful of many of its citizens. A separatist curricula also educates by exclusion by fostering a sense of superiority among some students at the cost of disparaging or degrading others. Neither response promotes mutual respect among citizens, which is still sorely lacking in our society, and many others.

Schools can teach mutual respect in at least two ways that meet the challenge of joining civic and multicultural aims to the benefit of both. Schools can create curricula that recognise the multicultural heritage of the United States as everyone's resource, belonging not only to all of us, but also to future immigrants and generations to come.

In addition, schools can teach about foreign cultures in a way that is more conducive to our remaining a society of immigrants. If we are to remain a haven for political and economic refugees, we need to respect not only the diverse cultures that are already ours, but also those that are not presently represented within our borders. Recognition of foreign cultures cannot of course be comprehensive In any case, cultivating a relatively deep appreciation of a few foreign cultures is likely to be more educationally effective than conveying a superficial familiarity with many.

But appreciation of cultural diversity is not enough to teach students the civic virtue of mutual respect, nor is it the toughest task now facing most schools. Expanding the knowledge of students meets only half the intellectual and moral challenge of the democratic ideal that have been defending. The second, pedagogically as well as politically more demanding, way in which schools can cultivate mutual respect is to teach students how to engage together in respectful discussions in which they strive to understand, appreciate, and, if possible, resolve political disagreements, including those that may be partly rooted in cultural differences. Mutual respect that rests only on the*recognition* of cultural diversity is an incomplete democratic virtue. Recognition needs to be accompanied by a willingness and ability to deliberate about politically relevant disagreements.

A culturally diverse citizenry dedicated to deliberation strives for reciprocity in political relationships. It seeks agreement on public policies that are mutually acceptable to all citizens who are bound by them. Reciprocity is a goal which is unlikely to be fully realised. As with many valuable ends, reciprocity is an aspirational ideal, one that is constitutive of the political ideal of democracy. By teaching the skills and virtues of deliberation among citizens, schools can contribute to bringing a democracy closer to its own ideal.

Even if reciprocity may never be fully realised, we can find partial ways of approaching its educational aims of cultivating an inclusive multiculturalism and a morally informed deliberation. We can find examples of promising practices in non-elite public schools in the United States. Deborah Meier's pioneering District 4 in East Harlem and California's statewide history curriculum offer models of inclusive multicultural curricula. Neither model is perfect, but both are better than what has gone before them. Meier's school is successful both by traditional measures and non-traditional measures.

Much more should be said about teaching morally-informed deliberation than this essay permits. I can only point to a good illustration of teaching the virtues and skills of morally informed deliberation. The example comes from an account of an American history class in a Brooklyn high school where students were asked whether it was moral for the United States to drop the atomic bomb on Japan.

The lesson was taught in a Socratic manner. Bruckner [the teacher] did not lecture. He asked questions and kept up a rapid-fire dialogue among the students. "Why?" "How do you know?" "What does this mean?" By the time the class was finished, the students had covered a great deal of material about American foreign and domestic politics during World War II; they had argued heatedly; most of them had tried out different points of view, seeing the problem from different angles.

Like this small but significant lesson in deliberation, a multicultural curriculum dedicated to teaching deliberation would encourage students to respect each other as equal citizens, regardless of the accomplishments of their ancestors, and to take different points of view seriously when thinking about politics. The practice of morally informed deliberation engages students in according each other the mutual respect and moral understanding that is too often lacking in contemporary politics.

Teaching mutual respect among citizens in these ways is a central aim of civic education in a multicultural democracy. Bolstering self-esteem by group identification is not — not because self-esteem is unimportant or insupportable by education, but because the self-esteem that is compatible with mutual respect among citizens cannot be acquired merely by means of group identification. Just as a civic education, unmodified by multiculturalism, represses cultural differences, multiculturalism, uninformed by civic values, discriminates among citizens on the basis of their group identities. Schools can meet this challenge of multiculturalism by allying common civic values with uncommon cultural appreciations.

Democratic Multicultural Education and "The Affair of the Scarf"

One speaks in the voice of a transcendent universalism, the other in the voice of a separatist particularism. A civic education cannot completely transcend particular cultures, and a multicultural education should not lose sight of the universalist principles of toleration and mutual respect that inform its commitment to cultural diversity. A democratic integration of civic education and multiculturalism can capture the partial truth in the two common perspectives by refusing to divorce the aims of civic education from those of multicultural education, at the same time recognising that there are potential tensions between these two inter-related strands of democratic education.

"Easier said than done," a critic might reply. This integration of multiculturalism and civic education has yet to confront the challenge of accommodating religious differences. To see if democratic education can meet this challenge, we should consider a controversy in which the aims of civic education are apparently at odds with religious freedom.

In 1989, three Muslim adolescent girls went to their local public high school in Creil, France wearing chadors. French public schools are, by law and centuries-long tradition, secular. A 1937 law prohibits the wearing of religious symbols, or at least conspicuous religious symbols, in government-run schools. Citing the 1937 law, the principal of the high school, a Catholic of Martinican origin, told the three students that they must remove their chadors in class. When they refused, the principal, supported by the school's teachers, forbade the girls to attend class.

Controversies like this one pose perhaps the toughest challenge of multiculturalism to civic education. The chador case divided not only French society, but French socialists, who consider themselves as universalist as anyone. Although the socialists could unite in criticising reactions like those of the conservative newspaper *Le Point*, whose headline read "Should We Let Islam Colonise Our Schools?" and the right-wing politician, Le Pen, who urged the repatriation of all immigrants who had arrived in France since 1974, they were bitterly divided among themselves. Some socialists found themselves allied with conservatives in defending the 1937 law, while others proclaimed it unjust. The debate among socialists helps demonstrate why transcendent universalism is inadequate as a public educational philosophy, and points us to a more defensible way of posing and provisionally resolving such problems.

Socialists who supported the 1937 law argued that the veil is "a sign of imprisonment that considers women to be subhumans under the law of Islam" and should therefore not be admitted by a public educational system committed to teaching gender equality. In opposition to the law, Prime Minister Michel Rocard argued that "tolerance must be put before principle." We might say instead that religious toleration itself is a universal principle to be considered alongside the principle of teaching gender equality. Invoking universal values alone therefore does not resolve the conflict, since religious toleration and gender equality both share the status of universal principles for the social context under consideration.

The indeterminacy of universalism is not a reason to abandon it, unless particularism carries with it better moral arguments. Does particularism get the better of universalism in this conflict? Should we give up looking for mutually-acceptable values in public education, and leave education to parents or religious groups? One attraction of particularism is that it offers religious parents effective access to schools that reflect their religious perspectives. Divide school systems into streams, particularists argue, and give every major cultural group the effective opportunity to shape the schooling of its own children.

The French government could then authorise each major community, including secularists, to run its own publicly subsidised schools. French secular schools could remain strictly secular, while orthodox Catholics, Muslims, and Jews could send their children to subsidised schools committed to reinforcing their particular communal values. If the government subsidises separate schooling for each group, then no group needs to compromise its particularist values for the sake of a common civic education.

Something more is missing from this particularist perspective that a more democratic perspective provides. The particularist response to religious diversity neglects, or at least downplays, the government's role in regulating the schools that it subsidises.

The particularist response is radically indeterminate when it comes to specifying what governments must do to ensure that schools adequately educate future citizens. It is this aim of educating future citizens that justifies massive state subsidies of schooling. So particularism cannot escape the question that it lacks the resources to answer: What may citizens reasonably expect of schools as a condition of their receiving public funding and accreditation? The silence of particularism in response to this question sustains the worry that separatist education is not designed to promote the civic values that justify public funding in the first place.

Unless schools serve civic purposes that citizens can share, their support should be left primarily to parents and private associations. Particularists who favor public support therefore should recognise that all streams of schooling must be publicly regulated to the extent necessary to ensure that they promote civic educational purposes. This recognition opens the door to giving precedence to democratic principles over and alongside particularistic purposes. Particularism, so modified, is far more defensible, but it no longer can claim the attraction of avoiding controversies over the content of civic education by ceding to each religious (or ethnic) group its own autonomous sphere of schooling. Nor is this kind of particularism easy to distinguish from a universalism that recognises the value of religious (or ethnic) diversity.

The problems of unregulated particularism are the mirror-image of those confronting a universalism that tries to transcend particularist cultures. While transcendent universalism expects too much uniformity in the content of public schooling, separatist particularism expects too little.

Public schools are the primary institution by which a democratic society educates future citizens, preparing them to share in responsible self-government. Teaching the elements of responsible self-government — which include mutual respect for basic liberty, opportunity, and a commitment to deliberate about politically relevant issues — is a major reason for mandating and publicly subsidising schooling for all children. These lessons are constitutive of the purposes of public schooling in contemporary liberal democracies, or aspiring liberal democracies.

Suppose we grant that teaching students the values of basic liberty, opportunity, and deliberation is a primary purpose of public education. We must still wonder whether any conception of education that recognises this purpose can find a way of resolving the chador case and similar conflicts that pit civic education and cultural diversity against each other. Is there a way of resolving the conflict between religious freedom and a civic education that aims to educate children for the rights and responsibilities of citizenship, where religious beliefs apparently conflict with the aims of civic education?

We cannot defer as a matter of principle to religious freedom regardless of its claims against civic education, as does a particularism unmodified by civic values. Nor can we defer as a matter of principle to a civic education that would expel religious dissenters, regardless of the content of their claims against civic education, as would one version of the universalism represented by the French left — a transcendent universalism that is unmodified by particularist values. This kind of universalism in effect denies that religious freedom, like freedom of conscience more generally, is a basic liberty, necessary to the integrity of persons as we know them.

Public schools have a responsibility to teach and practice religious toleration as *part* of civic education. Both a universalism that respects particular values and a particularism that respects civic values can recognise this responsibility. The critical question remains: To what extent can schools teach and practice religious toleration without sacrificing civic equality and mutual respect among men and women?

We can begin to answer the question by recognising that there are principled limits to the religious freedom that the law must respect, and therefore also limits to the religious practices that a public school must tolerate. (Insisting on wearing a chador is not the same as insisting on being taught in classes that are segregated by religion, gender, ethnicity, or race.) We need to determine the substantive limits of religious toleration in a particular context of public schooling and therefore to consider in the chador case whether the wearing of conspicuous religious symbols — especially religious symbols of gender inequality in a public school classroom —exceeds those limits.

We can locate religious practices that lie beyond the legally protected realm of religious freedom and toleration. The legally protected realm excludes religious practices that conflict with other basic democratic rights and which are themselves less valuable than the particular rights with which they conflict. Examples of religious practices that may be outlawed in order to protect more valuable rights are ritual human sacrifice and the denial of essential health care to children.

In harder cases where rights conflict, we encounter more uncertainty. These conflicts must be resolved, at least provisionally, but they cannot be even provisionally resolved without our rendering some substantive judgment, which will not be neutral, among particular ways of life. The position of deferring, either to established religious practices or established state policy, is not morally neutral, nor does liberal democracy establish a presumption in favor of either position. We have no better alternative than to assess the conflict as carefully as we can and at the most specific level that public policy can handle. We cannot legitimately counterpoise teaching gender equality against protecting religious freedom in its entirety. Instead, we need to focus on the specific aspects of gender equality and religious freedom that are at issue — that is, the school's obligation to teach students, regardless of their religion or gender, to associate as civic equals in the classroom, and the students' freedom to wear conspicuous religious symbols to school, including those that are commonly associated with gender subordination. We now must ask: Is there any way to reconcile these two apparently conflicting values? If not, which value is the more important to secure in this context?

If we recognise the school's dual responsibility — to teach the civic equality of men and women, and to respect individuals regardless of religious differences insofar as these differences are consistent with civic values — we can develop an alternative way of viewing the conflict, a principled integration of the central purposes of the two perspectives.

The liberal democratic values that give public schooling its primary social purpose guide the integration. Schools should tolerate the religious difference represented by the chadors without acquiescing in the gender segregation and subordination that typically accompanies this dress in religious practice outside of schools. The French public schools could have made an educational opportunity out of the girls' wearing of the scarves in school in order to express a democratic commitment to educate all students, regardless of their gender and the religious convictions of their parents.

Schools can teach these democratic lessons in different ways, but the way in which the French government recently resolved the chador controversy is not one of them. In September 1994, the government reversed an earlier ruling by the *Conseil d'Etat* that would have allowed the wearing of chadors in public schools. Under the new policy, students are not permitted to wear "ostentatious religious signs" in the classroom, and chadors count as ostentatious signs. Crucifixes and yarmulkes, on the other hand, are considered discrete and are therefore permitted. Thus, Catholic boys and girls who wear crucifixes or Jewish boys who wear yarmulkes will be welcome within French public schools, while Muslim girls who insist on wearing chadors will not.

The previous ruling by the *Conseil d'Etat* had been more defensible on democratic grounds, though it too fell short of a fully principled integration of particularism and universalism. The wearing of religious symbols, the

Conseil had said, is permissible so long as it does not involve one of the four *P*s: "pressure on others, provocation, propaganda, or proselytism."

The ruling raised a critical question concerning moral responsibility in an educational context: What if the wearing of chadors provokes some students to taunt the girls? The ruling suggested that discipline may be directed to the girls rather than the taunters. Yet this way of resolving the problem of provocation would be unjust to the girls, who should not be held responsible for the uncivil behavior of students who fail to respect their right to religious freedom.

Educators should be able to distinguish such uncivil behavior from another kind of reaction among students, which would be fully consistent with democratic education. The wearing of chadors might provoke criticism among some students for being a symbol of women's second-class citizenship. This criticism, in turn, might provoke the Muslim girls to respond with a defense of their tradition. These forms of civil provocation might be discomforting to all parties, but such discomfort is not unwelcome to democratic education. While multiculturalism, informed by democratic principles, encourages us to understand the value that different ways of life have for people who live them, it also exposes every way of life to civil criticism.

The democratic rationale for opening schools to the display of religious difference, along with other kinds of cultural difference, is therefore not to protect each particular way of life from criticism or even from erosion. The rationale is rather to encourage citizens to understand, appreciate, and evaluate politically relevant differences among ways of life. Because some ways of life are more open to criticism and change than others, reflection on politically relevant differences is bound to be more unsettling to some students and citizens than to others, but the non-neutrality of a democratic education is a virtue as well as a necessity.

Non-neutrality is a necessity because an educational program would be empty were it to rest upon neutrality among different conceptions of the good life. Non-neutrality, more interestingly, is a virtue because citizens should support an educational system only if it is *not* neutral between those ways of life that respect basic liberty, opportunity, and deliberation, and those that do not. A liberal democracy should take its own side in arguments about teaching the skills and virtues that are constitutive of its own flourishing.

Among the various responses in France to the chador case, the one that best reflects the democratic aim of integrating particularism and universalism was that of Souad Benani, a spokesperson for *Les Nanas Beurs,* an organisation of women of North African descent. "As Arab feminists of Muslim culture," Benani said,

> we believe that fundamentalism in all its forms is dangerous and the scarf is oppressive. But it should not be used as a pretext to exclude twelve- or thirteen-year-old girls from school when it is precisely these secular schools that should offer them the opportunity to learn, grow, and make their own choices.

Informed by a larger conception of democratic education, this response does not simply defer to the religious beliefs of Muslim parents or students, nor does it claim to be transcendent in its universalism. Its guiding principles — which include basic liberty and opportunity for all individuals, and their effective freedom to deliberate as civic equals about collective choices — are arguably universal for our world as we now know it, but these principles are also importantly open-ended in their content. Not only will their implications vary with the facts of particular societies, but the principles themselves are also legitimately subject to interpretation by the ongoing public deliberation that democratic education ideally supports.

The principles of democratic education do not comprehensively specify what constitutes a *good* education independently of particular cultures, life projects, and democratic deliberations. Democratic education rejects the separatist strand of particularism, which would give up on the project of educating all children for the rights and responsibilities of citizenship, regardless of their familial culture. But it respects the widest range of cultural differences compatible with teaching those rights and responsibilities. These differences include cultural practices that you or I may judge wrong, or of lesser value than competing practices, but that we can still recognise as reasonable for those who adopt them.

Democratic education would not force the girls to give up wearing chadors in class, but it would expose them to a public culture of gender equality in public school. This exposure gives them reasons why women should view themselves as the civic equals of men, and it opens up opportunities that are not offered by their families and religious communities. By opening up such opportunities, democratic education may lessen the likelihood that certain kinds of cultural practices will perpetuate themselves. A democratic government should not go out of its way to perpetuate cultural practices that conflict with its constitutive principles.

Some critics suggest that this position of partial accommodation is little more than a pretense of accommodation with ways of life that dissent from liberal democratic orthodoxy. "Funny-hat liberalism," it is sometimes disparagingly called. Why? Because the price paid by orthodox Muslim parents for accepting the accommodationist position of democratic education may be a serious weakening of the hold of their religious convictions and inherited way of life on their children.

The critics are correct in suggesting that democratic education does not grant illiberal ways of life nearly all that they claim for themselves, nor even all that they may need in order to perpetuate themselves in their present form. Democratic education does not claim to support any cultural way of life on its own terms, or even to the extent necessary to guarantee its survival as such. Nor should it. Cultures do not have rights to survival. People have rights to religious freedom, along with other basic liberties and opportunities, that place demands on democratic education. The right to religious freedom, as we have seen, has principled limits. Among those limits is the right of children to be educated for full citizenship in a democratic society, and the responsibility of publicly-supported schools to secure that right for students, even when it conflicts with religious commitments of their parents.

Moreover, the critics' disparagement of accommodating the wearing of chadors in public schools is not true to the experience of the Muslim parents and the girls themselves. The Muslim parents and the girls in this case preferred, and had good reason to prefer, the earlier accommodation by the *Conseil d'Etat* to the more recent banning of chadors. The parents argued for the right of their children, *dressed in accordance with their religious convictions,* to be educated as future French citizens within the public schools. They did not argue for their right to be *religiously* educated, as fundamentalist Muslims, in public schools.

The critics seem to assume that religious education in publicly subsidised schools is the only consistent position available to any truly religious parents. Many religious parents reasonably believe otherwise, and it is the willingness of the vast majority of citizens to draw some line of separation between civic education and religious education that permits any religiously pluralistic democracy to pursue liberty and justice for all.

The critics are therefore correct in claiming that the earlier ruling by the *Conseil d'Etat* did not provide the Muslim girls with a public education that conformed to their religious convictions, but the critics fail to defend their presumption that public education should be judged by its conformity with the religious convictions of parents. The critics offer no reason to reject the view that publicly subsidised education should serve distinctively civic purposes, which can be shared by a diverse citizenry, not distinctively religious purposes which divide us.

Democratic education respects religious differences that are consistent with expecting all citizens, regardless of their religious beliefs, to honor a set of civic responsibilities. Those civic responsibilities include allowing one's children to be educated for democratic citizenship. Democratic education thereby integrates particularist and universalist values. A religiously diverse citizenry can honor this integration as long as they are willing to share a society together on terms that they can justify to one another.

Liberalism, Multiculturalism, and Education

Raging debate over multiculturalism has permeated virtually every facet of academic endeavor. Appropriately, political philosophers and philosophers of education are as embroiled in these discussions as any other academicians. Theoretical traditions are being reexamined in light of demands for group representation in political participation and resource distribution. Scholarly attention to the "recognition" and "difference" of cultural groups suggests that a multicultural agenda must address histories of exclusion and domination. Multiculturalism aspires to replace discriminatory practices with equal status relationships in an inclusionary public realm. For political philosophers this agenda raises the question:

What theoretical orientation is most hospitable to the ideals of multiculturalism? For philosophers of education the question becomes: What educational practices are consistent with a multicultural public ethos?

While many traditions are drawn upon in multicultural discourse, this paper will explore the fruitfulness of a marriage between liberal theory and multiculturalism.

Standards Objections to Liberal Theory

Possibly the most frequent critique of modern liberalism is that of abstract individualism. Detractors contend that the liberal emphasis on individual rights is non-relational, failing to recognise the essential embeddedness of persons in social contexts. Accordingly, the role of culture is seen to be subsumed under a definition of self preoccupied by individual interests and autonomous free choice.

In response to these charges, Kymlicka claims that, within modern liberalism, people are not abstract individuals, but *social beings,* whose essential interest is in living a good life. He contends that what is important for liberals is not abstracting the individual from society, but providing social conditions under which people can choose their essential good. It is this provision of social conditions, by way of a formulation of the basic structure of society, that Rawls is concerned with in positing the concept of "justice as fairness." Rawls's idea of justice as the first virtue of political society does not necessarily abstract the individual from his/her social context by ruling out important virtues such as bonding, love, and identification.

Accordingly, he refers to society, not as a union of individuals, but as a *"union of social unions."* He also insists that justice is not a comprehensive metaphysical ideal, but a political conception appropriate for a partitioning of societal realms, whereby justice may be most appropriate for the public realm, but an ideal such as loyalty or caring might be better suited for other "nonpublic" realms.

An emphasis on the social conditions which necessitate a political conception of justice indicates that modern liberals are not so naive as to consider the "self" as atomistic or existing prior to social relationships. But, aside from abstract individualism and of equal concern to multiculturalism, modern liberalism may also seem vulnerable to charges of Eurocentrism. Critics argue that, both historically and metaphysically, liberalism rests on particular notions of the self and society that pass as universal in the interests of Western cultural imperialism.

Yet, modern liberals have taken great pains to separate a political conception of justice from metaphysical foundationalism. Rawls's move — from conceiving of justice as an overarching moral or philosophical ideal to grounding it as a workable political principle for constitutional regimes — allows for the concept to be claimed from within many doctrines, rather than being imperialistically imposed from a Eurocentric vantage point. Rawls argues that this capacity for different traditions to share a political conception of justice as consistent with their own ideals augments both social unity and stability. Hence, Rawls's conception of justice as fairness addresses both charges of universalism and doctrinal imperialism.

Associated with charges of Eurocentrism are more pragmatic concerns that the liberty and equality of opportunity espoused by liberals have never been realised in American institutions. Such concerns oversimplify the complex relationship between political ideals and contextual implementation and mistakenly place fault with the ideals. As Parens asserts: "Our failure is not in adopting such principles but in failing to live up to them." The argument that liberal tenets have never been entirely realised is not a sufficient reason to abort the project. The following reconciliation of the ideals of liberalism and multiculturalism represents an attempt to address both theoretical discrepancies and structural inequities in our current sociopolitical context.

Attractions of Liberal Theory for Multiculturalism

Multiculturalism's foci on the politics of recognition and difference seem to require at least two things of liberal theory: first, an acknowledgment of the importance of culture to the exercise of individual rights; and second, protection of many different conceptions of the good for individuals and groups alike. Modern liberal theory addresses these concerns by positing an impartial or neutral public sphere for the adjudication of justice claims, basic rights of individuals that take into account the importance of cultural membership, and necessary conditions for the examination and pursuit of various cultural goods.

Critics charge that liberal neutrality and impartiality neglect, or even disallow, certain conceptions of the good and that public/private distinctions maintain relations of domination. But liberal theorists are not blind to these issues. More recent works of Rawls and Kymlicka address some of the weaknesses within modern liberal theory that are of preeminent concern to multiculturalism. Whereas Rawls's work informs the relationship between difference and the public sphere, Kymlicka's work illuminates the relationship between the individual and his/her cultural background.

Tolerance for Diversity

The liberal ideal of neutrality allows for tolerance of many different visions of the good life. Liberals acknowledge that modern constitutional regimes are comprised of different groups with varying notions of the good life, which are often conflicting and sometimes incommensurable. Hence, public agreement regarding the good is not sought. Instead, liberal political theorists seek to provide grounds which legitimate the power of the state, or the public, in mediating conflicting interests. The project of legitimation is generally conceived of in terms of rules for participation in public discussions in which legitimate political decisions are made.

Rawls's offers the idea of a free-floating, overlapping consensus to describe what can be talked about, how it should be talked about, and the level of agreement that should be sought in liberal public discourse. He is interested in providing some grounds for stability and unity among the disparate groups of the state. Thus, his overlapping consensus is intended to narrow the range of disagreements between different groups who support multiple visions of the good. But he does not seek to get rid of disagreement by searching for deeper commonalties which might subsume or ignore differences. Where Ackerman has been criticized for advocating silence surrounding disagreements, Rawls suggests instead:

> that questions are not removed from the political agenda, so to speak, solely because they are a source of conflict. We appeal instead to a political conception of justice to distinguish between those questions that can be reasonably removed from the political agenda and those that cannot. Some questions still on the agenda will be controversial, at least to some degree; this is normal with political issues.

Rawls's reassurance that conflictual issues may remain on the table is important for protecting the degree of diversity, and possibly incommensurability, suggested by the politics of difference. But his emphasis on what *can* be removed is still somewhat troubling. Can we really expect the dialogic process to be so straightforward that we will reasonably agree to remove such weighty issues that those remaining will only cause "some degree" of conflict?

Benhabib is concerned about a model of discourse that takes some conceptions of the good life and privatises them by removing them from the table of public debate. Benhabib concedes that public conversations need to be *constrained,* but disagrees that any substantive issues should be beyond the realm of discussion. She advocates a model of practical discourse ethics in which "no issues of debate and no conceptions of the good life are precluded from being voiced in the public arena of the liberal state."

Benhabib's concerns are important to the multicultural agenda for a number of reasons. She is particularly suspicious of two tendencies within liberalism: the ideal of impartiality and the insistence on strict separation between public and private spheres. Benhabib is uncomfortable with impartiality because it denies the essential embeddedness of the self in social relationships. In addition, Benhabib's suspicion of the public/private distinction is firmly rooted in a feminist critique of historical exclusion of women from the public sphere. Benhabib asserts that it is too convenient to label issues as "private" when they are uncomfortable to discuss and/or reflect oppressive power relations.

Strike's conception of the overlapping consensus presents a more realistic picture of the depth of struggle surrounding not only how to engage in public discourse, but what can be talked about. Like Rawls, he suggests that differences cannot be ignored nor subsumed under commonalty. But Strike seems more willing to account for the importance of what Rawls would label "private" concerns. For Strike, substantive discourse is required, surrounding what can be agreed upon given the depth of diverse outlooks.

The question is not "On what do we all currently agree that can serve as a basis of political discussion?" Nor is it an answer to the question, "What can we agree on once we have bracketed such differences as religion, gender, race and ethnicity?" It is more like "What can we agree on, given ample time for debate, that allows us to meet in the commons and that does not require us to abandon or bracket those background convictions on which we differ?" This means that the construction of a fabric of public reason, of a commons, requires *real arguments* between *real interlocutors* with *real substantive moral convictions.*

One strength of Strike's interpretation of the overlapping consensus for multiculturalism is his acknowledgment that actual people with deeply held beliefs will be coming to the table to engage in substantive discussion. This emphasis is more consistent with the rootedness of social identities suggested by Benhabib and Young and suggests a more meaningful model of public discourse than that of Rawls's — one capable of grappling with issues that are controversial, rather than merely pushing them aside.

Strike's willingness to grant that convictions accompany individuals into the commons seems to move away from the strict separation of public/private and political/non-political apparent in Rawls's work. Rawls's insistence that associational ties are voluntary and apolitical seems antithetical to the politics of recognition and difference.

Commonly held notions regarding the interrelationships between culture, socialised identities and ascribed biological attributes suggest that cultural associations are not always voluntary. Nor, if one believes that selves are socialised or dialogically constituted beings, does it seem likely that either associational or affectional ties can be left at the door of the political arena. This separation of public versus nonpublic identity in Rawls's theory of justice raises questions about where culture fits in. Is culture essential to the equal rights of the individual as a basic or primary good? Or is it on the same level as voluntary associations? Resolution of such questions is crucial to the discourse between multiculturalism and liberal theory. It is precisely this weighty issue that Kymlicka addresses.

Culture as a Primary Good

A large part of Kymlicka's project in *Liberalism, Community, and Culture* is to reconcile modern liberal theory with the notion of culture as a primary good. Kymlicka bases the importance of this project around the protection of minority rights — particularly within the Canadian context — on both philosophical and pragmatic grounds. He acknowledges that for liberalism to remain a dynamic and robust political philosophy, it must respond to eminent and immanent concerns regarding its supposed lack of theoretical attention to the relationship between individual and community.

From without liberalism, critiques of abstract individualism articulated by feminists and communitarians require liberals to demonstrate at least a "basic understanding of the importance of cultural membership." From within, insufficient attention to culture raises problems when balancing equality of opportunity with minority rights. Kymlicka suggests that this inherent tension can be addressed in one of two ways: one can discard liberalism as incomplete and inhospitable to minority rights, or one can "attempt to reconcile minority rights and liberal equality." He undertakes such a project of reconciliation, arguing that this endeavor also makes sense on pragmatic political grounds in terms of appealing to political decision makers who have power over issues of group rights.

Kymlicka asserts that defending minority rights within liberalism requires two things: 1) showing that cultural membership has a more important status in liberal thought than is explicitly recognised; and 2) showing that the members of minority cultures may face particular kinds of disadvantages with respect to the good of cultural membership which require and justify minority rights. For our purposes, we will focus on his exploration of the first provision — an argument for the reconciliation between modern liberal theories of justice, and substantive recognition of the importance of cultural membership.

Kymlicka grounds his discussion within the parameters of Rawls's conception of the "liberties of equal citizenship." He acknowledges that Rawls's insistence on the priority of liberties of citizenship appears to make his theory of justice incompatible with minority rights. But he pursues *why* Rawls places such great emphasis on these liberties in the first place, suggesting that the salient point for emphasis is that "the freedom to form and revise our *beliefs* about value is a crucial precondition for pursuing our essential interest in leading a good life". Crucial prerequisites to guarantee this freedom are posited as 1) the social conditions to make intelligent decisions about value; and 2) self-respect as a precondition "of any rational plan of life."

Within this framework, Kymlicka makes his crucial move to demonstrate the inextricable links between cultural membership and the liberties of citizenship. Since the work of J.S. Mill, the importance of free exchange and debate surrounding the good life has been a cornerstone of modern liberalism. Kymlicka follows Rawls's lead in releasing this quest from any comprehensive moral ideals. He argues:

> Liberals should be concerned with the fate of cultural structures, not because they have some moral status of their own, but because it's only through having a rich and secure cultural structure that people can become aware, in a vivid way, of the options available to them, and intelligently examine their value.

Kymlicka suggests here that culture is crucial to and necessary for individual freedom. He argues that we must look more closely at where beliefs, self-respect, and ideas about value come from and concludes:

The decision about how to lead our lives must ultimately be ours alone, but this decision is always a matter of selecting what we believe to be most valuable from the various options available, selecting from a *context of choice* which provides us with different ways of life.

This is important because the range of options is determined by our cultural heritage. Kymlicka goes on to assert that the relationship between cultural membership and self-respect urges parties to "original position" to grant cultural membership status as a primary good. Hence, in his conception, culture is not merely associational nor voluntary, but fundamental to individual well-being and the exercise of basic rights of equality and liberty.

At the same time that Kymlicka makes a case for the importance of cultural membership, he continues to stress liberal choice. By emphasizing both cultural membership and cultural choice, Kymlicka is simultaneously advocating and downplaying culture's importance — it is necessary for the individual to make choices, hence the individual can choose to opt out of his or her cultural membership. In accordance with deontological liberalism, the examination of value is freed from particular ends, but not from any standards of relative worth. Cultural choice is implicitly valued over cultural reproduction.

The tension between cultural choice versus cultural reproduction, found within both multiculturalism and liberalism, indicates a key difference between conditions that allow freedom to *examine* the good and conditions that allow freedom to *pursue* the good. Kymlicka's argument suggests that, for examination of the good, culture is essential as a context for choice; for pursuit of the good, culture must be viewed as an object of choice. Before exploring what this tension means for the relationship between multiculturalism and liberalism, let us see how it plays out in the arena of education.

Multicultural Education and Conditions for Choice

Many multicultural educators are concerned with students' capacities to move beyond their cultural boundaries to a position of cultural choice. However, according to one multiculturalist critique, students are not currently free to pursue cultural choice. Because society and schools are dominated by mainstream or Eurocentric interests, one notion of the good life prevails over alternatives. The crux of the problem is identified in terms of *representation* of various cultures within the educational process.

The argument for representation proceeds as follows. Without accurate and adequate portrayal of marginalised groups' experiences, free choice is disallowed for two reasons. First, omitted or distorted information affects students self-esteem, having negative consequences for academic success. Second, such alienation from schooling becomes a vicious cycle during which marginalised students are denied access to "high status" knowledge, which may afford them future opportunities. Thus, students from certain groups do not have equal opportunity to pursue their vision of the good.

The first issue has to do with representation of alternative conceptions of the good and primarily impacts students ability to *examine* their own conception of the good. The second issue has to do with access to educational resources to enable students equal opportunity to *pursue* a vision of the good which they see as most valuable. Multiculturalists are concerned with reforming educational institutions to address these inequities. In terms of representation, for the liberal conditions of free choice to be met, it seems that students need two main things: 1) the *means* to make intelligent choices, and 2) various *ends* to choose from.

In terms of means, remembering Rawls's and Kymlicka's emphasis on the importance of self-respect for determining value, recognition becomes essential for free choice. According to multiculturalists, students need to see their cultural selves reflected in schools in order for self-esteem, motivation, and academic success to increase.

Places to see such reflection include content, approaches to knowledge, teaching styles, and personnel. Accurate cultural representations in these areas will improve conditions for students to gain skills to make informed choices between cultural goods. In terms of ends, accurate cultural representation becomes a requirement for equal consideration of different conceptions of the good. Portraying various visions of the good expands the options of choice for all students, not only those from culturally marginalised backgrounds.

Is accurate representation of groups enough to secure the conditions for examination and pursuit of the good? For liberals, the principle of *equal protection* has been a primary tool for providing free conditions under which different views of the good can be pursued. However, in a society where one cultural group is dominant, treating everyone the same may not be an execution of justice nor fairness. For example, success demands sacrifices from marginalised groups that it does not require of the mainstream group.

Fordham's research suggests that "African American students who become high academic achievers resolve the conflict caused by the interaction of their personal cultural knowledge with the knowledge and norms within schools by becoming "raceless" or by "ad hocing a culture." If, in fact, enculturation predisposes students toward different approaches to learning, equal conditions would require *different treatment*, because treating all groups the same systematically disadvantages some. Hence, equal opportunity may require certain rights and protections for students from minority groups. To be consistent with liberalism's own principles, treating students equally may require treating them differently.

Multiculturalists' advocacy of cultural representation and special status treatment suggests the importance of recognition to making choices about the good life. But this emphasis on culture is still undermined by the insistence that students can and should choose whatever vision of the good life seems most valuable. A deeper notion of culture would limit one's ability to forfeit cultural identity, but would be more consistent with arguments for the rootedness of selves and the importance of culture as a context or screen for making choices about other, perhaps less weighty, goods. At this point, let us return to the theoretical realm to explicate the tensions between liberalism and multiculturalism that we have seen played out in the educational arena.

Potential problems with a marriage between liberalism and multiculturalism

The liberal emphasis on conditions to examine and pursue one's ends is problematic for three reasons when considering cultural goods. First, insistence on a *political* identity which values basic *individual* equality and liberty may pose problems for groups whose comprehensive doctrines place more value on a *social self*. Second, the notion of individual choice assumes that a culture, or parts of it, can be forfeited for something else that is more valuable. This assumption undermines the idea of a culture as a coherent whole. Choice is also at odds with the importance of culture in identity formation, as asserted by many multiculturalists. For someone like Asante who emphasizes "psychological and cultural dislocation," the inextricable linkage between a person's cultural affiliation and psychological well being seems to minimise choice surrounding cultural goods.

Third, the notion of free choice presumes some level of autonomy; it seems to be based on the assumption that people have definite interests of their own that can be clearly delineated from other people's interests. Kymlicka and Rawls attempt to defend liberalism against charges of abstract individualism by stressing social conditions for choice. But, continued division between public and nonpublic identities, and the abstraction required for parties to the original position are problematic. Are liberals still abstracting individual interests out of social contexts in ways that do not mesh with identity formation and social interaction?

All of these questions revolve around key relationships between self, culture and choice. For a lasting relationship between multiculturalism and liberalism to be forged, such questions need to be resolved. Further exploration of the relationship between individuals and culture, and of congruence between substantive diversity and the public sphere, will help to illuminate these issues.

Identity, Plurality, and Education

Many theorists of education have defined school as a place where competencies, knowledge, and attitudes are transmitted to a new generation, and family education as the locus for the transmission of cultural and moral ideals, values and norms. Such a view, of course, leaves out the most important element of education, and reduces educational theory to an applied developmental psychology and a sociology of education. Unless cultural transmission is understood as a totally mechanistic and determined form of socialisation, the aim of this transmission is always that the pupil learn to give meaning to "things" and "facts," and to act socially in an autonomous way according to his or her own judgment. Besides the acquisition of competencies, this calls for the development of personal identity which includes being aware of oneself as a consistently and continuously judging and acting person. Without this quality, human agency seems unthinkable.

In educational theory, however, this aim of personal identity has often gone unanalysed in the sense that it has been accepted without questioning its validity. The possibility of a contribution of education to its attainment has normally been seen as self-evident. Only recently, since the quality of the cultural resources to be transmitted has come into question, and the "postmodern" plurality of culture has come to be seen as a potential problem in reaching identity, has educational theory begun to be interested in analysing and questioning the assumptions behind the idea of personal identity.

The Concept of Identity

Erikson suggests that in the course of ontogeny, learning "a group's basic ways of organising experience", in combination with becoming aware of one's own physiological and psychological traits, leads to the development of "ego identity." This he describes alternately as "the awareness of a style of individuality" and "the sense of being capable of acting effectively within a group." Thus, it is clear that identity is a concept which refers both to individual and group characteristics, to differences and to communalities, and to the way an individual learns to combine these characteristics into a more or less stable and consistent whole. In psychoanalytic theory, which underlies Erikson's model, the ego is a term for describing the process of maintaining this consistency.

For Rorty and Wong, "a person's identity is constituted by a configuration of central traits..that typically make a systematic difference to the course of a person's life, to the habit-forming and action-guiding social categories in which she is placed, to the way that she acts, reacts, and interacts." They distinguish traits that have to do with body awareness and somatic self-confidence; individual temperament and psychological characteristics; social and institutional roles; group or collective identity; ideals, norms, and ideal self images. Such traits can have a more or less central position in a hierarchy of traits; moreover, the "objective" centrality of a trait may not correspond to its "subjective" centrality. The role of the ego is replaced here by the concept of hierarchy.

It is important to realise the importance of what Erikson calls the ego process. Personality traits may, and usually will, be in conflict, both between and within categories. The hierarchy of traits is seldom a perfect one. Even if we conceive of needs, interests, and psychological characteristics as "authentic," not socially influenced personality traits, these will contain conflicting elements. This is, for instance, recognised in the "psychological" anthropology of Plato who suggests that conflicting desires should be "tamed," moderated by will and rationality.

Generally speaking, the fact of potential conflict seems to require some sort of governing instance which insures self-identity over time and in different contexts. In the view not only of Plato, but of many theorists, such self-identity can only be warranted by a second "part" of the concept of identity — the ego or self — which differs from, and is placed above, the hierarchy of personality traits.

Education is habitually seen as an important factor in the construction of a social identity, or in the terms of Rorty and Wong, of the communal aspects of individual trait hierarchies. Education has the task of providing the group's "basic ways of organising experience" which includes ideals and norms as well as accepted ways of interpreting and giving meaning to phenomena. It also provides the cultural resources which constitute models both of traits and of their possible relationships. Schooling, as a societal enterprise, has been charged with the task of providing elements for a national or even universal identity. In any country where curriculum decisions have been made at a central level, or a general education program has been discussed, one of the suggested aims of such a program has been the creation of communality, of a common "expectation horizon," to facilitate the coordination of behavior for the members of a nation, or of all people.

It is a common position among educational theorists that in traditional societies, because of their cultural consistency, group identity was enough to ensure internal consistency of the person as well, and autonomy was hardly an issue. This also means that, in such societies, a systematic introduction to the communal knowledge and values base should be enough to produce a coherent personality. In this traditional view of education, then, rationality is thought to coincide with "the group's basic ways of organising experience"; and the development of will serves to ascertain that reason will indeed prevail over the more individual traits and desires. As self and rationality coincide in this view, it is clear that education does not have to worry about the development of the self as a separate task.

Our present society, however, distinguishes itself from traditional ones precisely by the fact that its culture is not consistent, but pluralistic. This has implications both for the development of identity and for the tasks of education.

Autonomy and Plurality

Two factors have been important in the rethinking of

identity. One is the realisation that, in our society, there is not one basic way of organising experience; there are many group cultural identities, and they are not easily reconciled or commensurated. The second is the discovery that power relations play an important part in creating an illusion of consistency and suppressing the free development of identity structures.

As a reaction to this, our culture attaches great value to the avoidance of indoctrination and the possibility of autonomous choice. Thus, if education provides the cultural resources for personality formation, our present educational ideal is not that children learn to internalise a prescribed cultural identity, but that they are enabled to pursue self-chosen goals and relationships and "create" their own personality by choosing between their possibilities. Self-identity as autonomy and being a subject is, thus, valued more highly than being a "good" or consistent personality. Autonomy and agency have become the primary aims of education.

In what way can education promote autonomy? The accepted view of "modern" education has been that it should counter the fragmenting tendencies of modern society with a universalising and formalising move. Rationality is no longer thought to exist in the traditional knowledge of a group; instead, it is thought of as a universal capacity which transcends particular thought systems. Adequate behavior is equated with behavior guided by universal principles.

This idea is behind the traditional view of school education. Schools are considered to have the task of teaching logical thinking procedures and universally valid facts on which these procedures can operate, producing "rational humans" who are able not only to rationally control their desires, but also to critically evaluate the prejudices and unwarranted ideas of everyday culture. Contrary to what I said earlier, this means that defining schools as places for information transmission does imply a specific view of identity. In fact, the idea of producing rational humans is central to what has been called the "project of modernity." In this model of identity, the upper, superior level of rationality controls the lower level of personality, the domain of choices, plurality and even contradictions.

In some views, this leads to a sharp distinction between school education as the domain of the rational, and family education as the domain of tradition and choices. As Marshall shows, in such a view, the range of rationality is twofold: critically testing for truth where applicable, as well as deliberating and choosing in accordance with a self-formulated scale of values where the truth criterion does not apply.

The latter aspect requires that the child be enabled to develop according to its own needs and desires. Progressive pedagogy has stressed that education should provide a stimulating and emotionally safe environment in which this development may take place. Some progressive theorists hold that personal identity will result more or less automatically from the growth of a principle innate in every human being.

In their learning and development process, pupils should be enabled to make their own choices between traditions or elements from traditions, based on their own authentic needs, interests, and preferences. "This..presupposes that needs and interests themselves are not socially constructed, or that decision making processes which underlie choosing between needs and interests are not problematic." Seen in this way, personality is a "product of nature," an outcome of natural growth, and learning about the physical and social environment is only made possible by the development of this personality.

Such educational philosophers as Peters and Scheffler have formulated a revised, "modern" version of this educational ideal, combining it with a cognitive developmental view of ontogeny. Theirs is a "formal education" view, in which pupils appropriate a number of forms of thinking which have a universal, or at least supra-traditional, validity. This extends the domain of rationality beyond the truth criterion. Because such forms of thinking do not have content, acquiring them presupposes that pupils have first appropriated the material contents of cultural traditions.

Learning the forms of thinking at the same time represents a later and higher, post-conventional stage of development which enables pupils to take a critical stance towards their social identity and, thus, to realise a "personalised" autonomous relation to that tradition. Plurality of values and views is therefore contained and subsumed under universal principles. The idea of incompatibility of different views is seen as characteristic of a prior developmental stage. Thus, Van Haaften and Snik consider the validity of the forms of thinking as ultimately warranted by the formal characteristics of language and communication, as elaborated in the "transcendental pragmatics" of Apel and Habermas.

While such a theory may be seen as an extension and reformulation of Piaget's epistemology, Habermas has given a version of it that is inspired by critical theory. Habermas endorses the position that, in our society, the structures of interaction in which individuals participate do not realise the ideals implicit in language use and are oppressive. Under such conditions, autonomy is repressed. The structure of our society is such that current educational situations can only produce either an internally divided, or an ideologically curtailed personality structure, depending on how one estimates the degree of dominance of hegemonic culture. Other theories consider the internally consistent person to be the self-evident aim of education; but this can, under current conditions in society, no longer be regarded as a factual or even a possible result of education.

In fact, education has deteriorated into what Adorno called "Halbbildung". Transmission of knowledge has displaced personality formation as the aim of education. Its primary function is to ensure the production of persons that fit into existing societal structures. Thus, critical theorists are pessimistic about the possibilities of education in our society. They understand education primarily as a means for continuing repression, not as a means for individual self-realisation.

The central category of critical pedagogy — emancipation — refers to the necessity of reclaiming a space for autonomy and subjectivity. As the structures of communication that individuals internalise are neither harmonious nor consistent, the implication for contemporary education is that, in order to reach individual rationality, the individual needs the competence to distance herself from internalised role positions and to reflect on and interpret these positions. Thus, identity no longer coincides with the internalised role patterns, the generalised other, but is elevated to a formal level. Identity presupposes distance from the self, and the ability to handle different, mutually inconsistent roles.

Whether in its classical or its modern form, the identification of autonomy with rationality is based on a harmonious world view. This holds true even for critical pedagogy, where harmony is seen as a counterfactual ideal. In such a view inconsistencies and contradictions are valued negatively and are seen as barriers to be overcome in the course of development and/or learning. They are not part of the "real" world, but only of our inadequate conceptions of it. Thus, such theories imply a form of Cartesian dualism, where "mind" in the course of the developmental process evolves to eventually reflect the "real" structures of the world — albeit in the "modern" version "world" implies culture and the structure of human communication. The implication is also that for every domain, there is ultimately only one way of "doing things right."

Other theories of autonomy tend in a totally different direction. Such theories are based on the view that the plurality of cultural traditions is fundamentally irreducible and should be dealt with as such. Basically, rationality in such views is understood to exist only within traditions, not above or outside them. This necessarily leads to the position that, where only one way of being and acting rationally is recognised, this must be the result of the suppression of other rationalities by power structures. Thus, Marshall comments on progressive education theory:

> The Western educational tradition emphasizes logic and truth, as if these notions have not themselves been constituted by various power structures and relationships of power. Once we admit such possibilities, especially in relation to the human sciences, then the notion of the autonomous chooser becomes problematic. Indeed it becomes possible that needs, interests and choice, the notion of autonomy, and even identity itself, have been constituted in various ways.

Thus, autonomy emerges as a political notion itself, instead of being the epitome of individual identity in the face of societal plurality and oppression. It is, of course, Foucault who has elaborated on this notion denying the existence of identity and rationality outside of power structures. Identity is the result of the exclusion of other possibilities. Larrosa elaborates on this argument translating it in terms of language structures. According to him, identity is reached by closing the mind to certain "experiences of language." Education is instrumental in this closing process:

> On the one hand, education is a matter of language...Thus, it has been necessary to control texts and textual practices from the point of view of their educational value. On the other hand, education is a matter of subjectivisation as well...Thus, it has been necessary to build up a normative idea of the good subjectivity, sometimes in terms of stability, unity and identity.

In such a view, then, education is conceptualised as an instrument for controlling the plurality of world views in order to achieve identity structures that will fit in with the existing power structures. It expresses a societal fear of plurality which is perceived as a threat to power structures and stability. This view also is at odds with the first category of theories about autonomy that I have discussed — those in which some form of rationality warrants autonomy. It sees these views as ideologies produced under those same power relations. But this, of course, evokes the question of whether autonomy and identity are not merely ideological concepts and humans are no more than products of existing powers and texts.

Many attempts to save the concept of human autonomy, including those of Foucault himself, have relied heavily on the idea that somewhere within the human individual, or in supra-individual structures like language, a "niche" can be found which can be the germ of a personality structure and a subject autonomy outside of power structures.

In fact, the theories of critical theorists like Habermas may be interpreted in this sense. In the next section, however, I will draw an outline of a discursive theory based on the work of Vygotsky and Bakhtin which takes plurality itself not as something to be mastered by autonomy, but as the very source of autonomy. It concentrates on the fact that the individual is not a passive recipient of cultural structures, but participates actively in constructing a system of meanings.

Plurality and Authorship

A discursive theory of autonomy, in fact, denies the existence of the self. That is, it does not recognise it as a stable, substantiated part of the person which acts as a consistent governing instance for thought and action. Instead, individual identity is seen as a continuous production in which a discursive position is created again and again in the course of participation in specific social activities and before a specific public.

Identity is not a given, but a project, the result of which is always only a temporary local stability. The task of maintaining an identity is not one of balancing between the expectations of others and those of the individual itself; rather, the balancing act is between different expectations, each of which have been partly internalised.

Every person has a feeling of belonging to different communities that can be in conflict with each other. Coordination of activities is not accomplished by some "deeper" ego level, but by the exigencies of joint activity in a social situation. Identity is not only produced dialogically; it always retains a dialogical character. This theory radicalises the position of Mead that thinking is equal to internalised conversation. Not the individual, but social activity is the basic unit in thinking about humanity. The boundary between inner and outer world does not coincide with the skin, but is situated within the individual. Moreover, the boundary is not fixed once and for all.

For some commentators on "the postmodern condition," the acceptance of this model of identity implies that postmodern human beings must be schizophrenics. They believe that, under postmodern conditions, no stable structures of society exist which could ensure identity, that is, make sense of the internal contradictions within the individual. Their views imply that only in an earlier stage in history was it possible for individuals to reach a unified identity.

In fact, such comments exhibit a false nostalgia for harmony characteristic of the modern, universalistic view of identity. A different interpretation would be that a stable identity, in this sense, has always been an ideological illusion, the true character of which only becomes visible under current historical conditions. This does not, of course, imply that humans have always been schizophrenic without knowing it. One can only come to that conclusion if one holds the "modern" view of personal identity. If, however, we are prepared to leave that view behind, the question becomes how people can learn to manage such contradictions and how, even under postmodern conditions, a stable identity can develop. If we are to understand identity in an different way, we also need a new theory of the development of identity.

In short, a theory of the discursive development of identity along Vygotskian lines would have the following characteristics. To begin with, the internalisation of the "ways of signifying" of the community should not be conceived as a transition from "outside" to "inside." It is, rather, the transition from what a child can or wants to do in the context of a social, joint activity — "going above itself" in the social relationship — to what it can or wants to do individually and independently. That is, the boundary between the not-yet and the already-internalised repertoires lies inside the individual. Such a theory, therefore, does not only deny that something like an "authentic" human subject exists and needs only to be developed, it goes on to deny that the *individual* is an adequate unity from which to understand human identity. Identity becomes understandable only in connection with social relations.

However, the human subject is not understood as just the inevitable product of social factors. It is not the social structures themselves that are internalised, but the meaning the individual learns to give to these structures in interacting with others and in relating this to what it has learned before. Internalisation is an activity of meaning-giving and digestion, not a process of transmission in which the individual is only a passive receiver. It is true that, in a way, socially existing positions are internalised; but these are empowering as much as limiting. And they are not internalised "as given."

Learning does not mean being fitted with a totally new repertoire of behavior, it consists of qualitative changes in an already existing repertoire. At the same time, learning means learning about yourself — building perspectives of yourself in relation to the learning situations you find yourself in. This generates a sense of identity over time — a sense of self — but does not presuppose the existence of a separate and always identical "self." In different situations, before different audiences, the individual may be guided by different perspectives which may be partially incompatible. Nor does learning have a definite end; as long as there is contradiction in the social relations, learning occurs and identity keeps changing.

The theory has a positive attitude toward such change. An individual who does not change anymore is dead, either literally or figuratively. The same holds true for a culture or a society. Continuous growth, not harmony and homeostasis is the ideal here. This holds true on the individual level as well as on the level of society. And the two levels interact: individual activities may generate societal change.

In the course of his or her development, each individual learns to handle the facts of change and contradiction in a certain way: either negating them or valuing them negatively, or understanding them as opportunities for development and using them in a positive way. Thus, people learn to manage their own development. Education can play a crucial part here by stimulating certain ways of handling contradictions. The universe of discourse of Vygotsky-oriented educators is not conceptualised in terms of consistency, but of openness. Contradictions should not be resolved or covered too soon. A "pluralist attitude" is a major aim of education here. Ideological critique is aimed at situations which impede openness.

Ultimately, in this theory autonomy is equated with the ability to not only handle change and plurality in a positive way, but also to contribute to the "writing" of the cultural "texts" that make up this plurality. Autonomous individuals are not just the product of these texts; they also are its *co-authors*. Creative participation in culture, that is, cultural (co-)authorship, characterises the truly autonomous person.

8

Women's Struggle for Education

Women are advancing, tho at present only a small minority strives to advance, and of these again only a few are fully conscious of their aims. They not only wish to measure their strength with that of men industrially and commercially, they not only wish to hold a more independent position in the family, they also wish to employ their intellectual abilities in higher positions and in public life. They are met time and again with the argument that they are unfit by nature for intellectual occupations. The question of the practice of learned professions only concerns a small number of women in present-day society, but it is important as a matter of principle.

The majority of men seriously believe that women must remain subjected to them intellectually also and that they have no right to seek equality; therefore they are vehemently opposed to the intellectual ambitions of women. The same men who do not object to women being employed in difficult and dangerous occupations that threaten their womanliness and injure their maternity, would bar them from professions that are far less difficult and dangerous and far better suited to their physical abilities.

In Germany, the lively agitation for the admission of women to universities, has called forth a great number of opponents who especially oppose the admission of women to the study of medicine. Among these are Pochhammer, Fehling, Binder, Hegar, and others. J. Beerenbach seeks to prove that women are not qualified for scientific study, by pointing out that no genius had as yet sprung up among women. This argument is neither valid nor convincing. Geniuses do not drop from the sky; they must have an opportunity for development, and such opportunity women have been lacking, for since thousands of years they have been oppressed and deprived of opportunity for intellectual development, and thereby their mental abilities have become atrophied. A considerable number of distinguished women exist even to-day, and if one denies the existence of potential geniuses among them, that is as far from being true as the belief that there were no more geniuses among men than those that were recognised as such.

Every country schoolteacher knows how many able minds among his pupils are never developed because they lack opportunity for development. Indeed we all have in our day met persons in whom we recognised rare ability and who, we felt, would have become a credit to the community, if circumstances had been more favorable to them. The number of talents and geniuses among men is far greater than could be revealed until now. The same is true of the abilities of women that have for thousands of years been far more hampered, repressed and cramped than those of men. We have no standard whereby we can measure the amount of intellectual strength and ability among men and women, that would unfold if they could develop under natural conditions.

To-day it is in human life as in plant life. Millions of precious seeds never achieve development because the ground on which they are cast is unfertile or is already occupied, and the young plant is thus deprived of air, light and nourishment. The same laws that apply to nature apply to human life. If a gardener or farmer would claim that a plant could not be perfected without having made an attempt to perfect it, his more enlightened neighbors would consider him a fool. They would hold the same opinion of him if he would refuse to interbreed one of his female domestic animals with a male of more perfect breed to obtain more perfect stock.

There is no peasant to-day who is so ignorant not to recognise the advantage of a rational treatment of his vegetables, fruit, and cattle; whether his means allow the application of advanced methods is another question. Only in regard to humanity even educated people will not admit what they regard as an irrefutable law with the rest of the organic world. Yet one need not be a scientist to derive instructive observations from life. How is it that peasant children differ from city children? How is it that children of the wealthier classes are, as a rule, distinguishable from the children of the poor by facial and bodily traits and by mental qualities? It is due to the difference in their conditions of living and education.

The one-sidedness of training for a certain profession leaves its particular imprint upon a person. As a rule a minister or a school teacher can easily be recognised by his bearing and the expression of his face, as also a military mail. even in plain clothes. A cobbler is easily distinguished from a tailor, a carpenter from a locksmith. Twin brothers who greatly resembled each other in their youth, will show marked differences in a more advanced age if their occupations have been very different from one another; if, for instance, one is a manual laborer, say a blacksmith, and the other has studied philosophy.

Heredity on the one hand and adaptation on the other, are decisive factors in human development as well as in the animal kingdom, and man, moreover, is the most adaptive of all creatures. Sometimes a few years of a different mode of life and a different occupation suffice to alter a person completely. External changes are never more clearly seen than when a person is transplanted from poor and narrow circumstances to greatly improved ones. His past can perhaps be disavowed least in his mental culture. When people have attained a certain age, they frequently have no ambition for intellectual improvement. and often they do not need it either. A parvenu rarely suffers from this shortcoming. In our day money is the chief asset, and people bow far more readily before the man with a great fortune than before the man of knowledge and great intellectual abilities, especially if it is his ill fortune to be poor. The worship of Mammon was never greater than in our day. Yet we are living in the "best of worlds."

Our industrial districts furnish a striking example of the influence of decidedly different conditions of life and education. Even externally, workers and capitalists differ to such an extent as if they were members of two different races. These differences were brought home to us in an almost startling manner at the occasion of a campaign meeting during the winter of 1877 in an industrial town of Saxony. The meeting, in which a discussion with a liberal professor was to take place, had been so arranged that an equal number of both parties were present. The front of the hall was occupied by our opponents, almost without exception healthy, strong, and some stately figures.

In the rear of the hall and on the galleries were the workingmen and small traders, nine-tenths of them weavers, mostly small, narrow-chested, hollow-cheeked figures whose faces bore the imprints of care and need. The one group represented the well-fed virtue and morality of the bourgeois world, the other represented the worker-bees and beasts of burden on whose labor the gentlemen waxed strong. If one generation were reared under equally favorable conditions of life the differences would be greatly decreased and would quite disappear among their progeny.

It is usually more difficult to determine the social position among women than among men. They easily accustom themselves to altered conditions and readily adopt more refined habits of life. Their adaptability is greater than that of the more clumsy man.

What good soil, air and light are to the plant, that to man are healthful social conditions, which enable him to develop his physical and mental qualities. The saying that "man is what he eats" expresses a similar thought somewhat too narrowly. Not only what a man eats, but his entire standard of life and his social environment advance or hamper his physical and mental development. and influence his feelings, his thoughts and his actions favorably or unfavorably, as the case may be. We see every day that persons living in good financial circumstances go to ruin mentally and morally, because outside of the narrow sphere of their domestic and personal relations, unfavorable influences, social in character. were brought to bear upon them and gained such control over them that they were driven into evil ways.

The social conditions under which we live are even more important than the conditions of family life. But when the social conditions of development will be the same for both sexes, when there will be no restriction for either, and when the general state of society will be a healthful one, woman will rise to a height of perfection that we can hardly conceive to-day, because until now no such conditions have existed in human evolution.

The achievements of individual women justify our highest expectations, for these tower above the mass of their sex just as male geniuses tower above the mass of men. If we apply the standard of rulership, for instance, we find that women have shown even greater talent for ruling than men. To mention just a few examples: There were Isabella and Blanche of Castilia, Elizabeth of Hungary, Katherine Sforza, Countess of Milan and Imola, Elizabeth of England, Katherine of Russia, Maria Theresa, and others. Basing his assertion on the fact that women have ruled well among all nations and in all parts of the globe, even over the wildest and most turbulent hordes, Burbach is led to remark that according to all probability women would be better qualified for politics than men. When in 1901 Queen Victoria of England died, a large English newspaper made the suggestion to introduce female succession exclusively in England, because the history of England showed that its queens ruled better than its kings.

Many a great man of history would shrivel considerably if we always knew how much was due to his own efforts and how much he owed to others. As one of the greatest geniuses of the French Revolution, German historians regard Count Mirabeau. Yet research has revealed the fact, that he owed the preparation of almost ail his speeches to the willing assistance of a few learned men who worked for him secretly and whose labor he skillfully made use of. On the other hand, women like Sappho, Diotima, at the time of Socrates, Hypatia of Alexandria, Madame Roland, Mary Wollstonecraft, Olympe de Gouges, Madame de Staël, George Sand, and others, merit our highest admiration. Many a male star pales beside them. The influence of women as mothers of great men is also well known.. Women have accomplished as much as they could accomplish under exceedingly unfavorable circumstances, and that entitles us to great expectations for the future. As a matter of fact, women were admitted to competition with men in various realms of activity only during the second half of the nineteenth century. The results obtained are very satisfactory.

But even should we take for granted that women, as a rule, are not as capable of development as men, that there are no geniuses and philosophers among them, we arc nevertheless led to ask whether this factor was considered among men when they, according to the wording of the laws, were given complete equality with the geniuses and philosophers. The learned men who deny the intellectual ability of women, are inclined to do the same in the case of workingmen. When persons of nobility pride themselves on their "blue" blood and their pedigree. they smile and contemptuously shrug their shoulders; but in the presence of the man of lowly birth they consider themselves an aristocracy that have achieved their favored position, not through their more advantageous circumstances, but only by their own peculiar talents.

The same men, who are unprejudiced in one respect and have a poor opinion of persons who are not as liberal-minded as they, become incredibly narrow-minded and fanatical when their class interests or personal conceit are involved. Men of the upper classes judge men of the lower classes unfavorably, and in the same way almost all men judge women unfavorably. The majority of men regard women only as a means to their comfort and enjoyment. To regard them as beings endowed with equal rights is repugnant to their prejudiced minds.

Woman should be modest and submissive; she should confine her interests to the home, and leave all other domains to the "lords of creation." Woman should check every thought and inclination, and wait patiently for what her earthly providence, father or husband, may decide. If she lives up to this standard she is praised for her good sense, modesty and virtue, even tho she may break down under the burden of physical and moral suffering. But if we speak of the equality of all human beings, it is preposterous to wish to exclude half of humanity.

Woman has the same right as man to develop her abilities and to employ them freely. She is a human being as well as man and should have the freedom of disposing of her own body and mind and he her own master. The chance of having been born a woman, must not affect her human rights. To exclude woman from equal rights because she has been born a woman and not a man — a fact of which both man and woman are innocent — is as unfair, as to make rights and privileges depend upon religious or political opinion; and it is as irrational as the belief that two persons are innate enemies because, by the chance of birth, they belong to different races or nationalities. Such views are unworthy of a free human being. Progress of humanity consists in removing whatever keeps one human being, one class or one sex in slavery and dependence upon another. No difference is justified except those differences established by nature to fulfill its purpose. But no sex will overstep the natural limits, because it would thereby destroy its own purpose in nature.

Differences in Physical and Mental Qualities of Man and Woman

One of the chief arguments of the opponents of equal rights is, that woman has a smaller brain than man and is less developed in other respects, and that therefore her lasting inferiority is proven. It is certain that man and woman are two human beings of different sex, that each has different organs adapted to the sexual purpose, and that, owing to the fulfillment of the sexual function, a number of differences in their physiological and psychological conditions exist. These are facts that no one can nor will deny; but they do not furnish any cause for social or political inequality between man and woman. Humanity and society consist of both sexes; both are indispensable to their maintenance and development. Even the greatest man was born by a mother to whom he may owe — his best qualities and abilities. By what right, then, can woman be denied equality with man?

According to the opinion of eminent authorities, the most marked differences in physical and mental qualities between man and woman are the following: In regard to stature, Havelock Ellis considers 170 centimeters the average height for men and 160 centimeters for women. According to Vierordt, it is 172 and 160, and in northern Germany, according to Krause, 173 and 163 centimeters.

The proportion of man's stature to woman's is as 100 to 93. The average weight of adult persons is 65 kilograms for men and 54 for women. The greater length of the trunk in a woman's body is a well-known difference; yet this difference is not as great as has been generally assumed, as careful measurements have shown. The legs if a woman of medium size are only by 15 millimeters shorter than those of a man of medium size, and Pfitzner doubts that this difference is noticeable. "The differences in the lengths of body and legs are influenced by the stature, and are independent of sex." But the female arm is decidedly shorter than the male arm (as 100 to 91.5). The male hand is broader and larger than the female hand, and with men the ring-finger is usually longer than the index, while the opposite is the case with women. By this the male hand becomes more ape-like, as the long arm also is a pithecoid (ape-like) characteristic.

In regard to the size of the head, the proportion of the absolute height of male and female heads may be set down as 100 to 94. But the relative sizes are 100 to 100.8. So actually woman's head is somewhat smaller, but in proportion to the size of her body, it is somewhat larger than man's. The bones of woman are smaller, finer, and more delicate in form and have a smoother surface, for the weaker muscles require less rough surface to fasten upon. The weaker muscular development is one of the most striking characteristics of woman. Each separate muscle of a woman's body is finer, softer, and contains more water. In regard to the adipose membrane the opposite proportion exists; it is much more amply developed with woman than with man. The chest is relatively shorter and narrower. Other differences are directly connected with the sexual purpose. The statements of various authors in regard to relative and absolute weight of the intestines, are very contradictory. According to Vierordt the proportion of the weight of the heart to the weight of the body is as 1 to 215 with men, and as 1 to 206 with women. According to Clendinning it is as 1 to 158 and as 1 to 149. Taken all in all, we may assume that the female intestines are absolutely smaller but relatively, in proportion to the weight of the body, heavier than the male.

The blood of women shows a larger percentage of water, a smaller quantity of blood-globules, and a smaller quantity of hemachrome. With woman the smaller size of the heart, the narrower vascular system, and probably also the larger percentage of water in the blood, cause a less intense assimilation of matter and an inferior nutrition. This may also account for the weaker jaws. "It may thus be explained that even civilised man in many respects is more closely connected with the animal world, especially the ape, than woman, that he possesses pithecoid traits which may be seen in the shape of the skull and the length of the limbs."

In regard to the differences of the skull of both sexes, let it be stated that, according to Bartels, there is no absolute indication whereby we could determine whether a skull belonged to a male or female person. Absolute comparison shows that the skulls of men are larger in all dimensions. Accordingly the weight is greater, too, and the interior space is larger.

As a medium weight of normally developed brains of adult persons, Grosser states 1388 grammes for the man and 1252 grammes for the woman. The great majority of male brains (34 per cent.) weigh between 1250 and 1550 grammes, and the great majority of female brains weigh between 1100 and 1450 grammes. But these weights are not subject to direct comparison since woman is smaller than man. It is, accordingly, necessary to determine the weight of the brain in proportion to the body. When we compare the weight of the brain with the weight of the body we find that with the man there are 21.6 grammes of the brain for every kilogram of the weight of the body, and with the woman there are 23.6 grammes. This outweighing is explained by the fact that woman's stature is smaller.

Different results are obtained by a comparison of equally large individuals of both sexes. According to Marchand the weight of the female brain is, without exception, lighter than that of men of the same size. But this method is as incorrect as a comparison with the size of the body. It takes for granted what remains to be proven: a direct relation between the size of the body and the weight of the brain. Blakeman, Alice Lee and Karl Pearson have determined on the basis of English data and measurements, that there is no noticeable relative difference in the weight of the brain between man and woman; that is, a man of the same age, stature and skull measurements as the average woman, would not differ from her in regard to the weight of his brain.

Even Marchand points out that the smaller size of woman's brain may be due to the greater fineness of her nerves. Grosser says: "Indeed, this has not yet been determined by means of the microscope, and would be difficult to determine. But we must point to the analogy that the eye-ball and the cavity of the ear are also somewhat smaller with woman than with man, yet these organs are no less fine and serviceable. Another, perhaps the chief reason, for the lighter weight of the woman's brain may be found in her weaker muscular development.

Inasmuch as the differences are rooted in the nature of sex, they can, of course, not be altered. But to what extent these differences in blood and brain can be changed by a different mode of life cannot be definitely determined for the time being. That modern woman differs from man to a greater extent than primitive woman or the woman of inferior races, seems to be established, and when we consider the social development of woman's position among civilised nations during the past 1000 or 1500 years, it seems only too obvious.

The following shows the capacity of the female skull according to Havelock Ellis :

Negro	984	Russian	884
Hottentot	951	German	838 to 897
Hindu	944	Chinese	870
Eskimo	931	English	860 to 862
Dutch	913	Parisian, 19 yrs.,	858

The conflicting statements among the Germans show that the measurements have been taken among greatly differing material, both in regard to quality and quantity, and that therefore they are not absolutely reliable. But the figures clearly show One thing: that Negroes, Hottentots and Hindu women have a considerably larger capacity of the skull than the German, English and Parisian women; and yet the latter are far more intelligent.

A comparison of the brain-weights of well-known deceased men shows similar contradictions and peculiarities. According to Professor Reclam, the brain of the scientist Cuvier weighed 1830 grammes; that of Byron, 1807; that of the famous mathematician Gauss, 1492; Of the philologist Hermann, 1358; Of the Parisian prefect

Hausmann, 1226. It is said that the weight of Dante's brain also was below the average weight of the male brains. Havelock Ellis gives us similar information. He reports that the brain of an unknown person, weighed by Bischoff, had a weight of 2222 grammes, while the brain of the poet Turgeniew weighed only 2012 grammes; the third largest brain was that of an imbecile; the brain of a plain workingman that was also examined by Bischoff, weighed 1325 grammes.

The heaviest female brains weighed between 1742 and 1580 grammes; two of these were taken from women who had suffered from mental derangement. On the congress of German anthropologists, which was held in Dortmund in August, 1902, Professor Waldeyer stated that an examination of the skull of the philosopher Leibnitz, who died in 1716, had shown that its contents only measured 1450 cubic centimeters, which corresponds to a brainweight of 1300 grammes.

According to Hausemann, who examined the brains of Mommsen, Bunsen and Adolph v., Menzel, Mommsen's brain weighed 1429.4 grammes; it accordingly did not exceed the average brainweight of an adult man. Menzel's brain weighed only 1298 grammes and Bunsen's less still — 1295 grammes, below the average male brainweight and not much above the brainweight of a woman Those are striking facts that completely overthrow the old assumption that intellectual abilities could be measured by the capacity of the skull. After an examination of the English data, Raymond Pearl comes to the following conclusion: "There are no proofs of a close relation between intellectual abilities and brainweight."

The English anthropologist, W. Duckworth, says: "There is no proof that a heavy brainweight is accompanied by great intellectual ability. Neither the brainweight, nor the capacity of the skull, nor the circumference of the head, where they could be determined, have been of any use as a measure of intellectual abilities."

Kohlbruegge, who has during recent years published the results of the examinations of human brains of many races, says: "Intelligence and brainweight are entirely dependent of one another. Even the greater brainweight of famous men is not sufficient proof, since it exceeds the general medium weight, but not that of the upper classes to which these men belonged. But by these statements I do not seek to deny that brainweight can be increased, especially by excessive study during youth, which may account for the heavier brainweights and the greater skull capacity of the upper classes and of scholarly persons, especially when — as is, usually the case among the well-to-do — excessive nourishment is added. This increase in weight by mental over-exertion has its dark sides also, as is well known. Lunatics often have very heavy brains. The main point is that it cannot be proven that intelligence has any relation to weight. It is true of the external formation also, that until now, no connection could be shown between certain forms and higher mental development, intelligence, or genius."

It is established, then, that we cannot draw conclusions from the brainweight as to mental qualities, as little as we can draw conclusions from the size of the body as to physical strength. The large mammals, such as elephant, whale, etc,, have larger and heavier brains; yet in regard to proportional brainweight they are excelled by most birds and small mammals. We have some very small animals (ant, bee) that are far more intelligent than much larger ones of small and insignificant appearance. According to all probability the mass of the brain is not the determining factor, but its organisation and the practice and use of its powers.

"In my opinion," says Professor L. Stieda, "the difference in psychic functions can doubtlessly be accounted for by the finer construction of the gray matter, the nerve cells, the white matter, the arrangement of the blood-vessels, the construction, form, size and number of nervecells, and last but not least, their nutrition, their metabolic assimilation."

If the brain is to attain the full development of its faculties, it must be exercised regularly, and the brain must be properly nourished, Just as every other organ; if this is left undone, or if the training is a faulty one, the normal development will be hampered, even crippled. One faculty is developed at the expense of another.

There are some anthropologists, as Manouvrier and others, who even seek to prove that woman is morphologically more highly developed than man. That is an exaggeration. Duckworth says: "When we compare the two sexes, we find that there is no constant difference that lets one sex appear morphologically superior to the other." Havelock Ellis only admits of one limitation. He believes that female characteristics show fewer variations than the male. But, in an anticritique, Karl Pearson has explicitly shown that this is only a pseudoscientific superstition.

No one who is acquainted with the history of the development of woman can deny, that woman has been sinned against. If Professor Bischoff asserts that woman was enabled to develop her brain and her intelligence as well as man, this assertion merely shows an incredible degree of ignorance upon the subject. The description we have given in this book of the position of woman during the course of civilisation, makes it appear quite natural, that thousands of years of male rule have brought about the difference in the physical and mental development of the sexes.

Our scientists ought to recognise that the laws of their sciences apply fully to man also. Heredity and adaptation prevail with man as with every other living creature. But if man constitutes no exception in nature, the law of evolution must apply to him also, whereby that becomes clear what otherwise remains wrapped in darkness, and then becomes an object of scientific mysticism or mystic science.

The brain formation of the sexes has developed in accordance with their different educations. Indeed during a great portion of the past, the word education could not be applied to woman at all. Physiologists are agreed that those parts of the brain which influence the intellect are situated in the fore-part of the head, while those that specially influence feeling and sentiment, are situated in the middle part. The conception of beauty for man and woman has developed accordingly. According to the Greek conception, which still prevails, woman is supposed to have a low forehead, while man is supposed to have a high and broad forehead. This conception of beauty, which is a symptom of her degradation, has been so impressed upon our women, that they consider a high forehead unbeautiful and seek to improve upon nature by combing their hair over their forehead to make it appear lower.

Darwinism and the Condition of Society

It has accordingly not been proven, that women are inferior to men as a result of the quantity of their brain; yet the present intellectual status of women is not surprising. Darwin is surely right in saying, that if a list of the ablest men on the subjects of poetry, painting, sculpture, music, science and philosophy were placed beside a list of the ablest women on the same subjects, the two could not compare with one another. But could it be otherwise? It would be surprising if it were not so. Very correctly Dr. Dodel (Zurich) says, that it would be different if for a number of generations men and women would be similarly educated. As a rule, woman is physically weaker than man also, which is by no means the case among many uncivilised peoples. How much can be attained by practice and training from childhood on, may, for instance, be seen with ladies of the circus and female acrobats, who achieve most astounding things in regard to courage, daring, skill and strength.

As all these things are conditioned by the mode of life and education, as they are — to use a scientific term — due to "breeding," it may be assumed as certain that the physical and intellectual life of man will lead to the best results, as soon as man will consciously and expediently influence his development.

As plants and animals depend upon conditions of existence, as they are fostered by favorable and hampered by unfavorable ones, and as compulsory conditions force them to change their nature and character — provided that their influence does not destroy them — thus it is also with man. The manner in which a human being obtains his means of subsistence not only affects his external appearance, but also his feelings, his thoughts and his actions. If unfavorable conditions of existence — that is, unfavorable social conditions — are the cause of insufficient individual development, then it follows that by a change of his conditions of existence — that is, his social condition — man himself will be changed. The point in question, then, is, so to organise social conditions that every human being will be given an opportunity for the untrammelled development of his nature; that the laws of development and adaptation — called Darwinism after Darwin — may be consciously and expediently applied to all human beings. But that will only be possible under Socialism. As a rational being, capable of judgment, man must so alter his social conditions and everything in connection with them, that equally favorable conditions of existence prevail for all. Every individual shall be enabled to develop his talents and abilities to his own advantage as well as to the advantage of society, but he must not have the power to harm other individuals or society at large. His own advantage and the advantage of all shall coincide. Harmony of interests must supercede the conflict of interests that dominate present-day society.

Darwinism, like every true science, is an eminently democratic science. If some of its representatives claim that the opposite is true, they fail to recognise the range of their own science. Its opponents, especially the clergy, who are always quick to perceive any advantage or disadvantage to themselves, have recognised this, and therefore denounce Darwinism as being Socialistic or atheistic. In this respect Professor Virchow agrees with his most vehement opponents, for at the congress of Scientists, held in Munich in 1877, he asserted in opposition to Professor Haeckel: "The Darwinian theory leads to Socialism.

Virchow tried to discredit Darwinism because Haeckel demanded, that the theory of evolution should be introduced into the school curriculum. The suggestion to teach science in the schools according to Darwin, and the results of modern scientific investigations, is vehemently opposed by all those who wish to maintain the present order. The revolutionary effect of these doctrines is well known; therefore it is deemed wiser to propagate them only among the chosen few. But we contend that if the Darwinian theories lead to Socialism, as Virchow claims, that is no argument against these theories, but an argument in favor of Socialism. Men of science should not question whether the consequences of a science lead to one form of the state or another, whether one social condition or another is justified by them; it is their sole duty to investigate whether the theories are in accordance with truth, and if they are, to accept them with all their consequences. Whoever acts otherwise, be it for personal gain or favor or to serve class or party interest, commits a despicable action and is no credit to science.

The representatives of corporate science, especially at our universities, can indeed only rarely lay claim to independence of character. The fear of financial loss, or the fear of being discredited with the powers that be and of being thereby deprived of title and rank and the opportunity of advancement, causes most of these representatives to bow down and either to conceal their conviction, or to say publicly the opposite of what they believe and know. At a ceremony of homage to the ruler held at the University of Berlin in 1870, Dubois-Reymond exclaimed: "The universities are institutions where the intellectual body-guards of the Hohenzollern are trained." If a Dubois-Reymond could express himself in this manner, we can imagine what conceptions in regard to the object of science are held by the majority of the others, who are very inferior to this eminent scientist. Science is degraded to serve the purposes of the ruling powers.

It is only natural that Professor Haeckel and his adherents, Professor 0. Schmidt, v. Hellwald and others, remonstrate energetically against the terrible accusation that Darwinism leads to Socialism. They claim that the opposite is true, that Darwinism is aristocratic, since it teaches that everywhere in nature the more highly organised and stronger living beings suppress the inferior ones; and since, according to their conception, the propertied and educated classes constitute these more highly organised and stronger living beings in human society, they consider the rule of these classes a matter of course, since it is justified by the laws of nature.

These, among our evolutionists, are ignorant of the economic laws which dominate bourgeois society. Otherwise they would know that the blind rule of these laws does not raise to social preeminence either the best or the ablest or the most competent, but frequently the worst and the most cunning, who thereby are placed in a position of making the conditions of life and development most favorable to their progeny, without the least effort on their part. Under no economic system did persons, possessing good and noble human qualities, have so little opportunity of attaining and maintaining an elevated position, as under the capitalistic system. Without fear of exaggeration it may be said, that this state of affairs increases with the development of this system.

Lack of consideration for others and unscrupulousness in the choice and application of means to attain one's end, prove far more effective than all human virtues combined. Only one who is ignorant of the nature of this society or who is so dominated by bourgeois prejudices that he cannot reason properly or draw correct conclusions, could regard a social system based upon such conditions as a society of the "fittest and best." The struggle for existence is always present with all organisms. It goes on without any knowledge on their part of the laws and conditions that shape it. This struggle for existence prevails among men also and among the members of each social group from which solidarity has disappeared, or where it has not yet been developed. This struggle for existence changes its form according to the various relations of men to one another in the course of human development. It assumes the character of class struggles on an ever higher scale. But these struggles — and thereby man is distinguished from all other human beings — lead to a growing understanding of the nature of society, and finally to a recognition of the laws which determine its development. Eventually man will but need to apply these laws to his social and political institutions and to transform them accordingly. The difference is that man may be called a reasoning animal, but the animal is not a reasoning human being. This many Darwinists fail to see, owing to their biased conceptions, and therefore arrive at false conclusions.

Professor Haeckel and his adherents also deny that Darwinism leads to atheism. Thus, after they have done away with the "creator" by all their scientific arguments and proofs, they mask desperate efforts to re-introduce him. To attain this purpose a new sort of individual "religion" is formed, that has been termed "higher morality," "moral principles," etc. In 1882 at the congress of scientists in Eisenach, in the presence of the Grand-duke of Weimar and his family, Professor Haeckel endeavored not only to save religion but also to represent his master, Darwin, as being a religious man. The attempt failed, as anyone can affirm who read the lecture and the letter from Darwin that was quoted in it. Darwin's letter expresses, though in careful terms, the opposite of what Professor Haeckel claimed it to express. Darwin was obliged to consider the piety of his fellow-countrymen, the English, therefore he never dared to express publicly his true views in regard to religion. But he did so privately, as became known shortly after the congress in Weimar, for he told Dr. L. Buechner that he had not believed since his fortieth year — since 1849 — because he had not been able to obtain proofs to justify belief. During the last years of his life Darwin also supported an atheistic newspaper, which was published in New York.

Woman and the Learned Professions

Women are justified in entering into intellectual competition with men, instead of waiting until it pleases the men to develop their intellectual faculties and to clear the path for them. The woman's movement is providing for this. Already women have removed many barriers and have entered the intellectual arena — in some countries with marked success. The movement to obtain admission to the higher institutions of learning and to the practice of learned professions is, in accordance with the nature of our conditions limited to the circles of bourgeois women.

The proletarian women are not directly concerned since, for the time being, these studies and the resulting positions are closed to them. Nevertheless, this movement and its success is an object of general interest. In the first place, it is a matter of principle, since it affects the general position of woman; in the second place, it is destined to show what women can accomplish even at present, under conditions that are highly unfavorable to their development. Moreover, all women are interested, for instance, in being able, in case of sickness, to be treated by physicians of their own sex, if they so choose, since many feel that they can confide with less reserve in a woman than in a man. To a great many of our women female physicians are a blessing, for the fact that they must turn to male physicians in the case of diseases or ailments connected with their sex functions, frequently prevents them from seeking medical aid in time. This leads to many troubles and serious results, not only to the women themselves, but to their husbands also. There is hardly a physician who has not had some experience with this reticence of women, that may sometimes be called almost criminal, and their aversion against confessing to their ailments. That is readily understood. But it is inconceivable that the men, and especially many physicians also, will not recognise how justifiable it is, therefore — indeed how necessary — for women to study medicine.

Female physicians are no novel factor. Among most of the ancients, especially among the ancient Germans, women practiced the art of healing. There were female physicians and surgeons of note during the ninth and tenth centuries in the kingdom of the Arabs, especially in Spain, under the rule of the Arabs (Moors), where they studied at the University of Cordova. The study of women at various Italian universities, as Bologna and Palermo, was also due to Moorish influence. When the "heathen" influence ceased in Italy, these studies were prohibited. In 1377 the faculty of the University of Bologna issued the following decree: "As woman is the source of sin, the devil's tool, the cause of the expulsion from paradise, and the cause of corruption of the old law, and as therefore every conversation with her should be carefully avoided, we distinctly forbid and interdict any one to venture to introduce any woman, no matter how respectable she may be, into this college. Should sonic one do so nevertheless, the rector shall punish him severely."

One good result of the study of women is, that female competition has a very stimulating influence on the studiousness of the male students, which has left much to be wished for, as has been affirmed by various sources. That alone would be a great gain. It would furthermore considerably improve their habits. The drunkenness, pugnacity, and beer-saloon habit of our students would become greatly checked. Those places from which our statesmen, judges, public attorneys, police officials, ministers, representatives of the people, etc., are chiefly recruited, would become more worthy of the objects for which they were founded and are being maintained. According to the impartial opinions of those competent to judge, such an improvement is exceedingly needful.

The number of states that admit women to their high-schools and universities are rapidly increasing since a few decades. None that lays claim to being a civilised state can offer continued resistance to this demand. The United States took the lead and Russia followed, two states that are diametrically opposed to one another in every respect. In the North American Union women have been admitted to high-schools and universities in all the states; in Utah since 1850; in Iowa since 1860; in Kansas since 1866; in Wisconsin since 1868; in Minnesota since 1869; in California and Missouri since 1870, and in Ohio, Illinois and Nebraska since 1871. Since then all the other states followed. Quite in accordance with their opportunity for study, the women in the United States have achieved their positions. According to the census of 1900 there were: 7399 female physicians and surgeons, 5989 writers, 1041 architects, 3405 ministers, 1010 lawyers, and 327,905 teachers. in Europe, Switzerland took the lead in opening its universities to women. The following shows the number of male and female students at Swiss universities:

	Total Enrolled	*female students*	*Total number of women attending courses*
1896-1897	7676	1502	2757
1900-1904	8521	1904	3156
1905-1906	4181	391	728
1906-1907	5301	854	1429

During the term 1906 to 1907 the female students were distributed as follows among the various faculties: law, 75; medicine, 1181; philosophy, 648. According to nationality there were 172 Swiss women, and 1732 foreigners. The number of German women students in Switzerland has decreased, since they are admitted to German universities now, although not without restrictions. During the term 1906 to 1907 the number of regularly enrolled female students constituted about 30 per cent. of all the students.

In England women are admitted to lecture at the universities, but at Oxford and Cambridge they are still barred from taking degrees. In France in 1905 there were 33,168 students, among these 1922 women. They were distributed as follows: Law, 57; medicine, 386; sciences, 259; literature, 838; miscellaneous, 382. The following are the countries in which women have been admitted to universities: United States, England, Holland, Belgium, Denmark, Sweden, Norway, Russia, Germany, Austria, Hungary, Italy, Switzerland, France, Turkey and Australia. Female physicians are admitted to the practice of their profession in India, Abysinnia, Persia, Morocco, China, etc. Especially in the Oriental countries female physicians are constantly gaining ground. The restrictions that custom and religion place upon women in these countries make female physicians an especially great boon.

After long struggles and great exertions, Germany, too, has at last taken a new course, though timidly at first. By a decision passed by the Federal Council on April 24, 1899, women have been admitted to examinations for the practice of medicine and dentristry, as well as pharmacy, upon the same terms as men. By another decision of the Federal Council of July 28, 1900, German women physicians who studied abroad are admitted to practice in Germany, and studies commenced abroad were accredited to them. Even since 1898 some German universities, as Heidelberg and Goettingen, had opened their doors to women. During the term 1901 to 1902, 1270 women attending courses were already ennumerated in the registers of the universities.

In a number of German cities girls' high-schools and colleges were founded; thus in Karlsruhe, Stuttgart, Hannover, Koenigsberg, Hamburg, Frankfort on the Main, Breslau, Berlin, Schoeneberg, Mannheim, etc. But in the spring of 1902, the senate of the University of Berlin again declined a request by female students, to be matriculated upon presentation of a certificate of admission from a German, college.

The opposition by very influential circles in Germany against the study of women had not yet been overcome. During March of 1902, the Prussian minister of public instruction delivered a speech in the Prussian diet, in which he said among other things, that they girls' colleges are an experiment that must be declined by the ministry of public instruction. He feared, so he said, that the differences between man and woman established by nature and developed by civilisation, would be impaired by the study of girls at colleges and universities, and that the characteristics of the German woman ought to be maintained for the welfare of the German family. That is quite in keeping with the old conception.

Many German professors also continue to oppose study for women, though others admit that many of the female students are well, some even excellently qualified, to meet the demands made upon them. What some of the students, perhaps a majority of them, thought in regard to the study of women, may be seen from the following protest of the clinical students at Halle, addressed to the medical students of Germany generally during March of 1902. After it states that the protest has been caused by the agitation, carried on by the "Society for Furthering the Education of Women in Berlin," to admit women to the study of medicine, it goes on to say: "Since this question has been called to public attention, the clinical students of Halle turn to those circles to whom the decision is of prime importance, the clinical students and physicians at German universities. They either know the resulting unpleasantness from personal experience, or can picture to what unwholesome situations, devoid of all modesty, this common clinical instruction must lead, situations that are too revolting to be described.

The medical faculty of the university of Halle was one of the first to admit women to the study of medicine, and the innovation may be regarded as a complete failure. Into these halls of earnest endeavor cynicism has entered with the women, and scenes frequently occur that are equally obnoxious to instructors, students and patients. Here the emancipation of woman becomes a calamity, conflicting with morality, and should be checked. Colleagues, who would dare, in the face of these facts, to oppose our just demands? We demand the exclusion of women from clinical instruction, because experience has taught us that a common clinical instruction of male and female students is incompatible with a thoroughgoing study of medicine, as well as with the principles of decency and morality. This question taken up by us is no longer a local one. Already it has been stated in government circles, that women are to be definitely admitted to the study of medicine. You all now are equally interested in our cause, and therefore we appeal to you: Express your opinion on this question and join with us in a common protest!"

This protest is a striking proof of the narrow-mindedness of the clinical students and also of their envy, for petty envy is at the bottom)f most of their moral considerations. How can an institution that has existed for years in other civilised countries, without injuring the morals and the sense of decency of male and female students, be considered a peril to Germany? The German students are not famed for their morality and ought to refrain from a moral outburst that seems like a jest. If it is not incompatible with decency and morality for female nurses to be present and to render assistance to the physicians during all kinds of operations upon male and female patients, if it is decent and proper for dozens of young men to surround, for the purpose of study, the bed of a woman in the throes of child-birth, and to witness operations upon female patients, then it is ridiculous to seek to exclude the female students.

Very different from the reasons given by the clinical students of Halle, was an argument advanced against the admission of women to the study of medicine by the late Professor Bischoff. The reason he gave was the brutality of the male students, which he was well qualified to judge. But, regardless of the narrow-mindedness or envy of men, the question has been decided in favor of the women. On August 18, 1908, an edict was published, decreeing the regular enrollment of female students at the universities of Prussia, where until then they had been admitted to the lectures. The only restriction is, that for the purpose of immatriculation German women require the consent of the minister in one case, and foreigners require it in all cases.

The admission of women to the universities necessitated a thoroughgoing reform of girls' high-schools. According to the provisions of May 31, 1899, a nine years' course had been set down as the rule for girls' high-schools, while a ten years' course was the exception. But development necessitated the regular introduction of a tenth class. According to statistics there were in 1901, 213 public high-schools for girls; among these go had a nine years' course and 54 a ten years' course. In October, 1907, the number of schools having a nine years' course had decreased from go to 69, and the number of schools having a ten years' course had increased from 54 to 132. Among the private schools for girls, too, there were, besides 110 with a nine years' course, 138 with a ten years' course. It only remained to add the bureaucratic seal to this actual development, and to preserve as much as possible of the "characteristics of German women." According to the reform of August 18, 1908, girls' high schools shall consist of ten grades. To "complete her education in regard to the future life's work of a German woman," it is planned to found a lyceum with a course from one to two years. In order to prepare young girls of the upper classes for academic training, colleges are being planned, which are to be under the same management as the girls' high-schools.

Thereby an experiment, which the board of education still refused to consider in March 1902, is now, six years later, under the pressure of economic development, being introduced by that same board on a, national scale. Let us consider the official argumentation! It reads as follows:

> "The rapid development of our civilisation and the resulting changes in social, economic and educational conditions, have brought about that, especially in the middle and upper classes, many girls remain unprovided

> for, and much ability reposing in woman, that may be valuable to the community, remains unapplied. The numerical superiority of the female population and the increasing bachelorhood of men of the tipper classes, compel a large percentage of educated girls to renounce their natural profession of wifehood and motherhood. It becomes necessary to open professions to them that are suited to their education, and to give them an opportunity to earn their living, not only by teaching, but also by other professions attainable by a university education." This almost reads like an extract from my book!

Be this as it may, the higher education of women can no longer be halted. There are female physicians in all civilised countries of the world, and even in some that are not yet regarded as civilised. The late Li Hung Chang had appointed as his family physician a Chinese woman doctor who practiced at the woman's hospital of her native town, Futchang. The late Sonia Kowalewska, the noted mathematician, was professor of mathematics at the University of Stockholm from 1889 until her death in 1891.

There are many women professors in the United States, and some also in Italy, Switzerland, England and France. In France the famous Marie Curie, who together with her husband discovered radium, and polonium, was, after the death of her husband in 1906, appointed his successor at the university. We see women acting as physicians, dentists, lawyers, chemists, physicists, geologists, botanists, teachers at higher institutions of learning, etc., and it is tip to the women themselves to prove by their achievements, that they are as competent to fill the positions entrusted to them as men. In Switzerland, during the summer of 1899, a majority of voters in the Canton of Zurich, favored the admission of women to the practice of law. The decision was passed by 21,717 against 20,046 votes. In the United States women are admitted to the bar in 34 states. They are also admitted in France, Holland, Sweden, Denmark, Finland, Russia, Canada and Australia.

Many men, especially learned men, are opposed to the higher education of women, because they believe that the sciences will become degraded if even women can practice them. They regard scientific study as a privilege reserved for the chosen few of the male sex.

Unfortunately our universities, as our entire educational system, still leave much to be wished for. As the children in the public schools are frequently robbed of the most valuable time to cram their brains with a lot of things that are not in conformity with reason and scientific knowledge, as they are burdened with a lot of learning that will prove useless in life and will rather hamper than help their development, thus it is also with our higher institutions of learning. In the preparatory schools the pupils are crammed with a lot of useless stuff, mostly learned by rote, that absorbs most of their time and strength, and in the universities the same method is generally pursued. Besides good and useful things, many that are antiquated and superfluous continue to be taught.

Most professors repeat the same lectures term after term even down to the interspersed jokes. To many the noble profession of teaching becomes a mere trade, and it does not require much intelligence on the part of the students to perceive this. The prevailing conceptions concerning college life also prevent the young people from taking their studies too seriously, and some who would like to take them seriously are repulsed by the pedantic and uninteresting methods of many professors. It is generally admitted that students at high-schools and universities are becoming less studious, a fact that has caused some alarm among the authorities.

Alongside of this we find toadyism and patronage playing an important part at our institutions of learning in this age, which is marked by a lack of character. To be of good family and to have "sound principles," is regarded as being of greater importance than knowledge and ability. A patriot — that is, one who has no convictions of his own, but takes his cue from his superiors and fawns upon them — is considered more than a man of character, wisdom and ability. When examinations come around, men of this type cram for a few months what is needful to attain the passing mark, and when the examinations have been passed successfully, and they have attained an official or professional position, many of these "scholars" merely continue to work in a mechanical way. Yet they are very insulted if a man, who is not a "scholar," does not treat them with utmost respect and fails to regard them as a superior species of human being.

The majority of our professional men, lawyers, judges, physicians, professors, public officials, artists, etc., are merely mechanics in their line, and their sole object is personal gain. Only the industrious man discovers later on how much superfluous knowledge he assimilated and how often he failed to learn that which he requires most, and then begins to learn anew. During the best part of his life he has been bothered with much that was useless or harmful; he requires a second part of his life to cast what is useless or harmful aside and to attain the heights of the views of his time, and then only can he become a useful member of society. Many do not surpass the first stage, others come to a standstill in the second, and only few have the energy to struggle on to the third.

But decorum demands that the mediaeval trash and superfluous learning should be maintained, and as women have been until now, and in many cases still are, excluded from the preparatory institutions, this fact furnishes a convenient excuse for excluding them from the lecture halls of the universities. In Leipsic, during the seventies, one of the most noted professors of medicine made the following frank confession to a lady: "A classical education is not essential to an understanding of medicine, but it must be made a condition of entrance to maintain the, dignity of science."

Opposition against an obligatory, classical education as being essential to the study of medicine, is gradually manifesting itself in Germany also. The tremendous advance of the sciences and their great importance to life in general, necessitates a scientific training. But the classical education, with its special preference of Greek and Latin, considers science unimportant and neglects it. It therefore frequently happens that young students are wanting in the most elementary scientific knowledge, that is of decisive importance for a study like medicine. Even teachers themselves are beginning to oppose this one-sided method of education. In other countries, for instance, in Switzerland, the study of science has long since been held as being of prime importance, and all who possess sufficient preliminary knowledge in the natural sciences and mathematics are admitted to the study of medicine, even without having had a so-called classical education. The same is true of Russia, the United States, and other countries.

In Russia, where suppression and persecution of the Jews is considered one of the maxims of government, an imperial ukase, in 1907, prescribed that in the newly established school of medicine for women, only 5 per cent. of the students might be of other than Christian faith. Of these Only 3 per cent. might be Jewesses, and the remaining 2 per cent. were to be reserved for students of Moslem origin. This is one of the retrogressive measures which are daily occurrences in Russia. The Russian government certainly had no cause for such provisions, because there is quite a dearth of physicians in that tremendous realm, and because the Russian women practitioners, regardless of their faith or origin, have been noted for the most unselfish devotion in the practice of their profession. Dr. Erismann, who practiced in Russia for many years, delivered a lecture at the 54th annual convention of the Medical Society in Olten, in which he said: Very favorable were the experiences gathered during the first years in regard to the activity of the female physicians. From the very beginning they were enabled to win the confidence of the people. In the noble competition with their male colleagues they even carried off the laurels. It was soon observed that the female physicians, on an average, treated more patients annually than the male physicians, although the latter proved very efficient and unselfish, likewise. Female patients especially, in great numbers, sought aid with the women doctors."

On the other band, female competition, so much feared by men, especially in regard to the practice of medicine, has not been in evidence. It seems that female physicians obtain a circle of patients from their own sex who apply to male physicians rarely, or only in cases of extreme necessity. It has, moreover, been observed that a great many women physicians abandon their profession as soon as they enter into marriage. It seems that in present-day society the domestic duties of married women are so numerous, especially where there are children, that many women find it impossible to have two professions simultaneously. A physician must be constantly prepared, by day and by night, to practice her profession, and to many that becomes impossible.

After England, the United States and France took lead in employing women as factory inspectors — an innovation that has become all the more necessary because, as has been shown, the number of women in industry is rapidly increasing, and the industries employing women, chiefly or exclusively, are increasing likewise — a number of German states have also followed their example. Baden, Bavaria, Hessia, the Kingdom of

Saxony, Weimar, Wurtemberg, and others have added women assistants to their factory inspectors, and some of these have already achieved much recognition by their activity. In Prussia there are three women factory inspectors in Berlin, and one each in Duesseldorf, Breslau and Wiesbaden. This proves again how the progress of Prussia has been retarded compared with other German states. There is not a single woman assistant in districts like Potsdam, Frankfort on the Oder, Liegnitz, and others, where their presence is extremely needful. Here, too, it has been seen that working women confide more readily in members of their own sex, and that female factory inspectors have been able to obtain much information that was denied to their male colleagues. One shortcoming of this institution is that the assistants frequently are not given the autonomy that is needful in their position, and their pay is not what it ought to be, either. The new institution is being tried out carefully and hesitatingly.

In Germany the prejudice and aversion against employing women in public offices is particularly strong, because so many retired military men annually seek appointments to all kinds of offices in the state and municipal administrations, that there is hardly any room left for applicants from other circles. When women are employed, nevertheless, their salary is considerably lower, whereby they immediately appear as being worth less than men, and whereby they also become a means to keep down wages and salaries.

The great variety of female ability could be observed especially well at the World's Fair in Chicago, in 1893. The splendid woman's building had been entirely planned by female architects, and the articles displayed that had been designed and made by women exclusively, were much admired for their tasty and artistic execution. In the realm of invention, too, women have achieved much and will achieve still more. An American trade-journal published a list of inventions by women; among them were: An improved spinning machine; a rotary loom, which produces three times as much as the usual kind; a chain elevator; a connecting-rod for a propeller; a fire-escape; an apparatus for weighing wool, one of the most delicate machines that have ever been invented, of immeasurable value to the wool industry; a fire extinguisher; a process of employing petroleum as a fuel for steam-engines instead of wood or coal; an improved spark-catcher for locomotives; a signal for grade-crossings; a system of heating cars without fire; a lubricating felt to diminish friction; a typewriter; a signal-rocket for the navy; a deep-sea telescope; a system for subduing the noise of the elevated trains; a smoke-consumer; a machine for folding paper bags, etc.

Many improvements on sewing machines have been made by women; for instance, an appliance for sewing canvas and coarse cloth; an apparatus for threading the needle while the machine is running; an improvement of machines for sewing leather, etc. The last-named invention was made by a woman who was a harness-maker in New York. The deep-sea telescope, invented by Mrs. Mather and improved by her daughter, is an invention of great importance, since it makes it possible to examine the keel of the largest vessel without bringing same into a dry-dock. With the aid of this telescope sunken wrecks may be examined from ship-board, obstacles to navigation and torpedoes may be located, and so forth.

A machine famed in America and Europe for its complicated and ingenious construction, is one for the manufacture of paper bags. Many men, among them noted mechanicians, had tried in vain to construct a machine of this sort. It was invented by a woman, Miss Maggie Knight. The same lady has since invented a machine for the folding of paper bags, which performs the labor of thirty persons. She personally conducted the construction of this machine in Amherst, Massachusetts.

9

Marxian Perspectives on Educational Philosophy

The theory associated with Marxism was developed in mid-19th century Europe by Karl Marx and Friedrich Engels. Although Marx and Engels did not write widely about education, they developed theoretical perspectives on modern societies that have been used to highlight the social functions of education and their concepts and methods have served to both theorise and criticise education in the reproduction of capitalist societies, and to support projects of alternative education.

MARX AND ENGELS: THE CLASSICAL PARADIGM

> The materialist doctrine that men are products of circumstances and upbringing, and that, therefore, changed men are products of other circumstances and changed upbringing, forgets that it is men who change cirumstances and that it is essential to educate the educator himself.
>
> —Karl Marx

Both Marx and Engels left comfortable bourgeois families to pursue a life of revolutionary scholarship and struggle. Meeting in Paris with Engels in 1843, Marx began studying economics and associated himself with communist groups, writing: "When communist *artisans* form associations, education and propaganda are their first aims. But the very act of associating creates a new need — the need for society — and what appeared to be a means has become an end. The most striking results of this practical development are to be seen when French socialist workers meet together. Smoking, eating, and drinking are no longer simply means of bringing people together. Company, association, entertainment which also has society as its aim, are sufficient for them; the brotherhood of man is no empty phrase but a reality, and the nobility of man shines forth upon us from their toil-worn bodies".

Marxís collaborator Engels grew up in the German capitalist town of Barmen, his family owned factories, and he experienced the industrial revolution and rise of the working class at first hand. In his early writings, Engels describes the lot of the new industrial working class as a miserable one: "Work in low rooms where people breathe in more coal fumes and dust than oxygen — and in the majority of cases beginning already at the age of six — is bound to deprive them of all strength and joy in life. The weavers, who have individual looms in their homes, sit bent over them from morning till night, and desiccate their spinal marrow in front of a hot stove. Those who do not fall prey to mysticism are ruined by drunkenness". Likewise, the "local-born leather workers are ruined physically and mentally after three years of work: "three out of five die of consumption." In sum, "terrible poverty prevails among the lower classes, particularly the factory workers in Wuppertal; syphilis and lung diseases are so widespread as to be barely credible; in Elberfeld alone, out of 2,500 children of school age 1,200 are deprived of education and grow up in the factories — merely so that the manufacturer need not pay the adults, whose place they take, twice the wage he pays a child".

The young Marx and Engels thus perceived that without education the working class was condemned to lives of drudgery and death, but that with education they had a chance to create a better life. In their famous 1848 "Communist Manifesto," Marx and Engels argued that growing economic crises would throw ever more segments of the middle classes, and the older peasant and artisan classes, into the impoverished situation of the proletariat and would thus produce a unified working class, at least one with interests in common. They declared that the bourgeois class is constantly battling against the older feudal powers, among its own segments, and against the foreign bourgeoisie, and thus enlists the proletariat as its ally. Consequently, the proletariat gains education and experience which it can use to fight the ruling class. As bourgeois society dissolves, a section of the bourgeoisie goes over to the proletariat, including a radical intelligentsia "who have raised themselves to the level of comprehending theoretically the historical movement as a whole".

In the *Manifesto,* expanded public education for the working class was one of the major demands, and henceforth both Marx and Engels saw themselves as providing education and theoretical guidance to the working class and socialist movement. Marx and Engels did not write much on educational institutions in bourgeois society, or develop models of education in socialist societies. Yet their historical materialist theory of history has been used to theorise and critique educational institutions within bourgeois society and to develop alternative conceptions of education, that are in accord with Marxian socialist principles. As the "Thesis from Feuerbach" which opens this section suggests, changing social conditions create new forms of education, so that the rise of capitalist-bourgeois societies would produce educational institutions that reproduce dominant social relations, values, and practices. Likewise, transforming capitalist societies and creating socialist ones requires new modes of education and socialisation.

The classical Marxian paradigm thus sees education as functioning within the hegemonic social system which is organised by and serves the interest of capital, while calling for alternative modes of education that would prepare students and citizens for more progressive socialist mode of social organisations. Marx and Engels envisaged education and free time as essential to developing free individuals and creating many-sided human beings. The sketch of socialism in *The German Ideology* — where one would "hunt in the morning, fish in the afternoon, rear cattle in the evening, criticise after dinner, just as I have a mind, without ever becoming hunter, fisherman, shepherd or critic"— reflects the ideals of a non-alienated life in which education is a key part of the life process.

Increasing free time under socialism, Marx argued in his 1857-8 notebooks collected under the name of the *Grundrisse,* would allow for more education and development of a social individual who can then enter "in the direct production process as this different subject. This process is then both discipline, as regards the human being in the process of becoming; and, at the same time, practice, experimental science, materially creative and objectifying science, as regards the human being who has become, in whose head exists the accumulated knowledge of society". For Marx, transforming social relations would produce the basis for a new society of non-alienated labor in which individuals could utilise their free-time to fully develop their human capacities and labor itself would be a process of experimentation, creativity, and progress. In the vision of a free society sketched out in the *Grundrisse,* the system of automation would produce most of societyís goods, and individuals could thus enjoy leisure and the fruits of creative work, whereby education would become an essential part of the life-process.

Such a society would be a completely different social order from that of capitalist society which is organised around work and the production of commodities. Marx acknowledges that the new society would have a totally "changed foundation of production, a new foundation first created by the process of history". In the third volume of Capital, Marx described this radically new social order in terms of a "realm of freedom," writing: "Freedom in this field can only consists in socialised man, the associated producers, rationally regulating their interchange with Nature, bringing it under their common control, instead of being ruled by it as by the blind forces of Nature; and achieving this with the least expenditure of energy and under conditions most favourable to, and worthy of, their human nature".

Marxís most distinctive vision of socialism thus envisages socialism as constituting a break in history as dramatic as the rupture between pre-capitalist and capitalist societies that produced modernity. While capitalism is a commodity-producing society organised around work and production, socialism would be a social order aiming at the full development of individual human beings. Marx formulated this radical vision of a new society in his late text *Critique of the Gotha Program* as the product of a transition to a higher phase of communism. In the first stage, the "prolonged birth pangs from capitalist society" would limit the level of social and individual development, but:

In a higher phase of communist society, after the enslaving subordination of the individual to the division of labor, and therewith also the antithesis between mental and physical labour, has vanished; after labour has become not only a means of life but lifeís prime want; after the productive forces have also increased with the all-round development of the individual, and all the spring of cooperative wealth flow more abundantly — only then can the narrow horizon of bourgeois right be crossed in its entirety and society inscribe on its banner: From each according to his ability, to each according to his needs!

Thus in Marxís utopian vision of communism, education would help fully develop socialised individuals, create a cooperative and harmonious society, and unleash creativity in all of its forms. In historical retrospect, however, the lack of a more fully articulated theory of education and subjectivity, and of the subjective conditions of revolutionary transformation, in the classical Marxian theory vitiated its theory and practice. Marx seemed to think that class and revolutionary consciousness would develop naturally, as a result of the workers" position in the process of production. Subsequent Marxian theorists, however, engaged in a heated debate concerning whether class consciousness developed spontaneously, or would have to be brought to the workers from outside. And later generations of neo-Marxian theorists would develop more sophisticated theories of consciousness, communication, and education, whereby political subjectivities could be formed which would strive for socialist and/or democratic social change.

Succeeding generations of Marxists perceived that the classical paradigm overemphasized the dimension of class, playing down the importance of gender, race, sexuality, and other key constituents of human experience, lacunae filled in by many neo-Marxian theories, as I note in the following sections. Moreover, many of Marxís texts also seem to place too heavy an emphasis on labor as the distinctly human activity, as the key to the development of the human being. Overemphasis on production is accompanied by an inadequate concept of intersubjectivity, lacking a fully developed theory of individual consciousness and its development in communication, symbolic action, and culture. Unlike later social theorists such as Durkheim, Mead, Dewey, and

Habermas, Marx failed to perceive the importance of wider communication in the development of new forms of association and solidarity. He thus put too much emphasis on class struggle, on direct action, and not enough on communication and democracy.

Indeed, Marx never grasped the significance of the institutions of liberal democracy as an important heritage of modern societies that should be absorbed into socialism. Although he espoused a model of radical democratic self-government in his writings on the Paris Commune, and while Marx long championed democracy as an ideal, he never properly appreciated the separation of powers and system of rights, checks and balances, and democratic participation developed within bourgeois society. Thus, Marx had an inadequate theory of education and democracy, and failed to develop an institutional theory of democracy, its constraints under capitalism, and how socialism would make possible fuller and richer democracy. These lacunae in the classical Marxian theory would be filled by later generations of Marxist theorists.

Within the Marxian tradition, a tremendous variety and diversity of different schools, movements, and positions have evolved. In the following narrative, I will trace developments within key neo-Marxian traditions, including those of the Frankfurt school, British cultural studies, and a diverse grouping of neo- and post-Marxian positions covered by the label of "critical pedagogy." In these traditions, certain positions overlap and there are also divergences based, in part, on responses to different socio-historical conditions in the trajectory from state and organised capitalism in the 1930s to the resurgence of neo-liberalism and return to market capitalism in the 1980s. The dynamics of globalisation and a variety of anti-globalisation movements in the 1990s to the present have also generated a global proliferation of the various formations of neo-Marxian theory which has produced a dizzying diversity of Marxian discourse.

Other narratives of the trajectory of Marxism and education have traced the development of different positions within education through the prisms of Gramsci, Althusser and structural Marxism, and reproduction theory, as well as the schools that I chart. There have also been studies of the role of Marxian ideas in curriculum and schooling in capitalist societies, as well as presentations of contemporary debates within Marxian theory on a vast range of topics in the field of education. I, however, will focus on the development of perspectives on education within the tradition of critical social theory and pedagogy developed by Western Marxism. This perspective and presentation is shaped by the work that I have done within the traditions I discuss and in the context of teaching at state universities in Texas and California in the U.S.

The Frankfurt School, Culture, and Regimes of Capital

Frankfurt School theorists have rarely explicitly addressed problems of education and pedagogy, although I will suggest that its critique of the culture industries provides an important model of Marxian cultural studies and pedagogy that anticipates the Birmingham School and that provides important contributions to educational philosophy today. The Frankfurt School stress on consciousness, ideology, culture, and socialisation highlights the importance of transforming individuals and societies through change of consciousness, culture, and the institutions of everyday life such as education.

In Weimar Germany in the early 1930s, the Frankfurt School were carrying out research into the family and authority, and were concluding that the family was declining as an agent of authority, giving way to the media, peer groups, schooling, and other institutions. In exile in the United States after 1934, the Frankfurt School focused on the role of the media in educating and socialising individuals. To a large extent, the Frankfurt school inaugurated critical studies of mass communication and culture, and thus produced an early model of cultural studies. In a wide-ranging set of studies and texts, the group developed a critical and transdisciplinary approach to cultural and communications studies, combining critique of political economy of the media, analysis of texts, and audience reception studies of the social and ideological effects of mass culture and communications.

The Frankfurt School theorists coined the term "culture industries" to signify the process of the industrialisation of mass-produced culture and the commercial imperatives which drove the system. The group analysed all mass-mediated cultural artifacts within the context of industrial production, in which the products of the culture industries exhibited the same features as other goods of mass production: commodification, standardisation, and massification.

The culture industries had the specific function, however, of providing ideological legitimation of the existing capitalist societies and of integrating individuals into the framework of its social formation. Adornoís analyses of popular music, Lowenthalís studies of popular literature and magazines, Herzogís studies of radio soap operas, and the critiques of mass culture developed in Horkheimer and Adornoís famous study of the culture industries provide many examples of the value of the critical theory approach. Moreover, in their theories of the culture industries and critiques of mass culture, they were the first to systematically analyse and criticise mass-mediated culture and communications within critical social theory. The critical theorists scrutinised the pedagogical and social functions the culture industries in the reproduction of contemporary societies. In their optic, mass culture and communications stand at the center of leisure activity, are important agents of socialisation and education, mediators of political reality, and should thus be seen as major institutions of contemporary societies with a variety of economic, political, cultural and social effects.

Furthermore, the critical theorists investigated the cultural industries in a political context as a form of the integration of the working class into capitalist societies. The group were among the first neo-Marxian theorists to examine the effects of mass culture and the rise of the consumer society on the working classes which were to be the instrument of revolution in the classical Marxian scenario. They also analysed the ways that the culture industries and consumer society were performing new kinds of pedagogy and stabilising contemporary capitalism. Accordingly, they sought novel strategies for political change, agencies of political transformation, and models for political emancipation that could serve as norms of social critique and goals for political struggle. This project required rethinking the Marxian project and produced many important contributions — as well as some problematical positions.

After World War II, the critical theorists examined how the state and public education produced a form of "Halb-Bildung," half-education, and themselves called for education that fully developed individual subjectivities. Their form of "critical theory" emphasized the importance of critique, reflexivity, and gaining emancipatory consciousness, free from indoctrination and socialisation. Although the Frankfurt School did not systematically explore the institutions of higher education, Adorno, Horkheimer, Marcuse, and Habermas wrote occasional critiques of the University and intervened frequently in educational debates.

In retrospect, one can see the Frankfurt groupís critical theory as articulation of a stage of state and monopoly capitalism which became dominant during the 1930s. In this era of "organised capitalism," the state and giant corporations managed the economy and individuals submitted to state and corporate control. This period is often described as "Fordism" to designate the system of mass production and the homogenising regime of capital which wanted to produce mass desires, tastes, and behavior. It was thus an era of mass production and consumption characterised by uniformity and homogeneity of needs, thought, and behavior producing a "mass society" and what the Frankfurt school described as "the end of the individual." No longer was individual thought and action the motor of social and cultural progress; instead giant organisations and institutions overpowered individuals. The era corresponds to the staid, ascetic, conformist, and conservative world of corporate capitalism that was dominant in the 1950s with its organisation men and women, its mass consumption, and its mass culture.

During this period, mass culture and communication were instrumental in generating the modes of thought and behavior appropriate to a highly organised and homogenised social order. Likewise, public education was creating standardised education and curricula which was serving as instruments of massification and social control. For instance, Herbert Marcuseís *One-Dimensional Man* criticised the ways that educational institutions, the media, and other forms of socialisation were creating conformist modes of thought and behavior, producing what he called "one-dimensional man."

Thus, the Frankfurt school theory of mass culture articulates a major historical shift to an era in which mass consumption and culture was indispensable to producing a consumer society based on homogeneous needs and desires for mass-produced products. In this context, the media and public education helped generate a mass society based on social organisation and homogeneity. It is culturally the period of highly controlled network radio and television, insipid top forty pop music, glossy Hollywood films, national magazines, and standardised public schooling.

Of course, media culture and schooling were never as massified and homogeneous as in the Frankfurt school model. Indeed, one could argue that the model was flawed even during its time of origin and influence and that other models were preferable, such as those of Walter Benjamin, Siegfried Kracauer, Ernst Bloch and others of the Weimar generation. Yet the original critical theory model of the culture industry and mass society did articulate the vital social roles of media culture and schooling during a specific regime of capital. It provided a model, still of use, of a highly commercial and technologically advanced culture that serves the needs of dominant corporate interests, plays a major role in ideological reproduction, and in enculturating individuals into the dominant system of needs, thought, and behavior. The Frankfurt school also influenced and helped produce other neo-Marxian approaches to culture, society, and education as we see in the following sections.

The Trajectories of Cultural Studies

British cultural studies, then, from historical perspective emerges in a later era of capital, on the cusp of what became known as "post-Fordism" and a more variegated and conflicted cultural formation. The forms of culture described by the earliest phase of British cultural studies in the 1950s and early 1960s articulated conditions in an era in which there were still significant tensions in England and much of Europe between an older working class-based culture and the newer mass-produced culture whose models and exemplars were the products of American culture industries. The initial project of cultural studies developed by Richard Hoggart, Raymond Williams, and E.P. Thompson attempted to preserve working class culture against onslaughts of mass culture produced by the culture industries.

Thompsonís historical inquiries into the history of British working class institutions and struggles, the defenses of working class culture and education by Hoggart and Williams, and their attacks on mass culture were part of a socialist and working class-oriented project that assumed that the industrial working class was a force of progressive social change and that it could be mobilised and organised to struggle against the inequalities of the existing capitalist societies and for a more egalitarian socialist one. Williams and Hoggart were deeply involved in projects of working class education and oriented toward socialist working class politics, seeing their form of cultural studies as an instrument of progressive social change.

The early critiques in the first wave of British cultural studies of Americanism and mass culture, in Hoggart, Williams, and others, thus paralleled to some extent the earlier critique of the Frankfurt school, yet valorised a working class that the critical theorists saw as defeated in Germany and much of Europe during the era of fascism and which they never saw as a strong resource for emancipatory social change. The early work of the Birmingham school, as I will now argue, was continuous with the radicalism of the first wave of British cultural studies as well, in important ways, with the Frankfurt school. Yet the Birmingham project also paved the way, as I suggest below, for a postmodern populist turn in cultural studies, which responds to a later stage of capitalism.

It has not yet been widely recognised that the second stage of the development of British cultural studies —

starting with the founding of the University of Birmingham Centre for Contemporary Cultural Studies in 1963/64 by Hoggart and Stuart Hall — shared many key perspectives with the Frankfurt school. During this period, the Centre developed a variety of critical approaches for the analysis, interpretation, and criticism of cultural artifacts.

Through a set of internal debates, and responding to social struggles and movements of the 1960s and the 1970s, the Birmingham group came to focus on the interplay of representations and ideologies of class, gender, race, ethnicity, and nationality in cultural texts, including media culture. Like the Frankfurt school, they analysed critically they pedagogical effects of newspapers, radio, television, film, music, and other popular cultural forms on audiences, as well as to develop critiques of schooling in Britain. They also focused on how various audiences interpreted and used media culture in varied and different ways and contexts, analysing the factors that made audiences respond in contrasting ways to media texts.

The now classical period of British cultural studies from the early 1960s to the early 1980s continued to adopt Marxian approaches to the study of culture, especially those influenced by Althusser and Gramsci. Yet although Hall and his colleagues usually omit the Frankfurt school from their narratives of their history and influences, some of the work done by the Birmingham group replicated certain classical positions of the Frankfurt school, in their social theory and methodological models for doing cultural studies, as well as in their political perspectives and strategies. Like the Frankfurt school, British cultural studies observed the integration of the working class and its decline of revolutionary consciousness, and studied the conditions of this catastrophe for the Marxian project of revolution. Like the Frankfurt school, British cultural studies concluded that mass culture was playing an important role in integrating the working class into existing capitalist societies and that a new consumer and media culture was forming a new mode of capitalist hegemony.

Both traditions focused on the intersections of culture and ideology and saw ideology critique as central to a critical cultural studies. Both viewed culture as a mode of ideological reproduction and hegemony, in which educational institutions and cultural forms help to shape the modes of thought and behavior that induce individuals to adapt to the social conditions of capitalist societies. Both also interpreted culture as a potential form of resistance to capitalist society and both the earlier forerunners of British cultural studies, especially Raymond Williams, and the theorists of the Frankfurt school perceived high culture as forces of resistance to capitalist modernity. Later, British cultural studies would valorise resistant moments in media culture and audience interpretations and use of media artifacts, while the Frankfurt school tended, with some exceptions, to view mass culture as a homogeneous and potent form of ideological domination — a difference that would seriously divide the two traditions.

From the beginning, British cultural studies was highly political in nature and focused on the potentials for resistance in oppositional subcultures, first, valorising the potential of working class cultures, then, youth subcultures to resist the hegemonic forms of capitalist domination. Unlike the classical Frankfurt school, British cultural studies turned to youth cultures as providing potentially new forms of opposition and social change. Through studies of youth subcultures, British cultural studies demonstrated how subcultural formations came to constitute distinct forms of identity and group membership and appraised the oppositional potential of various youth subcultures.

British cultural studies also investigated how schooling integrates youth into capitalist societies and the ways that working class youth rebel and resist. Paul Willisí now classic *Learning to Labor* carried out ethnographic and critical studies of how working class youth confront disciplinary schooling that tries to get them to conform to authority and middle class values and mores. Willis documents both modes of disciplinary schooling and resistance, showing how working class youth rebel and construct identities outside of schooling and middle class norms.

Within the University, British cultural studies developed interdisciplinary programs to study the intersection of culture, society, and politics, and developed critiques of academic fragmentation and disciplinarity. British cultural studies — like the Frankfurt school — insists that culture must be studied within the social relations and system through which culture is produced and consumed, and that thus study of culture is intimately bound up with the study of society, politics, and economics.

British cultural studies and the Frankfurt school were thus both founded as fundamentally transdisciplinary enterprises which resisted established academic divisions of labor and implicitly revolutionise University education. Indeed, their boundary-crossing and critiques of the detrimental effects of abstracting culture from its socio-political context elicited hostility among those who are more disciplinary-oriented and who, for example, believe in the autonomy of culture and renounce sociological or political readings. Against such academic formalism and separatism, cultural studies insists that culture must be investigated within the social relations and system through which culture is produced and consumed. From this perspective, analysis of culture is intimately bound up with the study of society, politics, and economics. Employing Gramsciís model of hegemony and counterhegemony, it sought to analyse "hegemonic," or ruling, social and cultural forces of domination and to seek "counterhegemonic" forces of resistance and struggle. The project was aimed at social transformation and attempted to specify forces of domination and resistance in order to aid the process of political struggle and emancipation from oppression and domination.

Some earlier authoritative presentations of British cultural studies stressed the importance of a transdisciplinary approach to the study of culture that analysed its political economy, process of production and distribution, textual products, and reception by the audience — positions remarkably similar to the Frankfurt school. For instance, in his classical programmatic article, "Encoding/Decoding," Stuart Hall began his analysis by using Marxís *Grundrisse* as a model to trace the articulations of "a continuous circuit," encompassing "production - distribution - consumption - production". Hall concretises this model with focus on how media institutions produce meanings, how they circulate, and how audiences use or decode the texts to produce meaning. Moreover, in a 1983 lecture published in 1985/1986, Richard Johnson provided a model of cultural studies, similar to Hallís earlier model, based on a diagram of the circuits of production, textuality, and reception, parallel to the circuits of capital stressed by Marx, illustrated by a diagram that stressed the importance of production and distribution. Although Johnson emphasized the importance of analysis of production in cultural studies and criticised *Screen* for abandoning this perspective in favor of more idealist and textualist approaches, much work in British and North American cultural studies has replicated the neglect of production and political economy.

In more recent cultural studies, however, there has been a turn — throughout the English-speaking world — to what might be called a "postmodern" problematic which emphasizes pleasure, consumption, and the individual construction of identities in terms of what McGuigan has called a "cultural populism." Media culture from this perspective produces material for identities, pleasures, and empowerment, and thus audiences constitute the "popular" through their consumption of cultural products. During this phase — roughly from the mid-1980s to the present — cultural studies in Britain and North America turned from the socialist and revolutionary politics of the previous stages to postmodern forms of identity politics and less critical perspectives on media and consumer culture. Emphasis was placed more and more on the audience, consumption, and reception, and displaced focus on production and distribution of texts and how texts were produced in media industries.

In context, the forms of cultural studies developed from the late 1970s to the present, theorise a shift from the stage of state monopoly capitalism, or Fordism, rooted in mass production and consumption to a new regime of capital and social order, sometimes described as "post-Fordism", or "postmodernism", and characterising a transnational and global capital that valorises difference, multiplicity, eclecticism, populism, and intensified consumerism in a new information/ entertainment society. From this perspective, the proliferating media culture, postmodern architecture, shopping malls, and the culture of the postmodern spectacle became the promoters and palaces of a new stage of technocapitalism, the latest stage of capital, encompassing a postmodern image and consumer culture.

What is described as the "new revisionism" severs cultural studies from political economy and critical social theory. During the current stage of cultural studies there is a widespread tendency to decenter, or even ignore completely, economics, history, and politics in favor of emphasis on local pleasures, consumption, and the construction of hybrid identities from the material of the popular. This cultural populism replicates the turn in postmodern theory away from Marxism and its alleged reductionism, master narratives of liberation and domination, and historical teleology.

The emphasis in postmodernist cultural studies arguably articulates experiences and phenomena within a new mode of social organisation. The emphasis on active audiences, resistant readings, oppositional texts, utopian moments, and the like describes an era in which individuals are trained to be more active media consumers, and in which they are given a much wider choice of cultural materials, corresponding to a new global and transnational capitalism with a much broader array of consumer choices, products, and services. In this regime, difference sells, and the diversities, multiplicities, and heterogeneity valorised in postmodern theory describes the proliferation of consumer choices in a new social order predicated on proliferation of products, desires, and needs.

Critical Pedagogy from Freire to North America and Beyond

Alongside of the proliferation of neo-Marxian theories of culture and society and globalisation of cultural studies, forms of an oppositional critical pedagogy emerged that explicitly criticised schooling in capitalist societies while calling for more emancipatory modes of education. In his now classic *The Pedagogy of the Oppressed*, Brazilian educator and activist Paulo Freire criticised the "banking concept of education" while calling for more interactive, dialogical, and participatory forms of pedagogy that are parallel in interesting ways to those of John Dewey. While

Dewey wanted education to produce citizens for democracy, however, Freire sought, in the spirit of Marxist revolutionary praxis, to develop a pedagogy of the oppressed that would produce revolutionary subjects, empowered to overthrow oppression and to create a more democratic and just social order.

Freireís pedagogy of the oppressed seeks to transform individuals from being objects of educational processes to subjects of their own autonomy and emancipation. Freire suggests that classical Marxism had not adequately developed the subjective and pedagogical dimension and that the oppressed must be educated so that they can perform their own self-emancipation. Setting up schools that practiced his critical pedagogy in his native Brazil, Freire was expelled when a military dictatorship took over his country, but continued his work in Chile and throughout the world until his death.

Freireís work found resonance on a global scale and by the 1980s there were many schools of critical pedagogy. In North America, a series of books on Freire appeared and groups and individuals took up his ideas in a variety of contexts. Theorists such as Henry Giroux, Donaldo Macedo, Carlos Torres, and Peter McLaren linked Freiren perspectives with those of Frankfurt school critical theory and other neo-Marxian approaches in works from the 1990s to the present. Cultural theorists and educators developed critical pedagogies of media and representation, and articulated neo-Marxian class perspectives with those of gender, race, and multiculturalism. Feminists, poststructuralists and others criticised what they saw as biases and limitations of critical pedagogy, and there were sharp debates over the value or limitations of the continuing role of Marxism within critical pedagogy.

Henry Girouxís early work was frequently linked to Michael Appleís attempts to link neo-Gramsci theories of hegemony to analyses of capitalist schooling as instruments of corporate power and domination, such as were produced by Bowles and Gintis. Apple was more influenced by Althusserian structural Marxism and Bowles and Gintis" critique of schooling in capitalist society. Both Giroux and Apple, however, saw the need for theories of resistance, transforming education in the interests of radical democracy, and bringing in multiculturalist problematics that would address issues of gender and race, as well as class. These moves led Marxist critics to suggest that they were abandoning Marxism for democratic populism, although one could argue that they are reconstructing Marxism for the present age, in the spirit of a revisionist dialectic.

Giroux urged movement from a language of critique to a language of hope and possibility, combining critique of the dominant mode of schooling with valorisation of resistance and alternative conceptions of education. After publishing a series of books that many recognise as major works on contemporary education and critical pedagogy, Giroux turned to cultural studies in the late 1980s to enrich education with expanded conceptions of pedagogy and literacy. This cultural turn is animated by the hope to reconstruct schooling with critical perspectives that can help us to better understand and transform contemporary culture and society in the contemporary era. Giroux provides cultural studies with a critical pedagogy missing in many versions and a sustained attempt to link critical pedagogy and cultural studies with developing a more democratic culture and citizenry. The result is an intersection of critical pedagogy and cultural studies that enhances both enterprises, providing a cultural and transformative political dimension to critical pedagogy and a pedagogical dimension to cultural studies.

In an ever-mushrooming profusion of books, Peter McLaren has been advocating a return to classical

Marxism as a strategy to transform educational practices within a project of social and cultural transformation. McLarenís most recent book *Che Guevara, Paulo Freire, and the Pedagogy of Revolution* sets out to introduce educators to the life and politics of Che Guevara; to recover the legacy of Paulo Freire from the interpretive efforts of educational humanists who have for the most part depotentiated the revolutionary import of Freireís teachings and have largely domesticated the Marxist trajectory of his politics; and to analyse the philosophical and political writings of these two figures in the context of their pedagogical theories and practices. In McLarenís view, the work of Marxist revolutionaries are too often overlooked in discussions of educational theory and pedagogical practice. Whereas such thinkers often occupy a prominent place in other disciplines such as philosophy and the social sciences, McLaren argues that educational theory is remiss in failing to discuss their important contributions. In setting forth his arguments, McLaren himself adopted Marxist-Humanist perspectives in his recent work.

The many works of Carlos Torres also navigate through the Marxian tradition and advance the positions of Paulo Freire and critical pedagogy. In addition to producing much on Freire, Torres has published important books in the political sociology of education and comparative education from neo-Marxian perspectives on topics such as education, the state, and power; the role of schooling in social and cultural reproduction; the role of social theory in comprehending the nature and conflicts in contemporary education; the problematics of globalisation; the interconnections between citizens, multiculturalism, and democracy; the ways that a democratic restructuring of schooling involve engaging the problematics of gender, race, and class in constructing pedagogies that promote agency, solidarity, respect for difference, and ultimately create a more just and democratic society; and the contributions of critical pedagogy to transforming education and democratising society.

Torres and his colleague Nicholas Burbules have co-edited a book on *Globalisation and Education. Critical Perspectives* that articulates an overview of the challenges to education from globalisation. Various contributors address the different components of globalisation and offer conflicting perspectives. They argue that the economic restructuring of the global economy suggests both the need to reconstruct education to make it relevant to the needs of a new economy, but also provides challenges to resisting the imposition of a market-based model of education that would impose similar business models and imperatives on educational institutions throughout the world, with problematic results. Indeed, one of the major thrusts of the collection is to present some of the dangers involved in the imposition of neo-liberalism and market models on the institutions of education, while benefiting from potential advances of globalisation, such as the Internet and new technologies, new forms of global and cosmopolitan culture, and a globalisation of democracy and human rights.

10

Media and Critical Pedagogy

A large number of educators and theorists recognise the ubiquity of media culture in contemporary society, the growing trends toward multicultural education, and the need for media literacy that addresses the issue of multicultural difference. There is growing recognition that media representations help construct our images and understanding of the world and that education must meet the dual challenges of teaching media literacy in a multicultural society and sensitising students and publics to the inequities and injustices of a society based on gender, race, and class inequalities and discrimination. Recent critical studies see the role of mainstream media in exacerbating these inequalities and the ways that media education and the production of alternative media can promote a healthy multiculturalism of diversity and more robust democracy. They thus confront some of the most serious challenges and problems that face us as educators and citizens as we move toward the twenty-first century.

Multiculturalism and Media Pedagogy

A recent reader *Shared Differences* demonstrates how media of cultural representation such as film, video, photography, and multimedia can be used to promote multicultural education. The text opens with a statement by co-editor Diane Carson that a sense of urgency concerning America's increasingly multicultural society drove her and Lester Friedman to investigate how multicultural education can help us invigorate education for the contemporary era: "A teacher's inclusion of multicultural pedagogy and an active engagement with diverse ethnic, racial, and national issues is critical to America's social well-being... We must put our beliefs into practice, aware that the defining characteristics and enabling understanding of ethnic, racial, and national groups can and ought to be taught. Teachers must acknowledge uniqueness and difference as they also applaud similarity, for the strength of small communities and also society at large derives from celebrating our diversity".

Carson expands her pitch for multicultural education as a response to deal creatively with growing diversity, which facilitates "strategies for sharing, understanding, and enjoying" our proliferating cultural multiplicities and differences. She urges developing strategies for action, that will promote multicultural understanding, that will empower students, and that will strengthen education. Carson's and Friedman's dual project is to argue that the issues of multiculturalism are central to academic disciplines from literature to anthropology, and that media pedagogy can serve to promote the goals of multicultural education and critical media literacy. They accordingly assemble a broad array of studies by teachers who use media technology to promote multiculturalism in a number of disciplines in two and four year colleges. Each of their 14 contributors outlines course goals, discusses how they use media and media education to promote these goals, and analyses their course experiences. Each also presents the syllabus used in the course to provide practical models of how to organise courses in multicultural education and media pedagogy.

The result is a very useful collection of models of practical criticism that will enable teachers in various fields to use media education to promote goals internal to their discipline. On the whole, the collection advances the social goals of making teachers and students sensitive to the politics of representation, to how media audiences' images of race, gender, sexuality, and cultural differences are in part generated by cultural representations, how negative stereotyping presents harmful cultural images, and the need for a diversity of representations to capture the cultural wealth of contemporary America. Teachers can gain insight into how media can serve their pedagogical goals and how they can both use media to promote multicultural education and to use this material to teach media literacy as well.

Following Carson's Preface and overview of the project, the collection opens with an essay by co-editor Lester Friedman, "Struggling for America's Soul: A Search for Some Common Ground in the Multicultural Debate." Friedman notes the current conflicts over multiculturalism in American society and the debates over multicultural education in the academic world. In this contentious and conflicted terrain, he suggests, we must seek common ground, to articulate what unites as well as divides us, and come to appreciate our commonalties as well as our differences. Indeed, the rancor in some of the education wars over curricula, pedagogy, and education in general are part and parcel of broader cultural wars between competing groups and ideologies fighting over the future of U.S. society and culture. Since educational debates are often intimately connected with political struggles, it is necessary to articulate clearly the different positions within the debates and if possible and appropriate to seek a common ground for consensus.

There is no necessary conflict between traditional and multicultural education, that the education process is strengthened with the incorporation of voices, viewpoints, and perspectives excluded from traditional canons, and that multicultural curricula, deployed wisely, can improve many academic courses. Friedman attempts to articulate some principles that would enable multicultural education to enrich rather than replace the traditional curriculum and that would provide a common ground for both traditionalists and multiculturalists to rethink education. Reaching a common and higher ground in the debates over education require, in Friedman's view: acknowledging that while knowledge is constructed and transmitted from specific locations that "knowledgeable, well-trained teachers can generate discussions about cultures other than their own,". For Friedman this entails accepting that multicultural curricula need not "be taught only, or even primarily, to members of ethnic minorities," nor that "one monocultural approach with another monocultural methodology.

If multicultural education is to promote genuine diversity and expand the curriculum, it is important both for groups excluded from mainstream education to learn about their own heritage and for dominant groups to explore the experiences and voices of minority and excluded groups. Moreover, as Friedman stresses, while it is important and useful to study cultures and voices excluded from traditional canons, dead white European male authors may have as much of importance to teach all students as excluded representatives of minority groups whom multiculturalists want, often with good reason, to include in the curriculum. Thus, Friedman convincingly argues that: "Western culture, despite its myriad faults, remains a crucial influence on American political, intellectual and social thought and, as such, should play an important role in classrooms".

Indeed, few advocates of multicultural education call for jettisoning the traditional canon and altogether replacing the classics with new multicultural fare. Genuine multicultural education requires expanding, not contracting, the curricula, broadening and enriching it, not impoverishing it. It also involves, as Friedman stresses, including white ethnic groups in the multicultural spectrum and searching out those common values and ideals that cut across racial and cultural boundaries. Thus, multicultural education can both help us understand our history and culture, and can move toward producing a more diverse and inclusive democratic society.

Shared Differences suggests how multicultural education can be used to enrich the subject matter of many traditional disciplines, ranging from literature to anthropology. In addition, traditional disciplines and texts can themselves be taken as the topic of critical scrutiny and inquiry, and can thus be used to promote the pedagogical goals of developing sensitivity to cultural difference. The emphasis in the reader is on using a medley of media material to present aspects and effects of the politics of representation from a variety of perspectives. Thus, an anthropologist discusses how media culture can be used to teach ethnography and cultural critique which is sensitive to cultural representation and difference; writing teachers present a course dedicated to writing about literature and various forms of popular media which helps make students aware of the forms of cultural rhetoric and difference; an English professor discusses how the English curriculum can be transformed by the addition of film and media culture; a public health professor discusses how negative media representations can contribute to problems of health and social well-being; and historian Carlos E. Cortes discusses how media education can contribute to better historical understanding and socio-political sensitivity.

These studies provide a variety of arguments for the importance of including media texts in the curricula and how using and studying the media can advance the aims of a variety of pedagogic practices. The teaching of writing, for example, as Himley and Temes stress, is enhanced by engaging students in analysing cultural rhetoric and difference in various domains of social discourses. Print journalism, film, television, photographic images, advertising, and political rhetoric are all forms of writing, all cultural texts that influence how we see the world, and the practice of critically dissecting these writings helps us to see how all of these cultural forms represent different modes of writing with their own biases and perspectives. Attending to the representation of difference within the broader field of society and culture can enable students to avoid manipulation by cultural rhetorics and to empower students to find their own voices within the cacophony of competing and conflicting discourses of the present age. Critically dissecting cultural materials also empowers students to reflect upon their own commonalties and differences, and to respect their differences from others, while becoming critical of those who would suppress differences or present some differences negatively, stereotypically, and pejoratively.

The authors in *Shared Differences* thus present arguments legitimating the use of media materials in a number of disciplines to promote both traditional pedagogic goals, as well as to contribute to the production of a more diverse democratic polity that appreciates and affirms differences between ethnic, racial, and cultural groups. On the other hand, many of the teachers who are using multicultural media as a tool to promote their own disciplines downplay the importance of cultivating media literacy as an important tool in developing students' critical and analytical skills. One needs to be aware that each media technology have their own biases, their own formal codes and rules, and that the ways in which the media themselves construct and communicate meaning needs to be an explicit focus of awareness and analysis.

Indeed, media culture constructs models of multicultural difference, privileging some groups, while denigrating others. Grasping the construction of difference and hierarchy in media texts requires learning how they are constructed, how they communicate, and how they influence their audiences. Textual analysis of media artifacts helps to reveal their codes and conventions, their values and ideologies, and thus their meanings and messages. In particular, a critical cultural studies should analyse representations of class, gender, race, ethnicity, sexual preference, and other identity markers in the texts of media culture, as well as attending to national, regional, and other cultural differences, how they are articulated in cultural representations, and how these differences among audiences create different readings and receptions of cultural texts.

On the whole, the contributions to *Shared Differences* focus on using media to promote multicultural education and downplay theorising and developing the skills of media literacy. Most of the contributors focus on the politics of positive/negative representations and do not present more complex methods of gaining media literacy, or articulate more general principles or models. Although many of the practical course curricula and syllabi present materials for developing media literacy, this topic is not overtly theorised and is merely mentioned in passing. In the next section, therefore, I will engage a series of books published over the past decade that contribute to developing a critical pedagogy of media literacy. The argument for developing such skills as part of standard educational training is that the media themselves are a form of cultural pedagogy and thus must be countered by a critical media pedagogy that dissects how media communicate and effect their audiences and how students and citizens can gain skills to critically analyse the media.

Media Literacy and the Challenges of Contemporary Education

While *Shared Differences* focuses on multicultural media pedagogy as a response to the challenge of developing multicultural education and understanding, a large number of books on media literacy over the past decade start from the premise of the ubiquity of media culture in contemporary society and produce a more general argument for critical media literacy as a response to media bombardment. "Media literacy" involves knowledge of how media work, how they construct meanings, how they serve as a form of cultural pedagogy, and how they function in everyday life. A media literate person is skillful in analysing media codes and conventions, able to criticise media stereotypes, values, and ideologies, and thus literate in reading media critically. Media literacy thus empowers people to use media intelligently, to discriminate and evaluate media content, to critically dissect media forms, and to investigate media effects and uses.

A critical media literacy is necessary since media culture strongly influences our view of the world, imparting knowledge of geography, of technology and the environment, of political and social events, of how the economy works, of what is currently going on in our society and the world at large. Media entertainment is also a form of cultural pedagogy, teaching dominant values, ways of thought and behavior, style and fashion, and providing resources for constituting individual identities. The media are both crucial sources of knowledge and information and sources of entertainment and leisure activity. They are our story tellers and entertainers, and are especially influential since we are often not aware that media narratives and spectacles themselves are a form of education, imparting cultural knowledge, values, and shaping how we see and live our social worlds.

Consequently, media literacy is an important part of multicultural education since many people's conceptions of gender, race, ethnicity, and class are constituted in part by the media which are often important in determining how people view social groups, conceive of gender roles of masculinity and femininity, and distinguish between good and bad, right and wrong, attitudes and behavior. Since the media also provide role models, conceptions of proper and improper conduct, and provide crucial cultural and political information, they are an important form of pedagogy and socialisation. A media literate person is thus able to read, understand, evaluate, discriminate and criticise media materials, and ultimately, as I shall suggest below, produce media artifacts, in order to use media as means of expression and communication.

Sometimes "the media" are lumped into one homogeneous category, but it is important to discern that there are many media of communication and forms of cultural pedagogy, ranging from print media such as books, newspapers, and magazines to film, radio, television, popular music, photography, advertising, and many other multimedia cultural forms, including video games, computer culture, CD-Roms, and the like. Media literacy thus requires traditional print literacy skills as well as visual literacy, aural literacy, and the ability to analyse narratives, spectacles, and a wide range of cultural forms. Media literacy involves reading images critically, interpreting sounds, and seeing how media texts produce meaning in a multiplicity of ways.

Since media are a central part of our cultural experience from childhood to the grave, training in media literacy should begin early in life and continue into adulthood, as new technologies are constantly creating new media and new genres, technical innovations, aesthetic forms, and conventions are constantly emerging.

Len Masterman has been associated with helping inaugurate a media literacy movement and his book *Teaching the Media* is frequently cited in the literature on the topic as a key text. Masterman makes the case that the ubiquity of the media in transmitting knowledge requires educators from primary schools to post-school to impart critical knowledge of how the media work, construct meaning, and function in everyday life. Yet Masterman's focus is on "delineation of a number of *general principles* for teaching across the media" and he does not really develop a concept or practical pedagogy of media literacy in his book. Rather, drawing heavily on British cultural studies, he provides a comprehensive overview of media education, discussing such topics as media institutions, text and rhetoric, ideology, audiences, and approaches to media education.

Masterman's text provides a useful general introduction to teaching the media, though his British-oriented approach might provide blocks to using his book in a North American setting. Moreover, while a general media literacy may be of some use in transmitting some general ideas and principles, one needs to develop a media literacy that is sensitive to the differences among the specific media, engaging students in critically analysing and dissecting a wide range of media materials, including such disparate phenomena as TV news, rock music, action-adventure film, advertising, and multimedia web sites. Hence, the principle of difference should not only be part of a multicultural education making students sensitive to social and cultural difference, but one should also see how different media construct their materials in different ways. One also needs to construct different forms of media literacy according to the age, interests, needs, and capacities of specific students. Obviously, teaching media literacy in kindergarten through the elementary grades is going to involve different strategies and pedagogy than teaching media literacy to high school, college, or adult audiences.

Contributions of a critical pedagogy of difference are found in recent contributions to expanding media literacy by scholars influenced by post-structuralist theory. Allan Luke and Carmen Luke have pointed to the usefulness of post-structuralist thought in rethinking education under contemporary conditions. Carmen Luke has shown how difference is often occluded in mainstream media culture and how cultural studies in the classroom can generate alternative readings and critically valorise difference. In turn, Allan Luke has shown how a post-structuralist-inspired discourse analysis can help dissect the construction of difference in cultural texts and be an important instrument in a critical pedagogy.

Although we are moving into an increasingly global media culture, critical media pedagogy should probably engage in classroom instruction media and cultural material familiar to students in different countries and parts of the world. In the 1990s, for instance, a series of books have been published in the United States dealing with various dimensions of media literacy and education which engages North American media material. Thus, whereas earlier cultural studies and models of media literacy often engaged material from English and Australian contexts that were not always accessible to individuals in the North American context, there is now a burgeoning tradition of cultural studies engaging material from a variety of cultures, ranging from the United States to Taiwan, in what might be seen as the globalisation of cultural studies. Thus, whereas John Fiske's earlier works primarily dealt with the English and Australian materials and the contexts in which he was himself living, teaching, and researching, his more recent books focus on North American media culture and contexts, reflecting his new domicile. In all of these cases, the issue of multiculturalism and the analysis of gender, race, and class in terms of the politics of representation and audience reception are stressed.

Other note-worthy attempts to develop a critical pedagogy focusing on cultivating media literacy and multicultural education include the work of James Schwoch, Mimi White, and Susan Reilly who recognise that the media are a form of pedagogy which construct social knowledge and requires critical dissection of its mode of teaching. The authors demonstrate how media images, discourse, symbols, and narratives constitute social meanings and subjectivities. Critically scrutinising the dominant forms of media culture, the authors develop a critical pedagogy of representation that dissects the values, meanings, and ideologies constructed in media texts. Combining analysis of news/information and entertainment, the authors see "media as perpetual pedagogy" and provide critical insights into the sort of pedagogy provided by mainstream media while providing a counterpedagogy of their own.

In the same critical spirit, David Sholle and Stan Denski discuss media education and the (re)production of culture, critically analysing the social production of knowledge through mass media of communication and proclaiming the need for a critical pedagogy that criticises its limitations, distortions, and biases. The authors stress the importance of building bridges across disciplines, using theory to connect media education with the empowerment of students and the promotion of radical democracy. Combining the critical theory of the Frankfurt school with British cultural studies, feminism, and postmodern theory, Sholle and Denski call for contextualising education within the framework of its functions in U.S. society, and they connect critical pedagogy and media education with transformative practice and the goal of producing a more democratic society.

In addition, Sholle, Susan Reilly, Peter McLaren, and Rhonda Hammer have published a co-authored text *Rethinking Media Literacy* which provide theoretical models of critical media literacy, practical studies that exemplify the project, and attempts to develop the literacies that will help make possible more critical and empowerment students and citizens. In particular, Hammer indicates how student video projects can empower students to learn the conventions and techniques of media production and use the media to advance their own aims. Whereas film production involves heavy capital investment, expensive technology, and thus restricts access, video production is more accessible to students, easier to use, and enables a broad spectrum of students to actually produce media texts, providing alternative modes of expression and communication. Video technology thus provides access to a large number of voices excluded from cultural production and expression, materialising the multicultural dream of democratic culture as a dialogue of a rainbow of voices, visions, ideas, and experiences.

There are indeed associations, groups, and texts that are oriented toward teaching multicultural education and media literacy to younger students. Survey of this vastly expanding material goes beyond the limits of this study, and here I merely want to mention the scope of importance of teaching media literacy and multiculturalism on all levels from kindergarten through graduate school and beyond. We live in a world of media and new technologies, and our social world is increasingly multicultural, providing new opportunities to enjoy richness and diversity, but also producing new social conflicts and problems.

It is the challenge of education and educators to devise strategies to teach media literacy while using media materials to contribute to advancing multicultural education. For, against McLuhan who claims that the younger generation are naturally media literate (1964), I would argue that developing critical media literacy requires cultivating explicit strategies of cultural pedagogy and models of media education. Yet within educational circles, there is a debate over what constitutes the field of media pedagogy, with different agendas and programs. A traditionalist "protectionist" approach would attempt to "inoculate" young people against the effects of media addiction and manipulation by cultivating a taste for book literacy, high culture, and the values of truth, beauty, and justice. Neil Postman in his books *Amusing Ourselves to Death* and *Technopolis* exemplifies this approach.

A "media literacy" movement, by contrast, attempts to teach students to read, analyse, and decode media texts, in a fashion parallel to the cultivation of print literacy. Media arts education in turn teaches students to appreciate the aesthetic qualities of media and to use various media technologies as tools of self-expression and creation. Critical media literacy, as I would advocate it, builds on these approaches, analysing media culture as products of social production and struggle, and teaching students to be critical of media representations and discourses, but also stressing the importance of learning to use the media as modes of self-expression and social activism.

Critical media literacy not only teaches students to learn from media, to resist media manipulation, and to empower themselves vis-a-vis the media, but it is concerned with developing skills that will empower citizens and that will make them more motivated and competent participants in social life. Critical media literacy is thus tied to the project of radical democracy and concerned to develop skills that will enhance democratisation and participation. Critical media literacy takes a comprehensive approach that would teach critical skills and how to use media as instruments of social change. The technologies of communication are becoming more and more accessible to young people and average citizens, and they should be used to promote education, democratic self-expression, and social progress. Thus, technologies that could help produce the end of participatory democracy, by transforming politics into media spectacles and the battle of images, and by turning spectators into cultural zombies, could also be used to help invigorate democratic debate and participation.

Indeed, teaching critical media literacy should be a participatory, collaborative project. Students are often more media savvy, knowledgeable, and immersed in media culture than their teachers and thus can contribute to the educational process through sharing their ideas, perceptions, and insights. On the other hand, critical discussion, debate, and analysis should be encouraged with teachers bringing to bear their critical perspectives on student readings of media material. Since media culture is often part and parcel of students' identity and most powerful cultural experience, teachers must be sensitive in criticising artifacts and perceptions that students hold dear, yet an atmosphere of critical respect for difference and inquiry into the nature and effects of media culture should be encouraged.

Another complexity in developing critical media pedagogy results from the fact that in a sense it is not a pedagogy in the traditional sense with firmly-established principles, a canon of texts, and tried-and-true teaching procedures. Critical media pedagogy is in its infancy, it is just beginning to produce results, and is thus more open and experimental than established print-oriented pedagogy. Moreover, the material of media culture is so polymorphous, multivalent, and polysemic, that it requires sensitivity to different readings, interpretations, perceptions of the complex images, scenes, narratives, meanings, and message of media culture which in its own ways is as complex and challenging to critically decipher as book culture.

I have, in fact, so far downplayed hostility toward media education and the media themselves. Educational traditionalists conceive of literacy in more limited print-media paradigms and, as I suggested above, often adopt a "protectionist" approach when they address the issue of the media at all, warning students against corruption, or urging that they limit media use to "educational" materials. Yet many teachers on all levels from kindergarten to the University have discovered that media material, judiciously used, can be valuable in a variety of instructional tasks, helping to make complex subject matter accessible and engaging. Obviously, media cannot substitute for print material and classroom teaching, and should be seen as a supplement to traditional materials rather than a magic panacea for the failures of traditional education. Moreover, as I argue in the next section, traditional print literacy and competencies are more important than ever in our new high-tech societies.

It is also highly instructive, I would argue, to teach students at all levels to critically engage popular media materials, including the most familiar film, television, music, and other forms of media culture. Yet, here one needs, however, to avoid an uncritical media populism, of the sort that is emerging within certain sectors of British and North American cultural studies. In a review of Rethinking Media Literacy, for instance, Jon Lewis attacked what he saw as the overly critical postures of the contributors to this volume, arguing: "If the point of a critical media literacy is to meet students halfway — to begin to take seriously what they take seriously, to read what they read, to watch what they watch —teachers must learn to love pop culture". Note the authoritarian injunction that "teachers must learn to love popular culture", followed by an attack on more critical approaches to media literacy.

Teaching critical media literacy, however, involves occupation of a site above the dichotomy of fandom and censor. One can teach how media culture provides significant statements or insights about the social world, positive visions of gender, race, and class, or complex aesthetic structures and practices, thus putting a positive spin on how it can provide significant contributions to education. Yet one should also indicate how media culture can promote sexism, racism, ethnocentrism, and other forms of prejudice, as well as misinformation, problematic ideologies, and questionable values. A more dialectical approach to media literacy engages students' interests and concerns, and should, as I suggested above, involve a collaborative approach between teachers and students since students are deeply absorbed in media culture and may know more about some of its artifacts and domains than their teachers. Consequently, they should be encouraged to speak, discuss, and intervene in the teaching/learning process. This is not to say that media literacy training should romanticise student views, however, that may be superficial, mistaken, uniformed, and full of various problematical biases. Yet exercises in media literacy can often productively involve intense student participation in a mutual learning process where both teachers and students together learn media literacy skills and competencies.

It is also probably a mistake to attempt to institute a top-down program of media literacy imposed from above on teachers, with fixed texts, curricula, and prescribed materials. Teachers and students will have very different interests and concerns, and will naturally emphasize different subject matter and choose examples relevant to their own and their student interests. Courses in critical media literacy should thus be flexible enough to enable teachers and students to constitute their own curricula to engage material and topics of current concern, and to address their own interests. Moreover, and, crucially, educators should discern that we are in the midst of one of the most intense technological revolutions in history and must learn to adapt new computer technologies to education, as I suggest in the following section.

New Technologies, Multiple Literacies, and Postmodern Pedagogy: The New Frontier

The studies on multicultural education and critical media literacy that I have examined up to this point neglect to interrogate computer culture and the ways that the Internet and new computer technologies and cultural forms are dramatically transforming the circulation of information, images, and various modes of culture. And so in this concluding section that is looking toward education in the next century, I want to argue that students should learn new forms of computer literacy that involve both how to use computer culture to do research and gather information, as well as to perceive it as a cultural terrain which contains texts, spectacles, games, and interactive media. Moreover, computer culture is a discursive and political location in which they can intervene, engaging in discussion groups, creating their web sites, and producing new multimedia for cultural dissemination. Computer culture enables individuals to actively participate in the production of culture, ranging from discussion of public issues to creation of their own cultural forms.

It is indeed a salient fact of the present age that computer culture is proliferating and so we have to begin teaching computer literacy as well from an early age on. Computer literacy, however, itself needs to be theorised. Often the term is synonymous with technical ability to use computers, to master existing programs, and maybe engage in some programming oneself. I want, however, to suggest expanding the conception of computer literacy from using computer programs and hardware to developing, in addition, more sophisticated abilities in traditional reading and writing, as well as the ability to critically dissect cultural forms taught as part of critical media literacy. Thus, on this conception, genuine computer literacy involves not just technical knowledge and skills, but refined reading, writing, and communicating ability that involves heightened capacities for critically analysing, interpreting, and processing print, image, sound, and multimedia material. Computer literacy involves heightened abilities to read, to scan texts and information, to put together in meaningful patterns mosaics of information, to construct meanings and significance, to contextualise and evaluate, and to discuss and articulate one's own views.

Thus, in my expanded conception, computer literacy involves technical abilities concerning developing basic typing skills, using computer programs, accessing information, and using computer technologies for a variety of purposes ranging from verbal communication to artistic expression. There are ever more implosions between media and computer culture as audio and video material becomes part of the Internet, as CD-Rom and multimedia develop, and as new technologies become part and parcel of the home, school, and workplace. Therefore, the skills of decoding images, sounds, and spectacle learned in critical media literacy training can also be valuable as part of computer literacy as well. Furthermore, print literacy takes on increasing importance in computer world as one needs to critically scrutinise and scroll tremendous amounts of information, putting new emphasis on developing reading and writing abilities. Indeed, Internet discussion groups, chat rooms, email, and various forums require writing skills in which a new emphasis on the importance of clarity and precision is emerging as communications proliferate. In this context of information saturation, it becomes an ethical imperative not to contribute to cultural and information overload, and to concisely communicate one's thoughts and feelings.

In a certain sense, computers are becoming the technological equivalent of Hegel's Absolute Idea, able to absorb everything into its form and medium. Indeed, computers are now not only repositories of text and print-based data, but also contain a wealth of images, multimedia sights and sounds, and interactive environments that, like the media, are themselves a form of education that require a critical pedagogy of electronic, digitised, culture and communication. From this conception, computer literacy is something like a Hegelian synthesis of print and visual literacy, technical skills, and media literacies, brought together at a new and higher stage. While Postman and others produce a simplistic Manichean dichotomy between print and visual literacy, we need to learn to think dialectically, to read text and image, to decipher sight and sound, and to develop forms of computer literacy adequate to meet the challenges of an increasingly high tech society.

Thus, a postmodern pedagogy requires developing critical forms of print, media, and computer literacy, all of crucial importance in the new technoculture of the present and fast-approaching future. Whereas modern pedagogy tended to be specialised, fragmented, and differentiated and was focused on print culture, a postmodern pedagogy involves developing multiple literacies and critically analysing, dissecting, and engaging a multiplicity of cultural forms, some of which are the products of new technologies and require developing new literacies to engage the new cultural forms and media. Indeed, contemporary culture is marked by a proliferation of image machines which generate a panoply of print, sound, environmental, and diverse aesthetic artifacts within which we wander, trying to make our way through this forest of symbols. And so we need to begin learning how to read these images, these fascinating and seductive cultural forms whose massive impact on our lives we have only begun to understand. Surely, education should attend to the new image culture and teach how to read images and narratives as part of media/computer/technoculture literacy. Such an effort would be part of a new critical pedagogy that attempts to critically empower individuals so that they can analyse and criticise the emerging technoculture, as well as participate in its cultural forums and sites.

Moreover, in addition to the critical media literacy, print literacy, and computer literacy, discussed above, multiple literacies involve cultural literacy, social literacy, and ecoliteracy. Since a multicultural society is the context of education in the contemporary moment, new forms of social interaction and cultural awareness are needed that appreciate differences, multiplicity, and diversity. Therefore, expanded social and cultural literacy is needed that appreciates the cultural heritage, histories, and contributions of a diversity of groups. Thus, whereas one can agree with E.D. Hirsch that we need to be literate in our shared cultural heritage, we also need to become culturally literate in cultures that have been hitherto invisible, as Henry Louis Gates and his colleagues have been arguing in their proposals for a multicultural education.

Social literacy should also be taught throughout the educational systems, ranging from focus on how to relate and get along with a variety of individuals, how to negotiate differences, how to resolve conflicts, and how to communicate and socially interact in a diversity of situations. Social literacy also involves ethical training in values and norms, delineating proper and improper individual and social values. It also requires knowledge of the contemporary societies and thus overlaps with social and natural science training. Indeed, given the tremendous role of science and technology in the contemporary world, given the threats to the environment, and need to preserve and enhance the natural as well as social and cultural worlds, it is scandalous how illiterate the entire society is concerning science, nature, and even our own bodies. An ecoliteracy should thus appropriately teach competency in interpreting and interacting with our natural environment, ranging from our own body to natural habitats like forests and deserts.

The challenge for education today is thus to promote multiple literacies to empower students and citizens to use the new technologies to enhance their lives and create a better culture and society based on respect for multicultural difference and aiming at fuller democratic participation of individuals and groups largely excluded from wealth and power in the previous modern society. A positive postmodernity would thus involve creation of a more egalitarian and democratic society in which more individuals and groups were empowered to participate. The great danger facing us, of course, is that the new technologies will increase the current inequalities based on class, gender, and racial divisions. So far, the privileged groups have had more immediate access to the new technologies. It is therefore a challenge of education today to provide access to the new technologies and the literacies needed for competence in order to overcome some of the divisions and inequalities that have plagued contemporary societies during the entire modern age.

Yet, there is also the danger that youth will become totally immersed in a new world of high-tech experience and lose its social connectedness and ability to communicate and relate concretely to other people.

Statistics suggest that more and more sectors of youth are able to access cyberspace and that college students with Internet accounts are spending as much as four hours a day in the new realm of technological experience. The media, however, has been generating a moral panic concerning allegedly growing dangers in cyberspace with lurid stories of young boys and girls lured into dangerous sex or running away from home, endless accounts of how pornography on the Internet is proliferating, and the publicising of calls for increasing control, censorship, and surveillance of communication — usually by politicians who are computer illiterate. The solution, however, is not to ban access to new technologies, but to teach students and citizens how to use these technologies so that they can be used for productive and creative rather than problematical ends.

To be sure, there are dangers in cyberspace as well as elsewhere, but the threats to adolescents are significantly higher through the danger of family violence and abuse than seduction by strangers on the Internet. And while there is a flourishing trade in pornography on the Internet, this material has become increasingly available in a variety of venues from the local video shop to the newspaper stand, so it seems unfair to demonise the Internet. Thus, attempts at Internet censorship are part of the attack on youth which would circumscribe their rights to obtain entertainment and information, and create their own subcultures. Consequently, devices like the V-chip that would exclude sex and violence on television, or block computer access to objectionable material, is more an expression of adult hysteria and moral panic than genuine dangers to youth which certainly exist, but much more strikingly in the real world than in the sphere of hyperreality.

New technologies are always demonised and in studying the exploding array of discourses which characterise the new technologies, I am rather bemused by the extent to whether they expose either a technophilic discourse which presents new technologies as our salvation, that will solve all our problems, or they embody a technophobic discourse that sees technology as our damnation, demonising it as the major source of all our problems. It appears that similarly one-sided and contrasting discourses greeted the introduction of other new technologies this century, often hysterically. To some extent, this was historically the case with film, radio, TV, and now computers. Film, for instance, was celebrated by early theorists as providing new documentary depiction of reality, even redemption of reality, a new art form, new modes of mass education and entertainment — as well as demonised for promoting sexual promiscuity, juvenile delinquency and crime, violence, and copious other forms of immorality. Its demonisation led in the United States to a Production Code that rigorously regulated the content of Hollywood film from 1934 until the 1950s and 1960s — no open mouthed kissing was permitted, crime could not pay, drug use or attacks on religion could not be portrayed, and a censorship office rigorously surveyed all films to make sure that no subversive or illicit content emerged.

Similar extreme hopes and fears were projected onto radio, television, and now computers. It appears whenever there are new technologies, people project all sorts of fantasies, fears, hopes, and dreams onto them, and I believe that this is now happening with computers and new multimedia technologies. It is indeed striking that if one looks at the literature on new technologies — and especially computers — it is either highly celebatory and technophilic, or sharply derogatory and technophobic. A critical theory of technology, however, and critical pedagogy, should avoid either demonising or deifying the new technologies and should inside develop pedagogies that will help us use the technologies to enhance education and life, and to criticise the limitations and false promises made on behalf of new technologies.

Indeed, there is no doubt that the cyberspace of computer worlds contains as much banality and stupidity as real life and one can waste much time in useless activity. But compared to the bleak and violent urban worlds portrayed in rap music and youth films like *Kids*, the technological worlds are havens of information, entertainment, interaction, and connection where youth can gain valuable skills, knowledge, and power necessary to survive the postmodern adventure. Youth can create new, more multiple and flexible selves in cyberspace as well as new subcultures and communities. Indeed, it is exciting to cruise the Internet and to discover how many interesting Web sites that young people and others have established, often containing valuable educational material. There is, of course, the danger that corporate and commercial interests will come to colonise the Internet, but it is likely that there will continue to be spaces where individuals can empower themselves and create their own communities and identities. A main challenge for youth is to learn to use the Internet for positive cultural and political projects, rather than just entertainment and passive consumption.

Reflecting on the growing social importance of computers and new technologies makes it clear that it is of essential importance for youth today to gain various kinds of literacy to empower themselves for the emerging new cybersociety. To survive in a postmodern world, individuals of all ages need to gain skills of media and computer literacy to enable ourselves to negotiate the overload of media images and spectacles; we all need to learn technological skills to use the new media and computer technologies to subsist in the new high-tech economy and to form our own cultures and communities; and youth especially need street smarts and survival skills to cope with the drugs, violence, and uncertainty in today's predatory culture.

It is therefore extremely important for the future of democracy to make sure that youth of all classes, races, genders, and regions gain access to new technology, receiving training in media and computer literacy skills in order to provide the opportunities to enter the high-tech job market and society of the future, and to prevent an exacerbation of class, gender, and race inequalities. And while multiple forms of new literacies will be necessary, traditional print literacy skills are all the more important in a cyberage of word-processing, information gathering, and Internet communication. Moreover, what I am calling multiple literacy involves training in philosophy, ethics, value thinking, and the humanities which I would argue is necessary now more then ever. Indeed, how the Internet and new technologies will be used depends on the overall education of youth and the skills and interests they bring to the new technologies which can be used to access educational and valuable cultural material, or pornography and the banal wares of cybershopping malls.

Thus, the concept of multiple literacy and the postmodern pedagogy that I envisage would argue that it is not a question of either/or, e.g. either print literacy or media literacy, either the classical curriculum or new curricula, but a question of both/and that preserves the best from classical education, that enhances emphasis on print literacy, but that also develops new literacies to engage the new technologies. Obviously, cyberlife is just one dimension of experience and one still needs to learn to interact in a "real world" of school, jobs, relationships, politics, and other people. Youth — indeed all of us! — needs to learn to interact in many dimensions of social reality and to gain a multiplicity of forms of literacy and skills that will enable us to create identities, relationships, and communities that will nurture and develop our full spectrum of potentialities and satisfy a wide array of needs. Our lives are more multidimensional than ever and part of the postmodern adventure is learning to live in a variety of social spaces and to adapt to intense change and transformation. Education too must meet these challenges and both use new technologies to promote education and devise strategies in which new technologies can be used to create a more democratic and egalitarian multicultural society.

11

Youth and Challenge of Pedagogy

For many youth, plurality and contingency, whether mediated through the media or through the dislocations spurned by the economic system, the rise of new social movements, or the crisis of representation and authority have resulted in a world with few secure psychological, economic, or intellectual markers. This is a world in which one is condemned to wander within and between multiple borders and spaces marked by excess, otherness, and difference. This is a world in which old certainties are ruptured and meaning becomes more contingent, less indebted to the dictates of reverence and established truth.

While the circumstances of youth vary across and within terrains marked by racial and class differences, the modernist world of certainty and order that has traditionally policed, contained, and insulated such difference has given way to a shared postmodern culture in which representational borders collapse into new hybridised forms of cultural performance, identity, and political agency. As the information highway and MTV condense time and space into what Paul Virilio calls "speed space" new desires, modes of association, and forms of resistance inscribe themselves into diverse spheres of popular culture. Music, rap, fashion, style, talk, politics and cultural resistance are no longer confined to their original class and racial locations.

Middle class white kids take up the language of gangsta rap spawned in neighborhoods turfs far removed from their own lives. Black youth in the urban centers produce a bricolage of style fashioned amid a combination of sneakers, baseball caps, and oversized clothing that integrates forms of resistance and style later to be appropriated by suburban kids whose desires and identities resonate with the energy and vibrancy of the new urban funk.

Music displaces older forms of textuality and references a terrain of cultural production that marks the body as a site of pleasure, resistance, domination, and danger. Within this postmodern culture of youth, identities merge and shift rather than become more uniform and static. No longer belonging to any one place or location, youth increasingly inhabit shifting cultural and social spheres marked by a plurality of languages and cultures.

Communities have been refigured as space and time mutate into multiple and overlapping cyberspace networks. Bohemian and middle class youth talk to each other over electronic bulletin boards in coffee houses in North Beach, California. Cafes and other public salons, once the refuge of beatniks, hippies, and other cultural radicals have given way to members of the hacker culture. They reorder their imaginations through connections to virtual reality technologies, and produce forms of exchange through texts and images have the potential to wage a war on traditional meaning, but also run the risk of reducing critical understanding to the endless play of random access spectacles.

This is not meant to endorse a Frankfurt School dismissal of popular culture in the postmodern age. On the contrary, The new electronic technologies with their proliferation of multiple stories and open ended forms of interaction have altered not only the pedagogical context for the production of subjectivities, but also how people "take in information and entertainment." Produced from the centers of power, mass culture has spawned in the name of profit and entertainment a new level of instrumental and commodified culture.

On the other hand, popular culture offers resistance to the notion that useful culture can only be produced within dominant regimes of power. This distinction between mass and popular culture is not meant to suggest that popular culture is strictly a terrain of resistance. Popular culture does not escape commodification, racism, sexism, and other forms of oppression, but it is marked by fault lines that reject the high/low culture divide while simultaneously attempting to affirm a multitude of histories, experiences, cultural forms, and pleasures. Within the conditions of postmodern culture values no longer emerge unproblematically from the modernist pedagogy of foundationalism and universal truths, or from traditional narratives based on fixed identities with their requisite structure of closure. For many youths, meaning is in rout, media has become a substitute for experience, and what constitutes understanding is grounded in a decentered and diasporic world of difference, displacement, and exchanges.

The intersection among cultural studies and pedagogy can be made more clear through an analysis of how the pedagogy of Hollywood has attempted in some recent films to portray the plight of young people within the conditions of a postmodern culture. The films—*River's Edge, My Own Private Idaho*, Slacker, and Juice are important as arguments and framing devices that in diverse ways attempt to provide a pedagogical representation of youth. These films point to some of the economic and social conditions at work in the formation of different racial and economic strata of youth, but they often do so within a narrative that combines a politics of despair with a fairly sophisticated depiction of the alleged sensibilities and moods of a generation of youth growing up amid the fracturing and menacing conditions of a postmodern culture. The challenge for progressive educators is to question how might a critical pedagogy be employed to appropriate the more radical and useful aspects of cultural study in addressing the new and different social, political, and economic contexts that are producing the twenty something generation. At the same time, there is the issue of how a politics and project of pedagogy might be constructed to create the conditions for social agency and institutionalised change among diverse sectors of youth?

White Youth and the Politics of Despair

For many youth, showing up for adulthood at the fin de siecle means pulling back on hope and trying to put off the future rather than take up the modernist challenge of trying to shape it. Popular cultural criticism has captured much of the ennui among youth and has made clear that "What used to be the pessimism of a radical fringe is now the shared assumption of a generation." Cultural studies has helped to both temper this broad generalisation about youth in order to investigate the more complex representations at work in the construction of a new generation of youth that cannot be simply abstracted from the specificities of race, class, or gender. And yet, cultural studies theorists have also pointed to the increasing resistance of a twenty something generation of youth who seem neither motivated by nostalgia for some lost conservative vision of America nor at home in the New World Order paved with the promises of the expanding electronic information highway. While "youth" as a social construction has always been mediated, in part, as a social problem, many cultural critics believe that postmodern youth are uniquely "alien," "strange" and disconnected from the real world. For instance, in Gus Van Sant's film, *My Own Private Idaho,* the main character Mike, who hustles his sexual wares for money, is a dreamer lost in fractured memories of a mother who deserted him as a child. Caught between flashbacks of Mom shown in 8mm color, and the video world of motley, street hustlers and their clients, Mike moves through his existence by falling asleep in times of stress only to awake in different geographic and spatial locations. What holds Mike's psychic and geographic travels together is the metaphor of sleep, the dream of escape, and the ultimate realisation that even memories cannot fuel hope for the future. Mike becomes a metaphor for an entire generation of lower, middle-class youth forced to sell themselves in a world with no hope, a generation that aspires to nothing, works at degrading McJobs, and live in a world in which chance and randomness rather than struggle, community, and solidarity drives their fate.

A more disturbing picture of white, working class youth can be found in *River's Edge.* Teen-age anomie and drugged apathy are given painful expression in the depiction of a group of working class youth who are casually told by John, one of their friends, that he has strangled his girlfriend, another of the group's members, and left her nude body on the riverbank. The group at different times visit the site to view and probe the dead body of the girl. Seemingly unable to grasp the significance of the event, the youths initially hold off in informing anyone of the murder and with different degrees of concern initially try to protect John, the teen-age sociopath, from being caught by the police. The youths in *River's Edge* drift through a world of broken families, blaring rock music, schooling marked by dead time, and a general indifference to life in general. Decentered and fragmented, they view death like life itself as merely a spectacle, a matter of style rather than substance. In one sense, these youth share the quality of being "asleep" that is depicted in *My Own Private Idaho.* But what is more disturbing in *River's Edge* is that lost innocence gives way not merely to teen age myopia, but to a culture in which human life is experienced as a voyeuristic seduction, a video game, good for passing time and diverting oneself from the pain of the moment. Despair and indifference cancel out the language of ethical discriminations and social responsibility while elevating the immediacy of pleasure to the defining moment of agency.

In *River's Edge,* history as social memory is reassembled through vignettes of 1960s types portrayed as either burned out bikers or as the ex-radical turned teacher whose moralising relegates politics to simply cheap opportunism. Exchanges among the young people in *River's Edge* appear like projections of a generation waiting either to fall asleep or to commit suicide. After talking about how he murdered his girlfriend, John blurts out "You do shit, its done, and then you die." Another character responds, "It might be easier being dead." To which her boyfriend, a Wayne's world type, replies, "Bullshit you couldn't get stoned anymore." In this scenario, life imitates art when committing murder and getting stoned are given equal moral weight in the formula of the Hollywood spectacle, a spectacle which in the end flattens the complex representations of youth while constructing their identities through ample servings of pleasure, death, and violence.

River's Edge and *My Own Private Idaho* reveal the seamy and dark side of a youth culture while employing the Hollywood mixture of fascination and horror to titillate the audiences drawn to these films. Employing the postmodern aesthetic of revulsion, locality, randomness, and senselessness, youth in these films appear to be constructed outside of a broader cultural and economic landscape. Instead, they become visible only through visceral expressions of psychotic behavior or the brooding experience of a self-imposed comatose alienation.

One of the more celebrated white, youth films of the 1990s is Richard Linklater's *Slacker*. A decidedly low-budget film, *Slacker* attempts in both form and content to capture the sentiments of a twenty-something generation of middle-class, White youth who reject most of the values of the Reagan/Bush era but have a difficult time imagining what an alternative might look like. Distinctly non-linear in its format, *Slacker* takes place in a twenty four hour time frame in the college town of Austin, Texas. Building upon an anti-narrative structure, *Slacker* is loosely organised around brief episodes in the lives of a variety of characters, none of whom are connected to each other except that each provides the pretext to lead the audience to the next character in the film. Sweeping through bookstores, coffee shops, auto-parts yards, bedrooms, and rock music clubs, *Slacker* focuses on a disparate group of young people who possess little hope in the future and drift from job to job speaking a hybrid argot of bohemian intensities and new age-pop cult babble.

The film portrays a host of young people who randomly move from one place to the next, border crossers with no sense of where they have come from or where they are going. In this world of multiple realities, youth work in bands with the name "Ultimate Loser," talk about being forcibly put in hospitals by their parents, and one neo-punker attempts to sell a Madonna pap smear to two acquaintances she meets in the street. "Check it out, I know it's kind of disgusting, but it's like sort of getting down to the real Madonna." This is a world in which language is wedded to an odd mix of nostalgia, pop-corn philosophy, and MTV babble. Talk is organised around comments like: "I don't know...I've traveled...and when you get back you can't tell whether it really happened to you or if you just saw it on TV." Alienation is driven inward and emerges in comments like "I feel stuck." Irony slightly overshadows a refusal to imagine any kind of collective struggle. Reality seems too despairing to care about. This is humorously captured in one instance by a young man who suggests: "You know how the slogan goes, workers of the world, unite? We say workers of the world, relax?" People talk, but appear disconnected from themselves and each other, lives traverse each other with no sense of community or connection. There is a pronounced sense in *Slacker* of youth caught in the throes of new information technologies that both contain their aspirations while at the same time holding out the promise of some sense of agency.

At rare moments in the films, the political paralysis of narcissistic forms of refusal is offset by instances in which some characters recognise the importance of the image as a vehicle for cultural production, as a representational apparatus that can not only make certain experiences available but can also be used to produce alternative realities and social practices. The power of the image is present in the way the camera follows characters throughout the film, at once stalking them and confining them to a gaze that is both constraining and incidental. In one scene, a young man appears in a video apartment surrounded by televisions that he claims he has had on for years. He points out that he has invented a game called a "Video Virus" in which through the use of a special technology he can push a button and insert himself onto any screen and perform anyone of a number of actions. When asked by another character what this is about, he answers: "Well, we all know the psychic powers of the televised image. But we need to capitalise on it and make it work for us instead of working for it." This theme is taken up in two other scenes. In one short clip, a history graduate student shoots the video camera he is using to film himself indicating a self-consciousness about the power of the image and the ability to control it at the same time. In another scene with which the film concludes a carload of people, each equipped with their Super 8 cameras drive up to a large hill and throw their cameras into a canyon. The film ends with the images being recorded by the cameras as they cascade to the bottom of the cliff in what suggests a moment of release and liberation.

In many respects, these movies largely focus on a culture of white, male youth who are both terrified and fascinated by the media, who appear overwhelmed by "the danger and wonder of future technologies, the banality of consumption, the thrill of brand names, [and] the difficulty of sex in alienated relationships." The significance of these films rest, in part, in their attempt to capture the sense of powerlessness that increasingly affects working class and middle class white youth. But what is missing from these films along with the various books, articles, and reportage concerning what is often called the Nowhere Generation, Generation X, 13thGen, or Slackers is any sense of the larger political, racial, and social conditions in which youth are being framed as well as the multiple forms of resistance and racial diversity that exists among many different youth formations. What in fact should be seen as a social commentary about "dead-end capitalism" emerges simply as a celebration of refusal dressed up in a rhetoric of aesthetics, style, fashion, and solipsistic protests. Within this type of commentary, postmodern criticism is useful but limited because of its often theoretical inability to take up the relationship between identity and power, biography and the commodification of everyday life, or the limits of agency in an increasingly globalised economy as part of a broader project of possibility linked to issues of history, struggle, and transformation.

In spite of the totalising image of domination that structures *River's Edge* and *My Own Private Idaho,* and the lethal hopelessness that permeates *Slacker,* all of these films provide opportunities for examining the social and cultural context to which they refer in order to enlarge the range of strategies and understandings that students might bring to them to create a sense of resistance and transformation. For instance, many of my students who viewed *Slacker* did not despair over the film, but interpreted it to mean that "going slack" was viewed as a moment in the lives of young people when, with the proper resources, offered them a period in which to think, move around the country, and chill out in order to make some important decisions about their lives. Going slack became increasingly more oppressive as the slack time became drawn out far beyond their ability to end or control it. The students also pointed out that this film was made by Linklater with his friends with a great deal of energy and gusto that offers in itself a pedagogical model for young people to take up in developing their own narratives.

Black Youth and the Violence of Race

With the explosion of rap music into the sphere of popular culture and the intense debates that have emerged around the crisis of black masculinity, the issue of black nationalism, and the politics of black urban culture, it is not surprising that the black cinema has produced a series of films about the coming of age of black youth in urban America. What is unique about these films is that unlike the black exploitation films of the 1970s which were made by white producers for black audiences, the new wave of black cinema is being produced by black directors and aimed at black audiences. With the advent of the 1990s, Hollywood has cashed in on a number of young talented black directors such as Spike Lee, Allen and Albert

Hughes, Julie Dash, Ernest Dickerson, and John Singleton. Films about black youth have become big business as exemplified by the fact that in 1991 "New Jack City" and "Boys N the Hood" pulled in over 100 million dollars between them. Largely concerned with the inequalities, oppression, daily violence, and diminishing hope that plagues black communities in the urban war zone, the new wave of black films has attempted to accentuate the economic and social conditions that have contributed to the construction of "black masculinity and its relationship to the ghetto culture in which ideals of masculinity are nurtured and shaped."

Unlike the many of the recent films about white youth whose coming of age narratives are developed within traditional sociological categories such as alienation, restlessness, and anomie, black film productions such as Ernest Dickerson's Juice depict a culture of nihilism that is rooted directly in a violence whose defining principles are homicide, cultural suicide, internecine warfare, and social decay. It is interesting to note that just as the popular press has racialised crime, drugs, and violence as a black problem, some of the most interesting films to appear recently about black youth have been given the Hollywood imprimatur of excellence and have moved successfully as crossover films to a white audience.

Juice is the story of four young Harlem Afro-American youth who are first portrayed as kids who engage in the usual antics of skipping school, fighting with other kids in the neighborhood, clashing with their parents about doing homework, and arguing with their siblings over using the bathroom in the morning. If this portrayal of youthful innocence is used to get a general audience to comfortably identify with these four black youths, it is soon ruptured as the group, caught in a spiraling wave of poverty and depressed opportunities, turn to crime and violence as a way to both construct their manhood and solve their most immediate problems. Determined to give their lives some sense of agency, the group moves from ripping off a record store to burglarising a grocery market to the ruthless murder of the store owner and eventually each other. Caught in a world in which the ethics of the street is mirrored in the spectacle of TV violence, Bishop, Quincy, Raheem, and Steel, decide after watching James Cagney go up in a blaze of glory in *White Heat* to take control of their lives by buying a gun and sticking up a neighborhood merchant who once chased them out of his store. Quincy is hesitant about participating in the stick up because he is a talented disc jockey and is determined to enter a local deejay contest in order to take advantage of his love of rap music and find a place for himself in the world.

Quincy is the only black youth in the film who models a sense of agency that is not completely caught in the confusion and despair exhibited by his three friends. Trapped within the loyalty codes of the street and in the protection it provides, Quincy reluctantly agrees to participate in the heist. Bad choices have major consequences in this typical big city-ghetto, and Quincy's sense of hope and independence is shattered as Bishop, the most violent of the group, kills the store owner and then proceeds to murder Raheem and hunt down Quincy and Steele since they no longer see him as a respected member of the group. Quincy eventually buys a weapon to protect himself and in the final scene of the film confronts Bishop on the roof where a struggle ensues and Bishop plunges to his death. As the film ends, one of onlookers tells Quincy "You got the juice," but Quincy rejects the accolade ascribing power and prestige to him and walks away.

Juice reasserts the importance of rap music as the cultural expression of imaginable possibilities in the daily lives of black youth. Not only does rap music provide the musical score which frames the film, it also plays a pivotal role providing a social context for the desires, rage, and independent expression of black, male, artistic expression. For Quincy, rap music offers him the opportunity to claim some "juice" among his peers while simultaneously providing him with a context to construct an affirmative identity along with the chance for real employment. Music in this context becomes a major referent for understanding how identities and bodies come together in a hip-hop culture that at its most oppositional moment is testing the limits of the American dream. But Juice also gestures, through the direction of Ernest Dickerson, that if violence is endemic to the black ghetto its roots lie in a culture of violence that is daily transmitted through the medium of television. This is suggested in one powerful scene in which the group watch on television both the famed violent ending of in James Cagney's White Heat, and the news bulletin announcing the death of a neighborhood friend as he attempted to rip off a local bar. In this scene, Dickerson draws a powerful relationship between what the four youths see on television and their impatience over their own lack of agency and need to take control of their lives. As Michael Dyson points out:

> Dickerson's aim is transparent: to highlight the link between violence and criminality fostered in the collective American imagination by television, the consumption of images through a medium that has replaced the Constitution and the Declaration of Independence as the unifying fiction of national citizenship and identity. It is also the daily and exclusive occupation of Bishop's listless father, a reminder that television's genealogy of influence unfolds from its dulling effects in one generation to its creation of lethal desires in the next, twin strategies of destruction when applied in the black male ghetto.

While Dyson is right in pointing to Dickerson's critique of the media, he overestimates the importance given in Juice to the relationship between black on black violence and those larger social determinants which black urban life both reflects and helps to produce. In fact, it could be argued that the violence portrayed in Juice and similar films such as Boys N' the Hood, New Jack City, and especially Menace II Society, "feeds the racist national obsession that black men and their community are the central locus of the American scene of violence." Although the violence in these films is traumatising as part of its efforts to promote an anti-violence message, it is also a violence that is hermetic, sutured, and sealed within the walls of the black urban ghetto. The counterpart of this type of violence in controversial, white films such as *Reservoir Dogs* is taken up by most critics as part of an avant garde aesthetic, but the violence in the recent wave of black youth films often reinforces for middle class viewers the assumption that such violence is endemic to the black community and the only salvation gained in portraying such inner city hopelessness is that it be noticed so that it can be stopped from spreading like a disease into the adjoining suburbs and business zones that form a colonising ring around black ghettoes. Because films such as Juice do not self-consciously rupture dominant stereotypical assumptions that make race and crime synonymous, they often suggest a kind of nihilism that Cornel West describes as "the lived experience of coping with a life of horrifying meaninglessness, hopelessness and lovelessness."

Unfortunately, West's notion of nihilism is too tightly drawn and while it may claim to pay sufficient attention to the loss of hope and meaning among black youth, it fails to connect the specificity of black nihilism to the nihilism of systemic inequality, calculated injustice, and moral indifference that operates daily as a regime of brutalisation and oppression for so many youth of color and class in this country. Itabari Njeri forcefully captures the failure of such an analysis and the problems that films such as Juice, in spite of the best intentions of their directors, often reproduce. Commenting on another coming-of-age black youth film, Menace II Society, he writes:

> The nation cannot allow nearly 50% of black men to be unemployed, as is the case in many African-American communities. It cannot let schools systematically brand normal black children as uneducable for racist reasons, or permit the continued brutalisation of blacks by police, or have black adults take out their socially engendered frustrations on each other and their children and not yield despair and dysfunction. This kind of despair is the source of the nihilism Cornel West described. Unfortunately, the black male-as-menace film genre often fails to artfully tie this nihilism to its poisonous roots in American's system of inequality. And because it fails to do so, the effects of these toxic forces are seen as causes.

In both pedagogical and political terms, the reigning films about black youth that have appeared since 1990 may have gone too far in producing narratives that employ the commercial strategy of reproducing graphic violence and then moralising about its effects. Violence in these films is tied to a self-destructiveness and senselessness that shocks but often fails to inform the audience about either its wider determinations or the audience's possible complicity in such violence. The effects of such films tend to reinforce for white middle class America the comforting belief that nihilism as both a state of mind and a site of social relations is always somewhere else-in that strangely homogenised social formation known as 'black' youth.

Of course, it is important to note that Juice refrains from romanticising violence, just as it suggests at the end of the film that Quincy does not want the juice if it means leading a life in which violence is the only capital that has any exchange value in African-American communities. But these sentiments come late and are too underdeveloped. One pedagogical challenge presented by this films is for educators and students to theorise why Hollywood is investing in films about black youth that overlook the complex representations that structure African-American communities. Such an inquiry can be taken up by looking at the work of black feminist film makers such as Julie Dash and the powerful and complex representations she offers black women in Daughters of the Dust or the work of Leslie Harris, whose film Just Another Girl on the IRT challenges the misogyny that structures the films currently being made about black, male youth. Another challenge involves trying to understand why large numbers of black, urban, male youth readily identify with the wider social representations of sexism, homophobia, misogyny, and gaining respect at such a high cost to themselves and the communities in which they live. Films about black youth are important to engage in order to both understand the pedagogies that silently structure their representations and how such representations pedagogically work to educate crossover white audiences. Most importantly, these films should not be dismissed because they are reductionistic, sexist, or one dimensional in their portrayal of the rite of passage of black, male youth; at most, they become a marker for understanding how complex representations of black youth get lost in racially coded films that point to serious problems in the urban centers but do so in ways that erase any sense of viable hope, possibility, resistance, and struggle.

Contemporary films about black youth offer a glimpse into the specificity of otherness, that is, they cross a cultural and racial border and in doing so perform a theoretical service in making visible what is often left out of the dominant politics of representations. And it is in the light of such an opening that the possibility exists for educators and other cultural workers to take up the relationship among culture, power, and identity in ways that grapple with the complexity of youth and the intersection of race, class, and gender formations.

Combining cultural studies with pedagogical theory would suggest that students take these films seriously as legitimate forms of social knowledge that reveal different sets of struggles among youths within diverse cultural sites. For white youth, these films mimic a coming of age narrative that indicts the aimlessness and senselessness produced within a larger culture of commercial stufpification; on the other hand, black youth films posit a not-coming-of-age narrative that serves as a powerful indictment of autogenocide among African-American youths. Clearly, educators can learn from these films and in doing so bring these different accounts of the cultural production of youth together within a common project that addresses the relationship between pedagogy and social justice, on the one hand, and democracy and the struggle for equality on the other. Clearly these films suggests that educators need to ask new questions, develop new models, and new ways of producing an oppositional pedagogy that is capable of understanding the different social, economic, and political contexts that produce youth differently within varied sets and relations of power.

Another pedagogical challenge offered by these films concerns how teachers can address the desires that different students bring to these popular cultural texts. In other words, what does it mean to mobilise the desires of students by using forms of social knowledge that constitute the contradictory field of popular culture. In part, it means recognising that while students are familiar with such texts, they bring different beliefs, political understandings, and affective investments to such a learning process. Hence, pedagogy must proceed by acknowledging that conflict will emerge regarding the form and content of such films and how students address such issues. For such a pedagogy to work, Fabienne Worth argues that "students must become visible to themselves and to each other and valued in their differences." This suggest giving students the opportunity to decenter the curriculum by structuring, in part, how the class should be organised and how such films can be addressed without putting any one student's identity on trail. It means recognising the complexity of attempting to mobilise students' desires as part of a pedagogical project which directly addresses representations that affect certain parts of their lives, and to acknowledge the emotional problems that will emerge in such teaching. At the same time, such a pedagogy must reverse the cycle of despair that often informs these accounts and address how the different postmodern conditions and contexts of youth can be changed in order to expand and deepen the promise of a substantive democracy. In part, this may mean using films about youth that capture the complexity, sense of struggle, and diversity that marks different segments of the current generation of young people. In this case, cultural studies and pedagogical practice can mutually inform each other by using popular cultural texts as serious objects of study that can be used to address the limits and possibilities that youth face in different social, cultural, and economic contexts; equally important is the need to read popular cultural texts as part of a broader pedagogical effort to develop a sense of agency in students based on a commitment to changing oppressive contexts by understanding the relations of power that inform them.

The pedagogical challenge represented by the emergence of a postmodern generation of youth has not been lost on advertisers and market research analysts. According to a 1992 Roper Organisation, Inc. study, the current generation of 18-29 year olds have an annual buying power of 125 billion dollars. Addressing the interests and tastes of this generation, "McDonald's, for instance, has introduced hip-hop music and images to promote burgers and fries, ditto Coca-Cola, with its frenetic commercials touting Coca-Cola Classic." Benetton, Esprit, The Gap, and other companies have followed suit in their attempts to identify and mobilise the desires, identities, and buying patterns of a new generation of youth. What appears as a despairing expression of the postmodern condition to some theorists, becomes for others a challenge to invent new market strategies for corporate interests. In this scenario, youth may be experiencing the indeterminacy, senselessness, and multiple conditions of postmodernism, but corporate advertisers are attempting to theorise a pedagogy of consumption as part of a new way of appropriating postmodern differences among youth in different sites and locations. The lesson here is that differences among youth matter politically and pedagogically, but not as a way of generating new markets or registering difference simply as a fashion niche.

What educators need to do is to make the pedagogical more political by addressing both the conditions through which they teach and what it means to learn from a generation that is experiencing life in a way that is vastly different from the representations offered in modernist versions of schooling. This is not to suggest that modernist schools do not attend to popular culture but they do so on very problematic terms, which often confine it to the margins of the curriculum. Moreover, modernist schools cannot be rejected outright. As I have shown elsewhere, the political culture of modernism with its emphasis on social equality, justice, freedom, and human agency needs to be refigured within rather than outside of an emerging postmodern discourse.

The emergence of the electronic media coupled with a diminishing faith in the power of human agency has undermined the traditional visions of schooling and the meaning of pedagogy. The language of lesson plans and upward mobility and the forms of teacher authority on which it was based has been radically delegitimated by the recognition that culture and power are central to the authority/knowledge relationship. Modernism's faith in the past has given way to a future for which traditional markers no longer make sense.

Cultural Studies and Youth: The Pedagogical Issue

Educators and cultural critics need to address the effects of emerging postmodern conditoins on a current generation of young people who appear hostage to the vicissitudes of a changing economic order with its legacy of diminished hopes, on the one hand, and a world of schisoid images, proliferating public spaces and an increasing fragmentation, uncertainty, and randomness that structures postmodern daily life on the other. Central to this issue is whether educators are dealing with a new kind of student forged within organising principles shaped by the intersection of the electronic image, popular culture, and a dire sense of indeterminacy. What cultural studies offers educators is a theoretical framework for addressing the shifting attitudes, representations, and desires of this new generation of youth being produced within the current historical, economic, and cultural juncture. But it does more than simply provide a lens for resituating the construction of youth within a shifting and radically altered social, technological, and economic landscape, it also provides elements for rethinking the relationship between culture and power, knowledge and authority, learning and experience, and the role of teachers as public intellectuals.

First, cultural studies is premised on the belief that we have entered a period in which the traditional distinctions that separate and frame established academic disciplines cannot account for the great diversity of cultural and social phenomena that has come to characterise an increasingly hybridised, post-industrial world. The university has long been linked to a notion of national identity that is largely defined by and committed to transmitting traditional, Western culture. Traditionally, this has been a culture of exclusion, one which has ignored the multiple narratives, histories, and voices of culturally and politically subordinated groups. The emerging proliferation of diverse social movements arguing for a genuinely multicultural and multiracial society have challenged schools that use academic knowledge to license cultural differences in order to regulate and define who they are and how they might narrate themselves. Moreover, the spread of electronically mediated culture to all spheres of everyday intellectual and artistic life has shifted the ground of scholarship away from the traditional disciplines designed to preserve a "common culture" to the more hybridised fields of comparative and world literature, media studies, ecology, society and technology, and popular culture.

Second, advocates of cultural studies have argued strongly that the role of culture, including the power of the mass media with its massive apparatuses of representation and its regulation of meaning, is central to understanding how the dynamics of power, privilege, and social desire structure the daily life of a society. This concern with culture and its connection to power has necessitated a critical interrogation of the relationship between knowledge and authority, the meaning of canonicity, and the historical and social contexts that deliberately shape students' understanding of accounts of the past, present and future. But if a sea change in the development and reception of what counts as knowledge has taken place, it has been accompanied by an understanding of how we define and apprehend the range of texts that are open to critical interrogation and analysis. For instance, instead of connecting culture exclusively to the technology of print and the book as the only legitimate academic artifact, there is a great deal of academic work going on which analyses how textual, aural, and visual representations are produced, organised, and distributed through a variety of cultural forms such as the media, popular culture, film, advertising, mass communications, and other modes of cultural production.

At stake here is the attempt to produce new theoretical models and methodologies for addressing the production, structure and exchange of knowledge. This approach to inter/post-disciplinary studies is valuable because it addresses the pedagogical issue of organising dialogue across and outside of the disciplines in order to promote alternative approaches to research and teaching about culture and the newly emerging technologies and forms of knowledge. For instance, rather than organise courses around strictly disciplinary concerns arising out of English and social studies courses, it might be more useful and relevant for colleges of education to organise courses that broaden student's understanding of themselves and others by examining events that evoke a sense of social responsibility and moral accountability. A course on "Immigration and Politics in Fin-de-Siecle America" could provide a historical perspective on the demographic changes confronting America and how such changes are being felt within the shifting dynamics of education, economics, cultural identity, and urban development. A course on the Los Angeles uprisings could incorporate the related issues of race, politics, economics, and education to address the multiple conditions underlying the violence and despair that produced such a tragic event.

Third, in addition, to broadening the terms and parameters of learning, cultural studies rejects the professionalisation of educators and the alienating and often elitist discourse of professionalism and sanitised expertise. Instead, it argues for educators as public intellectuals. Stuart Hall is instructive on this issue when he argues that cultural studies provides two points of tension that intellectuals need to address:

> First, cultural studies constitutes one of the points of tension and change at the frontiers of intellectual and academic life, pushing for new questions, new models, and new ways of study, testing the fine lines between intellectual rigor and social relevance....But. secondly...cultural studies insist on what I want to call the vocation of the intellectual life. That is to say, cultural studies insists on the necessity to address the central, urgent, and disturbing questions of a society and a culture in the most rigorous intellectual way we have available.

In this view, intellectuals must be accountable in their teaching for the ways in which they address and respond to the problems of history, human agency, and the renewal of democratic civic life. Cultural studies strongly rejects the assumption that teachers are simply transmitters of existing configurations of knowledge. As public intellectuals, academics are always implicated in the dynamics of social power through the experiences they organise and provoke in their classrooms. In this perspective, intellectual work is incomplete unless it self-consciously assumes responsibility for its effects in the larger public culture while simultaneously addressing the most profoundly and deeply inhumane problems of the societies in which we live. Hence, cultural studies raises questions about what knowledge is produced in the university and how it is consequential in extending and deepening the possibilities for democratic public life. Equally important is the issue of how to democratise the schools so as to enable those groups who in large measure are divorced from or simply not represented in the curriculum to be able to produce their own representations, narrate their own stories, and engage in respectful dialogue with others. In this instance, cultural studies must address how dialogue is constructed in the classroom about other cultures and voices by critically addressing both the position of the theorists and the institutions in which such dialogues are produced. Peter Hitchcock argues forcefully that the governing principles of any such dialogic exchange should include some of the following elements:

1) attention to the specific institutional setting in which this activity takes place;
2) self-reflexivity regarding the particular identities of the teacher and students who collectively undertake this activity;
3) an awareness that the cultural identities at stake in 'other' cultures are in the process-of-becoming in dialogic interaction and are not static as subjects; but
4) the knowledge produced through this activity is always already contestable and by definition is not the knowledge of the other as the other would know herself or himself.

Fourth, another important contribution of cultural studies is its emphasis on studying the production, reception, and use of varied texts, and how they are used to define social relations, values, particular notions of community, the future, and diverse definitions of the self. Texts in this sense do not merely refer to the culture of print or the technology of the book, but to all those audio, visual, and electronically mediated forms of knowledge that have prompted a radical shift in the construction of knowledge and the ways in which knowledge is read, received, and consumed. It is worth repeating that contemporary youth increasingly rely less on the technology and culture of the book to construct and affirm their identities; instead, they are faced with the task of finding their way through a decentered cultural landscape no longer caught in the grip of a technology of print, closed narrative structures, or the certitude of a secure economic future. The new emerging technologies which construct and position youth represent interactive terrains that cut across "language and culture, without narrative requirements, without character complexities....Narrative complexity way to design complexity; story way to a sensory environment." Cultural studies is profoundly important for educators in that it focuses on media not merely in terms of how it distorts and misrepresents reality, but also on how media plays "a part in the formation, in the constitution, of the things they reflect. It is not that there is a world outside, 'out there,' which exists free of the discourse of representation. What is 'out there' is, in part, constituted by how it is represented."

On the contrary, as youth are constituted within languages and new cultural forms that intersect differently across and within issues of race, class, gender, and sexual differences, the conditions through which youth attempt to narrate themselves must be understood in terms of both the context of their struggles and through a shared language of agency that points to a project of hope and possibility. It is precisely this language of difference, specificity, and possibility that is lacking from most attempts at educational reform.

Fifth, it is important to stress that when critical pedagogy is established as one of the defining principles of cultural studies, it is possible to generate a new discourse for moving beyond a limited emphasis on the mastery of techniques and methodologies. Critical pedagogy represents a form of cultural production implicated in and critically attentive to how power and meaning are employed in the construction and organisation of knowledge, desires, values and identities.

Critical pedagogy in this sense is not reduced to the mastering of skills or techniques, but is defined as a cultural practice that must be accountable ethically and politically for the stories it produces, the claims it makes on social memories, and the images of the future it deems legitimate. As both an object of critique and a method of cultural production, it refuses to hide behind claims of objectivity, and works effortlessly to link theory and practice to enabling the possibilities for human agency in a world of diminishing returns. It is important to make a distinction here that challenges the liberal and conservative criticism that since critical pedagogy attempts both to politicise teaching and teach politics that it represents a species of indoctrination.

Political education, which is central to critical pedagogy, refers to teaching "students how to think in ways that cultivate the capacity for judgment essential for the exercise of power and responsibility by a democratic citizenry....A political, as distinct from a politicising education would encourage students to become better citizens to challenge those with political and cultural power as well as to honor the critical traditions within the dominant culture that make such a critique possible and intelligible." A political education means decentering power in the classroom and other pedagogical sites so the dynamics of those institutional and cultural inequalities that marginalise some groups, repress particular types of knowledge, and suppress critical dialogue can be addressed. On the other hand, politicising education is a form of pedagogical terrorism in which the issue of what is taught, by whom, and under what conditions is determined by a doctrinaire political agenda that refuses to examine its own values, beliefs, and ideological construction. While refusing to recognise the social and historical character of its own claims to history, knowledge, and values, a politicising education silences in the name of a specious universalism and denounces all transformative practices through an appeal to a timeless notion of truth and beauty. For those who practice a politicising education, democracy and citizenship become dangerous in that the precondition for their realisation demands critical inquiry, the taking of risks, and the responsibility to resist and say no in the face of dominant forms of power.

Border Youth and Postmodern Education

For many theorists occupying various positions on the political spectrum, the current historical moment signals less a need to come to grips with the new forms of knowledge, experiences, and conditions that constitute postmodernism than the necessity to write its obituary. The signs of exhaustion are in part measured by the fact that postmodernism has gripped two generations of intellectuals who have pondered endlessly over its meaning and implications as a "social condition and cultural movement". The "postmodern debate" has spurned little consensus and a great deal of confusion and animosity. The themes are, by now, well known: master narratives and traditions of knowledge grounded in first principles are spurned; philosophical principles of canonicity and the notion of the sacred have become suspect; epistemic certainty and the fixed boundaries of academic knowledge have been challenged by a "war on totality" and a disavowal of all- encompassing, single, world-views; rigid distinctions between high and low culture have been rejected by the insistence that the products of the so-called mass culture, popular, and folk art forms are proper objects of study; the Enlightenment correspondence between history and progress and the modernist faith in rationality, science, and freedom have incurred a deep-rooted skepticism; the fixed and unified identity of the humanist subject has been replaced by a call for narrative space that is pluralised and fluid; and, finally, though far from complete, history is spurned as a unilinear process that moves the West progressively toward a final realisation of freedom.

While these and other issues have become central to the postmodern debate, they are connected through the challenges and provocations they provide to modernity's conception of history, agency, representation, culture, and the responsibility of intellectuals. The postmodern challenge constitutes not only a diverse body of cultural criticism, it must also be seen as a contextual discourse that has challenged specific disciplinary boundaries in such fields as literary studies, geography, education, architecture, feminism, performance art, anthropology, sociology, and many other areas. Given its broad theoretical reach, its political anarchism, and its challenge to "legislating" intellectuals, it is not surprising that there has been a growing movement on the part of diverse critics to distance themselves from postmodernism.

While postmodernism may have been elevated to the height of fashion hype in both academic journals and the popular press in North America during the last twenty years, it is clear that a more sinister and reactionary mood has emerged which constitutes something of a backlash. Of course, postmodernism did become something of a fashion trend, but such events are short lived and rarely take any subject seriously. But the power of fashion and commodification should not be underestimated in terms of how such practices bestow on an issue a cloudy residue of irrelevance and misunderstanding. There is more at stake in the recent debates on postmodernism than the effects of fashion and commodification; in fact, the often essentialised terms in which critiques of postmodernism have been framed suggest something more onerous. In the excessive rhetorical flourishes that dismiss postmodernism as reactionary nihilism, fad, or simply a new form of consumerism, there appears a deep-seated anti-intellectualism, one that lends credence to the notion that theory is an academic luxury and has little to do with concrete political practice. Anti- intellectualism aside, the postmodern backlash also points to a crisis in the way in which the project of modernity attempts to appropriate, prescribe, and accommodate issues of difference and indeterminacy.

Much of the criticism that now so blithely dismisses postmodernism appears trapped in what Zygmunt Bauman refers to as modernist "utopias that served as beacons for the long march to the rule of reason visualised a world without margins, leftovers, the unaccounted for-without dissidents and rebels". Against the indeterminacy, fragmentation, and skepticism of the postmodern era, the master narratives of modernism, particularly Marxism and liberalism, have been undermined as oppositional discourses. One consequence is that "a whole generation of postwar intellectuals have experienced an identity crisis. . . . What results is a mood of mourning and melancholia".

The legacy of essentialism and orthodoxy seems to be reasserting itself on the part of left intellectuals who reject postmodernism as a style of cultural criticism and knowledge production. It can also be seen in the refusal on the part of intellectuals to acknowledge the wide-ranging processes of social and cultural transformation taken up in postmodern discourses that are appropriate to grasping the contemporary experiences of youth and the wide-ranging proliferation of forms of diversity within an age of declining authority, economic uncertainty, the proliferation of electronic mediated technologies, and the extension of what consumer pedagogy into almost every aspect of youth culture.

A resistant or political postmodernism seems invaluable to me in helping educators and others address the changing conditions of knowledge production in the context of emerging mass electronic media and the role these new technologies are playing as critical socialising agencies in redefining both the locations and the meaning of pedagogy. My concern with expanding the way in which educators and other cultural workers understand the political reach and power of pedagogy as it positions youth within a postmodern culture suggests that postmodernism is to be neither romanticised nor casually dismissed.

On the contrary, it is a fundamentally important discourse that needs to be mined critically in order to help educators to understand the modernist nature of public schooling in North America. It is also useful for educators to comprehend the changing conditions of identity formation within electronically mediated cultures and how they are producing a new generation of youths who exist between the borders of a modernist world of certainty and order, informed by the culture of the West and its technology of print, and a postmodern world of hybridised identities, electronic technologies, local cultural practices, and pluralised public spaces.

Welcome to the Postmodern Backlash

While conservatives such a Daniel Bell and his cohorts may see in postmodernism the worst expression of the radical legacy of the 1960s, an increasing number of radical critics view postmodernism as the cause of a wide range of theoretical excesses and political injustices. For example, recent criticism from British cultural critic John Clarke argues that the hyper-reality of postmodernism wrongly celebrates and depoliticises the new informational technologies and encourages metropolitan intellectuals to proclaim the end of everything in order to commit themselves to nothing. Dean MacCannell goes further and argues that "postmodern writing [is] an expression of soft fascism". Feminist theorist Susan Bordo dismisses postmodernism as just another form of "stylish nihilism" and castigates its supporters for constructing a "world in which language swallows up everything".

The backlash has become so prevalent in North America that the status of popular criticism and reporting seems to necessitate proclaiming that postmodernism is "dead." Hence, comments in forums ranging from the editorial pages of the *New York Times* to popular texts such as 13THGEN to popular academic magazines such as the Chronicle of higher Education alert the general public in no uncertain terms that it is no longer fashionable to utter the "p" word.

Of course, more serious critiques have appeared from the likes of Jrgen Habermas, Perry Anderson, David Harvey, and Terry Eagleton, but the current backlash has a different intellectual quality to it, a kind of reductionism that is both disturbing and irresponsible in its refusal to engage postmodernism in any kind of dialogical, theoretical debate. Many of these left critics often assume the moral high ground and muster their theoretical machinery within binary divisions that create postmodern fictions, on the one side, and politically correct, materialist freedom fighters on the other. One consequence is that any attempt to engage the value and importance of postmodern discourses critically is sacrificed to the cold winter winds of orthodoxy and intellectual parochialism. All critics of postmodernism fall prey to such a position suggesting that concerns about the relationship between modernity and postmodernity, the status of ethics, the crisis of representation and subjectivity, or the political relevance of postmodern discourses should not be problematised. But viewing postmodernism as a terrain to be contested suggests theoretical caution rather than reckless abandonment or casual dismissal.

What is often missing from these contentious critiques is the recognition that since postmodernism does not operate under any absolute sign, it might be more productive to reject any arguments that position postmodernism within an essentialised politics, an either/or set of strategies. A more productive encounter would attempt, instead, to understand how postmodernism's more central insights illuminate how power is produced and circulated through cultural practices that mobilise multiple relations of subordination. Rather than proclaiming the end of reason, postmodernism can be critically analysed for how successfully it interrogates the limits of the project of modernist rationality and its universal claims to progress, happiness, and freedom. Instead of assuming that postmodernism has vacated the terrain of values, it seems more useful to address how it accounts for how values are constructed historically and relationally, and how they might be addressed as the basis or "precondition of a politically engaged critique".

In a similar fashion, instead of claiming that postmodernism's critique of the essentialist subject denies a theory of subjectivity, it seems more productive to examine how its claims about the contingent character of identity, constructed in a multiplicity of social relations and discourses, redefines the notion of agency. One example of this type of inquiry comes from Judith Butler, who argues that acknowledging that "the subject is constituted is not that it is determined; on the contrary, the constituted character of the subject is the very precondition of its agency". The now familiar argument that postmodernism substitutes representations for reality indicates less an insight than a reductionism that refuses to engage critically how postmodern theories of representation work to give meaning to reality.

A postmodern politics of representation might be better served through an attempt to understand how power is mobilised in cultural terms, how images are used on a national and local scale to create a representational politics that is reorienting traditional notions of space and time. A postmodern discourse could also be evaluated through the pedagogical consequences of its call to expand the meaning of literacy by broadening "the range of texts we read, and . . . the ways in which we read them". The fact of the matter is that the mass media plays a decisive role in the lives of young people, and the issue is not whether such media perpetuate dominant power relations but how youth and others experience the culture of the media differently.

Postmodernism pluralises the meaning of culture, while modernism firmly situates it theoretically in apparatuses of power. It is precisely in this dialectical interplay between difference and power that postmodernism and modernism inform each other rather than cancel each other out. The dialectical nature of the relationship that postmodernism has to modernism warrants a theoretical moratorium on critiques that affirm or negate postmodernism on the basis of whether it represents a break from modernism. The value of postmodernism lies elsewhere. Acknowledging both the reactionary and progressive moments in postmodernism, anti-essentialist cultural work might take up the challenge of "writing the political back into the postmodern," while simultaneously radicalising the political legacy of modernism in order to promote a new vision of radical democracy in a postmodern world.

One challenge in the debate over postmodernism is whether its more progressive elements can further our understanding of how power works, how social identities are formed, and how the changing conditions of the global economy and the new informational technologies can be articulated to meet the challenges posed by progressive cultural workers and the new social movements. More specifically, the issue for critical educators lies in appropriating postmodernism as part of a broader pedagogical project which reasserts the primacy of the political while simultaneously engaging the most progressive aspects of modernism. Postmodernism becomes relevant to the extent that it becomes part of a broader political project in which the relationship between modernism and postmodernism becomes dialectical, dialogic, and critical. First, there is the challenge of understanding the modernist nature of existing schooling and its refusal to relinquish a view of knowledge, culture, and order that undermines the possibility for constructing a radical democratic project in which a shared conception of citizenship simultaneously challenges growing regimes of oppression and struggles for the conditions needed to construct a multiracial and multicultural democracy. Second, there is a need for cultural workers to address the emergence of a new generation of youth who are increasingly constructed within postmodern economic and cultural conditions that are almost entirely ignored by the schools. Third, there is the challenge to critically appropriate those elements of a postmodern pedagogy that might be useful in educating youth to be the subjects of history in a world that is increasingly diminishing the possibilities for radical democracy and global peace.

Modernist Schools and Postmodern Conditions

A clip from War Games: David Lightman see a brochure of a computer company promising a quantum leap in game technology coming this Christmas . . . breaks into a system and, thinking it's the game company computer, asks to play global thermonuclear war . . . Sees on TV that for three minutes Strategic Air Command went on full alert thinking there had been a Soviet sneak attack . . . is arrested and interrogated . . . breaks back into the system and asks the computer, "Is this a game or is it real?" The computer answers: "What's the difference?"- Walter Parkes.

Wedded to the language of order, certainty, and mastery, public schools are facing a veritable sea change in the demographic, social, and cultural composition of the United States for which they are radically unprepared. As thoroughly modernist institutions, public schools have long relied upon moral, political, and social technologies that legitimate an abiding faith in the Cartesian tradition of rationality, progress, and history. The consequences are well known. Knowledge and authority in the school curricula are organised not to eliminate differences but to regulate them through cultural and social divisions of labor. Class, racial, and gender differences are either ignored in school curricula or subordinated to the imperatives of a history and culture that is linear and uniform.

Within the discourse of modernism, knowledge draws its boundaries almost exclusively from a European model of culture and civilisation and connects learning to the mastery of autonomous and specialised bodies of knowledge. Informed by modernist traditions, schooling becomes an agent of those political and intellectual technologies associated with what Ian Hunter terms the "governmentalising" of the social order. The result is a pedagogical apparatus regulated by a practice of ordering that views "contingency as an enemy and order as a task". The practice of ordering, licensing, and regulating that structures public schooling is predicated on a fear of difference and indeterminacy. The effects reach deep into the structure of public schooling and include: an epistemic arrogance and faith in certainty sanctions pedagogical practices and public spheres in which cultural differences are viewed as threatening; knowledge becomes positioned in the curricula as an object of mastery and control; the individual student is [illegible] as a unique source of agency irrespective of iniquitous relations of power; the technology and culture of the book is treated as the embodiment of modernist high learning and the only legitimate object of pedagogy.

While the logic of public schooling may be utterly modernist, it is neither monolithic nor homogeneous. But at the same time, the dominant features of public schooling are characterised by a modernist project that has increasingly come to rely upon instrumental reason and the standardisation of curricula. In part, this can be seen in the regulation of class, racial, and gender differences through rigid forms of testing, sorting, and tracking. The rule of reason reveals its Western cultural legacy in highly centered curricula that more often than not privilege the histories, experiences, and cultural capital of largely white, middle class students. Moreover, the modernist nature of public schooling is evident in the refusal of educators to incorporate popular culture into the curricula or to take account of the new electronically mediated, informational systems in the postmodern age that are generating massively new socialising contexts for contemporary youth.

The emerging conditions of indeterminacy and hybridity that the public schools face but continue to ignore can be seen in a number of elements that characterise call postmodern culture. First, the United States is experiencing a new wave of immigration which, by the end of this century, may exceed in volume and importance the last wave at the turn of the twentieth century. Key geographic areas within the country-chiefly the large metropolitan regions of the Northeast and Southwest, including California-and major public institutions are grappling with entirely new populations that bring with them new needs. In 1940, seventy percent of immigrants came from Europe, but in 1992 only fifteen percent came from Europe while 44 percent came from

Latin America and 37 percent came from Asia. National identity can no longer be seen through the lens of cultural uniformity or enforced through the discourse of assimilation. A new postmodern culture has emerged marked by specificity, difference, plurality, and multiple narratives.

Second, the sense of possibility that has informed the American Dream of material well-being and social mobility is no longer matched by an economy that can sustain such dreams. In the last two decades, the American economy has entered a prolonged era of stagnation, punctuated by short-term growth spurts. In the midst of an ongoing recession and declining real incomes for low- and middle-income groups, the prospects for economic growth over the next period of US history appear extremely limited. The result has been the expansion of service economy jobs and an increase in the number of companies that are downsizing and cutting labor costs in order to meet global competition. Not only are full-time jobs drying up, but there has also been a surge in the "number of Americans-perhaps as many as 37 million-[who] are employed in something other than full-time permanent positions". These so-called "contingent workers" are "paid less than full-time workers and often get no health benefits, no pensions and no paid holidays, sick days or vacations". Massive unemployment and diminishing expectations have become a way of life for youth all over North America. *Maclean's Magazine* reports that in Canada, "People ages 15 to 24 are currently facing unemployment rates of more than 20 percent, well above the national average of 10.8 percent". For most contemporary youth, the promise of economic and social mobility no longer warrants the legitimating claims it held for earlier generations of young people. The signs of despair among this generation are everywhere. Surveys strongly suggest that contemporary youth from diverse classes, races, ethnicities, and cultures "believe it will be much harder for them to get ahead than it was for their parents-and are overwhelmingly pessimistic about the long-term fate of their generation and nation".

Clinging to the modernist script that technological growth necessitates progress, educators refuse to give up the long-held assumption that school credentials provide the best route to economic security and class mobility. While such a truth may have been relevant to the industrialising era, it is no longer sustainable within the post-Fordist economy of the West. New economic conditions call into question the efficacy of mass schooling in providing the "well-trained" labor force that employers required in the past. In light of these shifts, it seems imperative that educators and other cultural workers reexamine the mission of the schools.

Rather than accepting modernist assumption that schools should train students for specific labor tasks, it makes more sense in the present historical moment to educate students to theorise differently about the meaning of work in a postmodern world. Indeterminacy rather than order should become the guiding principle of a pedagogy in which multiple views, possibilities, and differences are opened up as part of an attempt to read the future contingently rather than from the perspective of a master narrative that assumes rather than problematises specific notions of work, progress, and agency. Under such circumstances, schools need to redefine curricula within a postmodern conception of culture linked to the diverse and changing global conditions that necessitate new forms of literacy, a vastly expanded understanding of how power works within cultural apparatuses, and a keener sense of how the existing generation of youth is being produced within a society in which mass media plays a decisive if not unparalleled role in constructing multiple and diverse social identities. As Stanley Aronowitz point out elsewhere:

> Few efforts are being made to rethink the entire curriculum in the light of the new migration and immigration, much less develop entirely different pedagogies. In secondary schools and community colleges for example, students still study "subjects"-social studies, math, science, English and "foreign" languages. Some schools have "added" courses in the history and culture of Asian, Latin American and Caribbean societies, but have little thought of transforming the entire humanities and social studies curricula in the light of the cultural transformations of the school. Nor are serious efforts being made to integrate the sciences with social studies and the humanities; hence, science and math are still being deployed as sorting devises in most schools rather than seen as crucial markers of a genuinely innovative approach to learning.

As modernist institutions, public schools have been unable to open up the possibility of thinking through the indeterminate character of the economy, knowledge, culture, and identity. Hence, it has become difficult, if not impossible, for such institutions to understand how social identities are fashioned and struggled over within political and technological conditions that have produced a crisis in the ways in which culture is organised in the West.

Bibliography

Barrow, Robin. An Introduction to Philosophy of Education, New York: Routledge, 1988.

Basham A.L., *The History and Doctrines of the Ajivikas*, 1951.

Beardsley, Monroe, *The Aesthetic Point of View*, Cornell University Press, 1982.

Benimadhab Barua, *Prolegomena to a History of Buddhist Philosophy*, 2nd ed., 1974.

Bernstein, Richard, *Beyond Objectivity and Relativism*, Philadelphia: University of Pennsylvania Press, 1983.

Berriedale Keith A., *Karma-mimamsa*, 1921, reprinted 1978.

Dale Riepe, *Early Indian Philosophical Materialism*, 1954.

Danto, Arthur, "The Transfiguration of the Commonplace: a Philosophy of Art", Harvard University Press, 1981.

Dasgupta, S.N., *The Study of Patanjali*, 1920.

David Rubenstein, ed., *Education and Equality*, Penguin Books, 1979.

Deutsch, Eliot, *Advaita Vedanta: A Philosophical Reconstruction*, 1969, reissued 1973.

Devereaux, Mary, "The Philosophical status of Aesthetics" http://www.aesthetics-online.org/ideas/devereaux.html, 1998.

Dickie, George, *Aesthetics: A Critical Anthology*, St Martin's Press, 1983

Edwa.d W. Hopkins, *The Great Epic of India*, 1901, reprinted 1973.

Eric J. Lott, *Vedantic Approaches to God*, a clear introduction to the religious philosophies of Vedanta, 1980.

Herman, A.L., *An Introduction to Buddhist Thought: A Philosophic History of Indian Buddhism*, 1983.

Heslep, Robert D., *Philosophical Thinking in Educational Practice*, Greewood Publishing Group, 1997.

Hutcheon, Linda, *The Politics of Postmodernism*, London: Routledge, 1989.

Ingalls D.H., *Materials for the Study of Navya-Nyaya Logic*, 1951.

Jean-Francois Lyotard, *The Postmodern Condition*, trans. Geoff Bennington and Brian Massumi, Minneapolis: University of Minnesota Press, 1984/1979.

Jones, Roger, 'Post Structuralism', in *Philosophy since the Enlightenment* <http://www.philosopher.org.uk>, accessed 18 December 2003]

Junankar, N.S., *Gautama: The Nyaya Philosophy*, 1978.

Karel Werner, *Yoga and Indian Philosophy*, a wide-ranging introduction, 1977.

Russell, B., *A History of Western Philosophy*, rev. ed. 1961.

Scruton, R., *Modern Philosophy: An Introduction and Survey*, 1995.

Shastri, P., *Introduction to the Purva Mimamsa*, 2nd ed., 1980.

Index